DUELLING LANGUAGES

*This book is dedicated
to two friends and mentors,
Leonard Doob and Murray Fowler*

Preface

The goal of this study is to describe and explain codeswitching, the accessing of multiple languages within the same sentence. The focus, therefore, will be on intrasentential codeswitching data and the principles behind their production.

The use of both the terms *code* and *switching* is traditional. *Code* is used because it is a relatively neutral term for linguistic varieties at any level of structural differentiation. Its use does not imply I am satisfied with equating *code* with all that is *communicated* when speakers interact. It will turn out that *switching* is something of a misnomer, since only one aspect of codeswitching will be characterized as actually involving the switching of the codes involved, and even this one aspect is better referred to as a switching of the underlying psycholinguistic procedures which yield the surface structures. I prefer to write *codeswitching* as one word, although many writers on the subject hyphenate the term. Others prefer the term *code-mixing*; and some differentiate *codeswitching* and *code-mixing*. This will be discussed in Chapter 1.

Most linguists who do *not* study codeswitching think of it as strictly in the domain of sociolinguistics. Most definitely, codeswitching has its sociolinguistic aspects; elsewhere I myself have written extensively on the social uses of codeswitching. However, many of the current studies of codeswitching are more appropriately also called studies in grammatical theory. This volume fits into this category: it approaches codeswitching as a product of the 'psycholinguistic stress' of two linguistic systems interacting. Looked at this way, codeswitching is especially well positioned to reveal the internal operations of language. Still, all codeswitching studies retain a social aspect because their basis is very empirical: at their best, they use naturally occurring performance data as their database.

The book claims to offer a comprehensive treatment of the morphosyntactic constraints on intrasentential codeswitching. The major structural adjustments which distinguish codeswitched discourse from monolingual discourse in the languages involved are at the morphosyntactic level. While phonological aspects of codeswitching also deserve attention, they will not be considered here.

The treatment is synchronic for the most part; however, later chapters discuss how some borrowing and codeswitching are diachronically related, and how codeswitching might contribute to language shift and language death.

The study is non-developmental: neither the acquisition of the bilingualism necessary for codeswitching to exist nor the development of codeswitching in children is included as a topic.

The treatment is intended to be theoretical, directed to linguists and psycholinguists concerned with morphosyntactic aspects of sentence structure and production, as well as sociolinguists, especially those studying aspects of language contact. Although its primary intended audience does not include applied linguists, specialists in language-teaching and language-planning should find its argument, that codeswitching is not a helter-skelter production, worth considering in their deliberations.

While the book offers a general structural model of codeswitching, it does not support any single current syntactic model. Still, its specific claims have implications for the validity of models both of syntax and of language production. Its special value is that it tests the fit of models in these areas for multi-language data.

The very fact that this is a study of the juxtaposition of two or more languages in the same conversation, and of the resulting structural patterns, demonstrates that I do not conceive of the core of linguistics as the study of single, invariant systems. The very existence—indeed, prevalence—of codeswitching is evidence that linguistic systems have the flexibility to execute 'alternative plans'.

Many examples are included to support the theoretical argument. The main database is a set of naturally occurring conversations audio-recorded in Nairobi, Kenya; but the codeswitching literature in general, representing typologically diverse languages and their pairings in codeswitching, is surveyed in the examples provided as tests for the proposed hypotheses.

I would like to acknowledge the help I have received in writing this book. Financial aid in order to conduct field-work in Africa was essential. While I have carried out such work intermittently since 1964, the database for this book is drawn especially from recent trips to Kenya and Zimbabwe. I received help under a Fulbright Research Grant (1983), a Social Science Council Grant (1988), and a Research and Productive Scholarship Award from the University of South Carolina (1988). I also am very grateful to Eugene Rowely for assistance with the computer programs used in the analysis. Iong Chen offered patient and expert assistance in many aspects of the production process. Lily Chen and

Curtis Amick deserve thanks for important help with statistical analyses of the Zimbabwe data.

Intellectual and psychological support has come from innumerable persons since I began working on structural constraints on codeswitching in the mid 1980s. I especially wish to thank the following for commenting on parts of earlier conceptions of the model or drafts of chapters of this book: Shoji Azuma, Janice Bernsten, Eyamba Bokamba, Hazel Carter, Carol Eastman, Janice Jake, Frances Karttunen, Georges Lüdi, John Singler, and Keith Walters. Kumbirai Mkanganwi of the University of Zimbabwe offered me welcome insights into the structure of Shona/English codeswitching in Zimbabwe. I am very grateful to Janice Bernsten for our pleasant and fruitful collaboration in field-work in Zimbabwe in 1988; she is to be credited with completing the task we began together. I also thank Nigel Crawhall for his help in gathering naturally occurring conversations in Zimbabwe. I appreciate the Wolof/French examples which Leigh Swigart gave me. I thank Shoji Azuma for introducing me to the idea (and the relevant literature) that differences in the class of morphemes considered might be responsible for differential accessing of morphemes in codeswitching. It is no exaggeration to say that discussions with Janice Jake about the relation of my model to current syntactic theories were invaluable.

Conversations with numerous colleagues at conferences helped me sharpen my ideas. I single out the London workshop (autumn 1990) and Barcelona symposium (spring 1991) sponsored by the European Science Foundation, since it was during this period that this manuscript was written. I wish to acknowledge the intellectual impetus and encouragement these meetings gave me, and I thank the Committee of the Network on Code-Switching and Language Contact for graciously including me in what was basically a European enterprise. My students have always been a source of encouragement: I single out Yuriko Kite, Ronald Sylvester Simango, and especially Wei Long Xing, who were also my research assistants during various stages of the writing of this book. I appreciated above all the efforts of my research assistants in Africa: without their skill in recording conversations, this study would have been impossible. Shem Lusimba Mbira, who has worked with me for many years and was instrumental in gathering the Nairobi corpus, has been a faithful friend. And, as always, my son, Kenneth Scotton, has been there to listen and to enhearten me.

Contents

Symbols and Abbreviations

[ ]	indicates broad phonetic transcription
/ /	indicates phonemic transcription
1, 2, 3	1st, 2nd, 3rd person
*	not grammatically acceptable
A, ADJ	adjective
ACC	accusative case
ADV	adverb
ADVP	adverb phrase
AGR	agreement
AOR	narrative tense
AP	adjectival phrase
APPL	applied
ART	article
AUX	auxiliary verb
B	borrowed
C	Cheŵa
CC	consonant cluster
CL	class
CM	code-mixing
COMP	complementizer
CONDIT	conditional mood
CONSEC	consecutive tense
CONT	continuous aspect
CONV	conversive
COP	copula
CP	complement
CS	codeswitching
DEM	demonstrative
DET	determiner
DO	direct object
DUR	durative aspect
E	English
EL	embedded language

EMPH	emphatic pronoun
ES	English + Swahili
F	feminine
F	functional level
FSG	feminine singular
FUT	future
GB	government and binding
HABIT	habitual aspect
I	inflection/INFL
$\bar{\text{I}}$	inflection/INFL bar (in X-bar theory)
INDIC	indicative mood
INFIN	infinitive
INFL	inflection
INTERROG	interrogative
IO	indirect object
IP	INFL phrase (= S)
L1	first language
L2	second language
LOC	locative
MANN	manner
MCA	modern classical Arabic
ML	matrix language
MLF	Matrix Language Frame
N	noun
N', N'', N'''	$= \bar{\text{N}}, \bar{\bar{\text{N}}}, \bar{\bar{\text{N}}}$: N bar, N double bar, N triple bar (in X-bar theory)
NC	nasal + consonant cluster
NC	noun complement
NEG	negative
NOM	nominative
NON-PAST	non-past tense
NP	noun phrase
OBJ	object
P	positional level
P	preposition
PART	particle
PASS	passive
PAST	past tense
PERF	perfective aspect

PL	plural
PLF	plural feminine
POSS	possessive
PP	prepositional phrase
PPART	past participle
PRES	present tense
PRO	pronoun
PROG	progressive aspect
RECIPR	reciprocal
REFL	reflexive
REL	relative pronoun
RO	rights and obligations
S	sentence
S	singular
SE	Swahili + English
SM	S in matrix language
SOV	subject + object + verb
SPEC	specifier
SS	Swahili + Swahili
SUBJ	subject
θ role	theta role = thematic role
V	verb
V′	*see* N′
VP	verb phrase

I
Introduction

Preliminaries

At some time or another, many readers of this volume have shaken their heads in amazement at overhearing speakers who were carrying out a conversation in two languages, apparently freely drawing from both linguistic systems at will. Some readers themselves produce such conversations regularly. Such naturally occurring conversations on everyday topics are the subject of this study.

These conversations are frequent all over the world wherever the participants are bilinguals, from Puerto Rican secretaries rapidly alternating Spanish and English while strolling on lunch-break on the sidewalks of New York City, to Kikuyu market vendors in Nairobi, Kenya, judiciously adding phrases in Luo to their Swahili while wooing a Luo-speaking customer, to university professors in Tamil Nadu, India, interchanging English and Tamil when relating what happened at a recent academic conference.

The Issues Involved

The research question which this book addresses is the following: when speakers alternate between two linguistic varieties, how free is this alternation from the structural point of view? That is, are there structural constraints on codeswitching, and, if so, what are those constraints? An additional question which the study answers indirectly is: do the social functions of codeswitching control in any way the types of structures occurring?

From the sociolinguistic point of view, codeswitching of languages offers bilinguals a way to increase their flexibility of expression, going beyond the style-switching of monolinguals. That is, switching is a means to index the nuances of social relationships by exploiting the socio-psychological associations of the languages employed (cf. Myers-Scotton, 1993).

From the psycholinguistic point of view, codeswitching represents flexibility in language production. One of the issues discussed by psycholinguists is 'the co-ordination problem'—how fluent speech is achieved. Codeswitching is a way to overcome difficulties in sentence-planning by making use of the resources of more than one language. At the same time, codeswitching, and also (at least) child language acquisition data and speech errors, are at once obvious symptoms and sources of psycholinguistic stress. While codeswitching in particular is a means of solving the coordination problem in fluent speech, it also creates stresses because of the special coordination codeswitching itself requires.

This book considers how those stresses on the grammars of the participating languages are handled. The general answer will be that they are attended to with little actual disruption of the linguistic systems involved. The overall argument will be that codeswitching data are not qualitatively different from other naturally occurring language structures. Thus, this study is an argument, supported by all the available empirical data, that codeswitching can be explained in a principled, general way. Codeswitching utterances everywhere conform to the grammars of their participating languages, subject only to the added constraints of the Matrix Language-Frame Model presented here.

This argument does not imply that codeswitching *performance* is the same everywhere. First, variable performance is obviously expected if one considers *why* speakers engage in codeswitching at all. From the point of view of *social motivations*, it becomes apparent that there are several different types of codeswitching; there is a large body of literature on this subject (cf. Scotton, 1988*a*; Myers-Scotton, 1993). Further, the types of codeswitching which occur (especially in terms of their frequency) are a function of the specific sociolinguistic profiles of the communities involved (cf. Scotton, 1986; 1988*b*). Second, because of *typological differences* between languages (e.g. word-order), not all grammatical constituents may be involved in codeswitching with the same frequency. Third, *lack of congruence* between languages regarding subcategorization features for certain grammatical categories or specific lexemes will also affect which configurations may occur in the codeswitching between specific language pairs. For example, such concerns as whether (in both the languages involved) pronouns are full forms or clitics, or whether a thematic role such as 'locative' is assigned by verbs or by prepositions, will make a difference. However, the claim here is that, no matter how diverse the linguistic repertoire of the community and speakers involved, no matter how diverse the social conditions which motivate codeswitching, and no matter how diverse languages are typologically or in regard to specific subcategorization procedures, the parameters limiting codeswitching are the same everywhere. Within these parameters, the *performance* of codeswitching (what structures actually occur) may vary across speakers and communities, but what is *possible* or *not possible* can be predicted. I return to this subject in Chapter 8.

Some Definitions

Codeswitching (hereafter CS) is the selection by bilinguals or multilinguals of forms from an embedded variety (or varieties) in utterances of a matrix variety during the same conversation. While CS may take place on any level of linguistic differentiation (languages, styles, or dialects/registers), this volume is concerned only with CS between languages. From now on, therefore, reference to the participating varieties in CS will be to languages.

The matrix language (hereafter ML) is the main language in CS utterances in a number of ways, as will become clear in the following chapters. Its identification is discussed in Chapter 3. The term 'embedded language' (hereafter EL) refers to the other languages[1] which also participate in CS, but with a lesser role. The argument of the model presented here is that the ML sets the morphosyntactic frame of sentences showing CS. In the most general terms, setting the frame means specifying the morpheme order and supplying the syntactically relevant morphemes in constituents consisting of morphemes from both participating languages. It also means determining when constituents within a sentence showing CS must occur entirely in the EL.

CS may be either intersentential or intrasentential. Examples [1] and [2] from naturally occurring conversations in Nairobi, Kenya, illustrate these types. Intersentential CS involves switches from one language to the other between sentences: a whole sentence (or more than one sentence)

---

[1] The Matrix Language-Frame Model uses descriptively the terms *matrix* and *embedded* languages, as well as *islands* (to be discussed in Ch. 5). Their primary references and connotations seem applicable (e.g. the matrix language is the 'principal' language in CS, the one 'around which something develops'; an 'embedded' language is 'fixed firmly in a surrounding mass', in this case the matrix language; an island is 'isolated' and 'a separate entity'). Their use is not intended to imply any theoretical bias; i.e. they are not islands in the sense of sentential subjects, complex NPs, co-ordinate structures, etc.

is produced entirely in one language before there is a switch to the other language(s) in use in the conversation. Note the sentence *You know, this is a Luyia land and therefore most of the people who live in rural areas do visit this town often* in [1]. Intrasentential switches occur within the same sentence or sentence fragment. Such switches produce three different types of constituent: those with material from two languages occurring within the same constituent, those entirely in the ML, or those entirely in the EL. Note *niko sure* 'I am sure', *ni-me-decide* 'I have decided', *kwa wingi* 'in abundance', and *white clothes* in [2].

[1] A Luyia man who now works in Nairobi is being interviewed about his job experiences elsewhere in Kenya. The interviewer is also a Luyia. The interviewee alternates between his Luyia variety (Lwidakho), Swahili, and English. At his job in Nairobi, he speaks both Swahili and English frequently. Lwidakho is printed in small capitals and English is italicized; the remainder is in Swahili, which can be identified as the matrix language of this conversational turn.

LUYIA MAN. NINDANGA NA KAKAMEGA, watu huko wanatumia Kiswahili, *English*, na Luyia. *You know, this is a Luyia land and therefore most of the people who live in rural areas do visit this town often.* Kwa hiyvo huwa sana sana wanatumia Kiluyia na Kiswahili. Lakini wale ambao wanaishi katika *town* yenyewe, wanatumia Kiswahili sana.
'To start with Kakamega, people there use Swahili, English, and Luyia . . . Therefore they use Luyia and Swahili very much. But those who live in the town itself, they use Swahili very much.'

(Swahili/Luyia/English;[2] Myers-Scotton, unpublished data)

[2] Two women in their twenties are talking at a Nairobi home about the problems of buying laundry detergent. They are educated to Form 4 level (the equivalent of high school). They come from different ethnic groups. Swahili is the matrix language here. English is italicized. The first speaker has said she could not find any Omo (a particular detergent) when shopping the previous day.

SPEAKER 2. Lakini ni-ko   *sure* ukienda *after two days* utaipata 'Uchumi'
                 1S-LOC COP
supermarket kwa wingi.
'But I'm sure if you go after two days you will get it [Omo] at "Uchumi" supermarket in abundance.'
SPEAKER 1. Hata siku hizi ni-me-*decide*   kwanza kutumia sabuni ya miti.
                 even days these 1S-PERF-decide first   to use   soap of stick
'[But] even these days I have decided first to use bar soap.'

---

[2] In citations following examples, the convention of listing the matrix language first will be observed.

SPEAKER 2. Hata hiyo inaweza kufanya. Ubaya wake ha-i-wez-i
                NEG-CL 9^3-able-NEG
fua[4] *white clothes.*
wash
'Even that can do. Its problem [is that] it can't wash white clothes.'

(Swahili/English; Myers-Scotton, unpublished data)

This volume will deal only with intrasentential CS. While the explanation of intersentential CS is by no means a trivial problem, accounting for where *within a sentence* a CS form or constituent may occur seems more immediately challenging. Note that it is an issue within CS research circles as to which EL material represents 'true' CS. The position taken here is that EL material of any size, from a single morpheme or lexeme to several constituents, may be regarded as CS material. This is why, for example, in [2] both *after two days* and *ni-me-decide* are referred to as constituents showing CS. The background to this issue will be discussed in Chapter 2 and my position on it will be explained in Chapter 6.

There is no question that singly occurring CS lexemes and single lexical borrowings resemble each other. In fact, I will argue in Chapter 6 that it is unproductive to try to distinguish them, *from the standpoint of the morphosyntactic processes which they undergo.* I will also argue, however, that CS and borrowed forms from an EL have different statuses in regard to the mental lexicon of the ML.

I will also discuss the relevance to CS of the fact that there are two different types of lexical borrowed forms. Cultural borrowed lexemes stand for objects or concepts new to the culture (e.g. *supermarket* in [2] above). Core borrowed lexemes are taken into the language even though the recipient language already has lexemes of its own to encode the concepts or objects in question (e.g. *town* in [1]).

Goals of This Study

The major goal of this study is to present a model to account for the structures in intrasentential CS. This is the Matrix Language-Frame

---

[3] References to 'classes' (e.g. CL 9) when morphemes are identified in examples refer to noun-class membership. Here, the verbal subject clitic governed by CL 9 nouns occurs, preceded by an invariant negative prefix (*ha-i-*). Bantuists number noun classes by convention, pairing up related classes, one of which signals singularity and the other plurality.

[4] Standard Swahili rules regarding well-formedness do not always apply in these conversations. Here, for example, standard Swahili would require the infinitival prefix *ku-* (*ku-fua*).

Model (MLF model). It is a production-based model which sees CS constraints as set by processes which operate well before the positional level at which surface orders and structures are realized. The model is supported with examples from naturally occurring conversations. Secondary goals are (1) to situate this model in relation to other attempts to explain CS structures, (2) to provide independent motivations for the model, and (3) to relate CS, as the model envisions it, to the other language contact phenomena of borrowing, language shift, and language death.

A Preview of the Matrix Language-Frame Model

The major premises of the MLF model are that the crucial generalizations about structural constraints on CS can be captured by recognizing the interplay of two hierarchies.

1. One of the languages involved in CS plays a more dominant role. This language is labelled the Matrix Language (ML), and its grammar sets the morphosyntactic frame for two of the three types of constituent contained in sentences showing intrasentential CS, ML + EL constituents (those showing morphemes from the two or more participating languages) and ML islands (constituents composed entirely of ML morphemes). The third type of constituent, the EL island, is entirely in the EL. It is produced when ML morphosyntactic procedures are inhibited and EL procedures are activated.

2. The major organizing device which the ML uses in setting the frame is the division between system and content morphemes. Whether a morpheme from the other language(s) involved in CS may appear in a ML + EL constituent depends on its status as a system or content morpheme; whether it must appear in an EL island (if it is to appear at all) also depends on this status. The congruence of an EL content morpheme with ML morphemes in various ways also determines whether that EL morpheme may be accessed in an ML + EL constituent.

In brief, three features distinguish content and system morphemes. Those with a plus setting for the feature [Quantification] are system morphemes. Categories with the feature [+ Quantification] pick out individuals or events. These prototypically include quantifiers, specifiers, and inflectional morphology. Morphemes with the feature [−Quantification] are potential content morphemes. To qualify as a content morpheme, however, a morpheme must have a plus setting for one of two other features [Thematic Role-Assigner] or [Thematic Role-Receiver].

Thematic roles (or theta roles) refer, of course, to the semantic relationships between verbs and their arguments: for example, the role of patient is typically assigned by the verb to the object argument. Prototypically, most verbs, prepositions, nouns, and descriptive adjectives will be content morphemes.

The provisions of the MLF model are contained in a set of interrelated hypotheses. Each hypothesis, however, also stands on its own in that it makes specific predictions. These predictions make clear the type of evidence which would falsify the hypothesis; data regarding what would constitute counter-examples are discussed at relevant junctures in Chapters 4 and 5.

The Matrix Language Hypothesis: The ML sets the morphosyntactic frame for ML + EL constituents.

This hypothesis is realized as two testable principles: the Morpheme-Order Principle ('Morpheme order must not violate ML morpheme order') and the System Morpheme Principle ('All syntactically relevant system morphemes must come from the ML').

The Blocking Hypothesis: The ML blocks the appearance of any EL content morphemes which do not meet certain congruency conditions with ML counterparts.

The EL Island Trigger Hypothesis: Whenever an EL morpheme appears which is not permitted under either the ML Hypothesis or the Blocking Hypothesis, the constituent containing it must be completed as an obligatory EL island.

The EL Implicational Hierarchy Hypothesis: Optional EL islands occur; generally they are only those constituents which are either formulaic or idiomatic or peripheral to the main grammatical arguments of the sentence.

How the MLF Model Views Speakers and Languages

The model presented here does not assume that speakers need be entirely fluent in the EL when they engage in CS. This claim rests on the provisions of the model, not on the fact that determining 'fluency' is an unresolved issue in second-language acquisition circles. As will become clearer when ML + EL constituents are discussed in detail, CS in such constituents takes the form of content morpheme insertion. Speakers do need to know some content morphemes from the EL in order to use them in these constituents, but they need not have mastered the system morphemes and phrase-structure rules necessary to produce well-formed sentences in the EL. Producing EL islands (well-formed constituents entirely in the EL) *does* require a higher level of ability in the EL, of course.

Because they must construct a morphosyntactic frame in the ML for ML + EL constituents, speakers must have more ability in the ML than the EL. That ML may be a second language, however, or, theoretically, it may even be what might be called a learner's interlanguage. What is required is that speakers have sufficient command of a set of principles of well-formedness for the ML—whether or not these principles coincide exactly with those of native speakers of the variety—in order to construct frames.

My assumptions regarding language activation and language-switching do not necessarily depend on treating languages themselves as 'discrete' in the sense of being closed or finite rule systems. Each language of a multilingual speaker *does* have its own internal rule system, but this is a dynamic system. Thus a language is thought of, not as a unitary object, but rather as an abstraction which is realized in a given community as a set of discrete subcategorization frames and morphosyntactic procedures. Is some overlap possible between languages? The answer is 'yes', especially if *overlap* is conceptualized abstractly as *congruence*. In fact, congruence in these frames and procedures between languages will be required for certain types of CS to occur. These ideas will come up again later in the volume.

Plan of This Volume

Following this chapter are two chapters offering some preliminaries to the presentation of the Matrix Language-Frame Model. Chapter 2 offers an overview of the major claims of other researchers about structural constraints on CS. It deals mainly with the 1970s and 1980s; however, some papers from 1990s are discussed here, while others are cited where relevant to the discussion in Chapters 4–6. Chapter 3 includes some motivations of the MLF model. It introduces research within psycholinguistics on language production which I see as especially relevant to CS. This chapter also discusses how the language designated as the matrix language in CS is identified. Chapters 4 and 5 present the MLF model. Chapter 6 contains an argument which, in some ways, is anterior to the MLF model, since it compares those EL forms which can be designated CS forms to those which are borrowed forms; however, this discussion depends on knowledge of the provisions of the MLF model. Chapter 7 discusses CS as a mechanism in contact-induced language change. Finally, Chapter 8 provides a synthesis of the earlier discussions. It also indicates some intersections between the claims of my model of the social motivations for CS (cf. Myers-Scotton, 1993 on the Markedness Model) and the MLF model presented here. This concluding chapter makes the important claim that, while what *may* occur as intrasentential CS is not subject to social and pragmatic pressures, these pressures are nevertheless important in providing the climate in which certain types of permissible CS utterances, in fact, *do* flower.

Overview of the Main Data Corpora

Data from a number of different sources will be used in the examples discussed in later chapters, but many of them will come from conversations audio-recorded in Nairobi.[5]

The capital of Kenya, Nairobi is a multi-ethnic city, even though it is located at the intersection of the traditional homelands of the Kikuyu and the Maasai ethnic groups. Kenya has about forty ethnic groups, and representatives from all of them can be found in Nairobi. All over Africa, urban areas are magnets to in-migrants from all over the country (and from other nations as well), because of the possibility of salaried work.

Both English and Swahili are the official languages of Kenya, with Swahili also designated as the *lugha ya taifa* 'national language'. English is the main language used in all official written work, however, and is also so used in the business community. English plays a major role in education, although Swahili is now a compulsory school subject, and was recently added to the roster of subjects included in the general examination at the end of primary school. Various indigenous languages (including Swahili) may be the media of instruction in the early primary years, but English then takes over as the medium through the upper primary years and onwards, including all higher education. In some urban schools, English is the medium even from primary 1 onwards.

When Kenya gained its independence from the United Kingdom in 1963, English was already in place as the language of higher education

---

[5] Numbers following examples from Swahili/English CS throughout the book refer to the interviews from the Nairobi corpus. These interviews are numbered 1–40.

and in higher-level governmental and business circles. As did most other African countries with an anglophone colonial heritage, Kenya named English its official language—largely because of its neutral status in comparison with the languages of any of the many indigenous ethnic groups. The idea behind selecting English was that all peoples theoretically were equal in their previous knowledge of English and their future ability to learn it. Further, there was no single ethnic group which was sufficiently numerous or politically dominant to impose its language on the new nation.

Swahili has a long history as a lingua franca in East Africa (cf. Nurse and Spear, 1985; Whiteley, 1969). It is spoken indigenously by a relatively small number of people along the East African coast and on the offshore islands, from just across the Kenya–Somalia border in the north to the Mozambique–Tanzania border in the south. In fact, one of the reasons it has been such a success as a lingua franca is that the small number of its indigenous speakers makes it unlikely that they will represent a major political force; therefore, other groups in Kenya and Tanzania have not felt they are making an important concession to a viable rival in bestowing a position of prominence on Swahili.

According to available records, Swahili was first spread across East Africa as far west as Zaïre by Arab trading caravans, many organized from the Swahili-speaking island of Zanzibar. The interior areas are inhabited by ethnic groups speaking many different languages; therefore, a lingua franca was needed. In the late nineteenth and early twentieth centuries, Swahili's position as a lingua franca was further enhanced when the colonials used it for lower-level administrative purposes (the British in Kenya, but first the Germans and then the British in the case of Tanzania).

Today, Swahili enjoys much currency in its role as a lingua franca all over East Africa and into neighbouring areas as well. Because the majority of peoples in these areas are speakers of Bantu languages, Swahili, which is also a Bantu language, is relatively easy to learn. While it has lost some of the proto-Bantu features which other Bantu languages retain (e.g. it does not show either morphological or lexical tone; and its noun-class system is slightly reduced, more so in up-country varieties), there is little evidence to support any argument that Swahili arose as a creole.[6] Thanks to the contacts between Bantu-speaking peoples along the coast and Arab

---

[6] See Nurse and Hinnebusch (1993) for a linguistic history of Swahili and its structural affinities with its closest neighbours in the Sabaki group.

sailors and traders, the Swahili vocabulary shows many lexical loans from Arabic. It also has many English loans as a result of the colonial period and the continuing eminence of English in large areas of Africa.

In 1930, a committee set up by the British colonial administration decided that the standard dialect of Swahili would be based on Ki-Unguja, the dialect of Zanzibar town. This is the dialect taught in Kenyan schools today. However, the Swahili of many Kenyans shows some non-standard features, most typically resulting from phonological interference from first languages and inflectional levelling. Speakers accept this feature of their Swahili for a number of reasons. First, one's ability to speak standard Swahili has never been considered an important socio-economic marker. A second and related reason is that Swahili has traditionally been acquired informally. It has not always been taught extensively in the schools, and therefore mastery of standard Swahili has not been a marker of education. How Swahili has been acquired by most speakers is a clue to the purposes for which it is valued: most adults pick up the variety of Swahili which they know from multiethnic co-workers. That is, Swahili has instrumental value as a tool of inter-ethnic communication. And even today, although they will study standard Swahili in school, many children acquire an urban variety of Swahili from playmates before they enter school.

Today, Swahili has official status in several nations. It is the sole official language of Tanzania (although English is the medium of education beyond primary school), and it is one of the four regional official languages in Zaïre. In Kenya, it became an official language jointly with English in 1984. Under the regime of Idi Amin, it was named the official language of Uganda; its status there today is in flux.

Since it is used daily in the corridors of governmental or business establishments, English in Kenya has associations with education and authority. And, of course, it is the order of the day in schools. Not surprisingly, many Nairobi residents are very accustomed to speaking English, although it is more associated with formal contexts than is the case for Swahili or their own first languages.

In contrast to English, Swahili is not linked with high socio-economic prestige. It retains its image from colonial times as the language used in a downward fashion to deal with subordinates. However, it also has a distinctly positive image as a language of solidarity among different ethnic groups, especially for their informal interactions. Even among some members of the same ethnic group, especially children and young adults who were raised in Nairobi, Swahili has a certain cachet as the *lugha ya town* 'language of town', with *town* meaning 'Nairobi'. It is no exaggeration to say that most Nairobi dwellers use Swahili every day for some interactions (cf. Myers-Scotton, 1993; Parkin, 1974; Scotton, 1982*b*; Scotton, 1988*b*).

Because the Nairobi corpus consists of casual conversations, it is no surprise that Swahili is the main language of those exchanges. English appears only in a CS pattern as the EL, with Swahili as the ML in all cases. In a few conversations, another Kenyan language is used briefly (e.g. Kikuyu) as another EL. As indicated above, Chapter 3 contains a lengthy discussion of how the ML is identified.

In almost all the conversations, the alternation between Swahili and English represents what I have labelled elsewhere as 'codeswitching itself as the unmarked choice' or 'unmarked codeswitching' (cf. Myers-Scotton, 1993; Scotton, 1988*a*). Note that I use 'unmarked choice' to indicate the *expected* choice among possible ways of speaking; therefore, where CS itself is the unmarked choice, this means that most conversations show much switching and little monolingual discourse. This type of switching is not found in all conversations where CS occurs in the world. Rather, unmarked CS is typical only of casual, ingroup conversations. This is why it is difficult to obtain examples of such switching through interviews, even if the interviewer is a member of the community. Speakers in any community have a sense of what constitutes the unmarked medium for interviews and it is often not the same medium which is unmarked for truly ingroup conversations. For example, in Nairobi either English on its own or Swahili on its own (depending on the social identity of the interviewer and the language he/she initiates) would be unmarked choices for an interview.

Further, unmarked CS is only typical of those communities where both the languages employed in switching are positively valued, and specifically so for ingroup identities. This is the case in Nairobi. By speaking some English, speakers associate themselves with the education, authority, and sophistication which this international language signifies in Nairobi. But by their use of Swahili they also show that they are cosmopolitan, urban dwellers who are proud of their East African heritage.

In this way, Nairobi contrasts with those communities where the languages which are candidates for use in CS represent ethnic groups in competition with each other. In such communities, unmarked CS is infrequent. Consider, for example, Flemish and French in Belgium or Catalan and Castilian for Catalonians in Barcelona (cf. Scotton, 1988*b*; Myers-Scotton, 1993). There, other types of CS may well occur, especially CS 'as a marked choice'; such switching is a negotiation to change the social distance between participants in a conversation.

I do not wish to leave the impression that unmarked CS is infrequent in the world. In fact, in many multilingual communities, it may be *the* major medium of casual, ingroup conversations. For example, it is prevalent all over Africa, as well as in India and elsewhere in south-east Asia. In Europe it is frequent in many bilingual populations, such as in Strasburg, France, between Alsatian and French. Everywhere it is common among immigrant populations, such as between Spanish and English among Hispanics in the United States; in Europe, recent immigrants alternate between their first languages and the official language where they live (e.g. Arabic/Dutch CS in the Netherlands, Turkish/ German in German-speaking Switzerland).

From a structural point of view, unmarked CS is characterized by a great deal of switching. Each individual switch is not intended to convey a special social message, as is the case with other types of CS. Rather, it is the overall pattern which is intended to index simultaneous identities, the very use of two languages, more or less at once. This is the type of conversation which produces many instances of intrasentential CS.

All conversations were transcribed and then portions showing CS were entered into Kwic-Magic, a computer-based concordance program (Whistler, 1988). A concordance was generated which includes frequencies and contexts of all material of English origin. When statistics are cited for the Nairobi corpus, they are based on this concordance.

The conversations used in this study were selected from a larger corpus of naturally occurring conversations gathered in Nairobi, with the criterion that they include use of Swahili. The first 40 conversations which showed any CS utterances were selected; others were entirely in Swahili. About 100 persons took part in these conversations. The makeup of participants is inter-ethnic in almost all cases, one of the factors promoting their use of Swahili and English rather than their own first languages.

Most speakers are not native speakers of Swahili. Some of the children from ethnically mixed marriages may consider Swahili as their first language; but all adults speak various Kenyan African languages as their first language, languages intimately associated with their ethnic groups. However, all speak Swahili fluently and, in fact, may use it as their main language. And while their Swahili does show some non-standard features, it never diverges far enough for it to be called a learner's interlanguage, and certainly not a pidgin. Most alternations are minor: for example, many second-language speakers of Swahili over-generalize noun class

9/10 agreements (e.g. *kitabu y-ake* instead of standard *kitabu ch-ake* for 'his/her book').

While care was taken to record naturally occurring conversations, topics and other situational circumstances were not a consideration. In most cases, speakers were unaware they were being recorded, since the research assistant making the recording was a friend or family member.[7] Speakers' permission to use the recorded material in an anonymous fashion was obtained after recording. The conversations vary in length from about ten minutes to over an hour, representing approximately twenty hours of material.

The conversations also vary considerably in the amount of CS they contain. Some contain only a handful of nouns as CS forms; others have few sentences not showing extensive switching, including that of an intraword nature (i.e. morphemes from different languages within a word). Speakers showing the most CS in this sample are the young school-age children and the young men and women who have just completed secondary school. The sample contains speakers of different ages. Their educational levels vary considerably, but the adults have no more than a secondary-school education at best. Even this level is more likely to characterize the younger speakers; the older ones tend to be at a lower level. The only exception is one conversation between university students.

Altogether, these conversations contain 328 individual lexeme types of CS forms, tabulated by form class in Table 1.1. Note that reference to 'CS forms' denotes singly occurring lexemes. Lexemes within 'islands' entirely of English (to be discussed in Chapters 4 and 5 as 'EL islands') are not counted as individual types; rather, islands themselves constitute a form class ($N = 121$). The relative frequency of the different form classes in CS is not especially surprising, given earlier tabulations by other CS researchers on other data sets; however, the number of verb stems ($N = 128$) may be comparatively high. This breakdown is not directly relevant to the predictions of the MLF model.

Recall that the model crucially distinguishes two types of morpheme, content and system morphemes. Therefore, what is highly relevant is that among the single lexeme/bound morpheme CS forms there are only content morphemes, system morphemes being absent with only one

---

[7] The value of being able to base an analysis on truly natural data cannot be overestimated. In this regard, I greatly appreciate the work of the research assistants who gathered the Nairobi data, especially Shem Lusimba Mbira, Edward Lusimba, and Nancy Gichohi.

Table 1.1. *Singly-occurring English lexemes (CS forms from EL) in Nairobi corpus of intrasentential codeswitching data*[a]

	Types	Tokens
Nouns	141	174
Verbs		
Finite	91	91
Infinitive	37	37
Past participle	13	15
Adjectives	27	36
Adverbs	11	11
Interjection	4	4
Conjunction	2	2
Pronoun	1	1
Possessive pronoun	1	3
TOTAL[b]	328	374

[a] Only lexemes occurring in fewer than three conversations are counted as CS forms.
[b] In addition: EL islands 121
   EL sentences (intersentential CS) 44.

exception.[8] Introduced above, the content versus system morpheme will be discussed extensively in Chapters 4 and 5.

In the corpus, there are only a few more tokens than types, since only lexemes occurring across fewer than three conversations are counted as CS forms. Those EL lexemes found in three or more conversations are counted as borrowed forms. From the standpoint of the morphosyntactic procedures which they undergo, CS forms do not differ in kind from borrowed forms; this is one of the major claims of Chapter 6. That is, the same procedures to be discussed here as applying to CS forms in constituents with morphemes from both languages also apply to borrowed forms. Still, to avoid the red herring of borrowed forms in the evaluation of the MLF model, an effort has been made to present only CS forms in the examples cited when the model is exemplified.

Reasons to distinguish CS forms from borrowed forms on other grounds are discussed in Chapter 6. Here, I briefly outline two heuristic devices I use to separate the two types of EL-origin material.

[8] The English pronoun *them* appears as a singly occurring lexeme. This is discussed in Ch. 5 as the single counter-example to the Blocking Hypothesis.

First, I suggest that a 'three-occurrence metric' can be used to distinguish the two. That is, I am suggesting that CS forms be separated, as 'lower-frequency forms', from borrowed forms, as 'higher-frequency forms'. The following reasons motivate this distinction. Lexical entries for CS forms are in the EL mental lexicon, not that of the ML. Borrowed forms, however, have become part of the ML lexicon; that is, by definition, they have been taken into the ML (while, of course, they also may remain active in the source language). Therefore, borrowed forms are predicted to have the same freedom of occurrence as any other ML lexeme. But when CS forms occur, they do so only under the restrictions discussed below. For these reasons, CS forms are predicted to occur less frequently than borrowed forms. Therefore, I suggest an admittedly arbitrary frequency metric to separate CS and borrowed forms. A type must occur in fewer than three different conversations to qualify as a CS form; otherwise, it is considered a borrowed form. (In Chapter 6, I show how *relative* frequency can be used as a metric: the frequency of a suspected borrowed form can be compared with that of the ML morpheme for the object/concept encoded by both.)

Second, 'cultural' forms are ruled out as CS forms. That is, any lexeme standing for an object or concept new to the culture is automatically considered a borrowed form, even if it occurs only once in the corpus (e.g. *engineer*, *steel wool*, *carrots*, *walkman* (tape-recorder), and *traffic jam*). The rationale for this move is discussed in Chapter 6. A few cases, admittedly, are problematic, but very few.

In examples drawn from other researchers' data corpora, I am unable to apply the 'three-occurrence metric' with potential CS forms, of course; however, I do not cite any examples as evidence for CS constraints if they are likely cultural borrowed forms (i.e. because they stand for new objects/concepts).

What Constitutes Data?

As mentioned above, CS takes two forms: intrasentential and intersentential. I include under intrasentential CS either bound EL morphemes or free-form, singly occurring EL lexemes which meet the criteria for CS forms sketched above and elaborated on in Chapter 6, as well as full EL phrases or clauses. Thus, any instances of juxtaposition of ML or EL material, at the morpheme, word, phrase, and clause level, are relevant data to test the proposed model. Altogether, there are 44 instances of intersentential CS in the Nairobi corpus; that is, there are 44 English sentences.

Treatment of data is limited in two ways. First, the phonology of CS constituents is not considered because it does not seem to figure in conditioning or explaining morphosyntactic constraints on CS, the subject here.[9] Second, the discussion does not take account of the difficulty of distinguishing ML from EL material in language-contact situations where syntactic convergence has taken place (cf. Clyne, 1987 on German/English CS among German immigrants to Australia), or where the switching is between dialects of the same language (cf. Heath, 1989 on modern classical Arabic/colloquial Moroccan Arabic, or Ramat, 1991 on standard Italian/regional dialects). Admittedly, in such cases it would be difficult (although not impossible) to test the claims of the model about the differential accessing of ML versus EL material. I comment briefly in Chapter 5 on CS in convergence situations.

Most of the examples of CS data come from Swahili/English CS in the Nairobi corpus discussed above (hereafter 'the Nairobi corpus'); but some come from Shona/English CS from other field-work of mine and of my associates. Also, data from interviews in Zimbabwe are the basis for a discussion of borrowing in Chapter 6. These come from interviews in Chitungwiza, a working-class suburb of Harare, the capital, and from the environs of the rural village of Mutoko, 120 km. east of Harare. These interviews represent field-work by Janice Bernsten and me. The sociolinguistic situation in Zimbabwe, the site of the Shona/English CS examples, will be discussed briefly in Chapter 6. Suffice it to say here that the use of such CS is even more an unmarked choice as an informal medium for many residents in Harare than is Swahili/English CS in Nairobi. English is the main official language of Zimbabwe, along with Shona and Ndebele. About 80 per cent of the population speaks a Shona dialect as a mother tongue.

In addition, many other CS examples from the literature are cited. The goal of including data from many languages is to test the model against typologically different languages and, when available, typologically mixed language pairs.

---

[9] As will be indicated in Ch. 2, in earlier studies on structural constraints, consideration of the phonological integration of EL material (into the ML) was part of many analyses because such integration was considered a criterion of status as a CS form or a borrowed form (i.e. forms showing phonological integration were classed as borrowed forms). However, discussion of that issue as part of the definitions issue was dropped later, when it must have been realized that not all borrowed forms show complete phonological integration, while some CS forms show some such integration.

Summary

This chapter has three major purposes. First, it introduces the material which will count as CS examples, while also offering something of the spirit of the conversations containing them. Second, it details the data set and the sociolinguistic background for the conversations from which the majority of CS examples will come. This is the Nairobi corpus. Third, it indicates that the goal of this volume will be to propose a structurally based model to account for where in a sentence switches from one language to the other may occur.

It is worth emphasizing that, while the data cited largely represent Swahili/English CS in Nairobi, this book is not intended primarily as a descriptive study of that data base. The main purpose in including these data is to provide a quantitative basis for testing the MLF model. That is, *all* instances of CS within the forty conversations constituting the Nairobi corpus are considered in the analysis. The very few instances which are exceptions to the claims of the MLF model are discussed along with the majority of examples, which support the model.

In addition, all relevant examples available in the general CS literature are also considered. Again, both potential counter-examples and examples supporting the MLF model are discussed.

2

The Search for Structural Constraints on Codeswitching

Introduction

Most research on CS in the 1970s and 1980s was fuelled by the recognition that CS properly should be considered as a type of skilled performance with social motivations (cf. Gumperz, 1982; Heller, 1988; Myers-Scotton, 1993). However, it soon occurred to researchers that quite another aspect of CS also might not be an accidental matter: where in an utterance a speaker might switch might well not be simply a whim of individual speakers or even a matter of habit for a specific speech community. This chapter surveys earlier answers to the constraints question: what are the limits on where the speaker may codeswitch within a sentence, and what motivates these limits? (Note that only intrasentential CS is relevant to the constraints question, as it has been addressed to date.)

Preliminaries

Three general approaches are apparent in the attempts to formulate constraints on CS. First, researchers articulated constraints on switching from the surface (e.g. largely using linear ordering, form class, or size of switched material). Second, some researchers proposed that constraints were driven by the same principles or rules formulated under current syntactic theories to explain syntactic structures within a single language. Third, simultaneously and then more recently as well, others suggested that a major linguistic constraint on CS is related to clashes in subcategorization restrictions between the languages involved.

In Chapters 4 and 5, I will argue instead that the source of constraints on CS is both more abstract and more specific: it lies at an even more non-representational level in message construction, within an even more hierarchical system of constituents than such dominant syntactic theories as government and binding offer for syntax. Constraints on CS are part of a lexically driven package of higher-order semantic and syntactic procedures which precede phrase-structure rules.

In the Matrix Language-Frame Model (MLF model) which makes these proposals, the participating languages in CS are labelled in the following way. The 'base' language is called the matrix language (ML) and the 'contributing' language (or languages) is called the embedded language (EL). This terminology will be used in this book. I follow Joshi (1985) in how the terms *matrix language* and *embedded language* are used in regard to CS,[1] while acknowledging that Jacobson (1977) seems to be the first to have used these terms in reference to CS, albeit in a different sense.

The important issue of how the ML is to be identified is discussed in Chapter 3. It will be argued that whatever language is the ML in CS between a given language pair, that language has a different sociolinguistic status from the EL in that pair, at least in the interaction type where the CS occurs and often in the community as a whole. However, in order to establish the ML in a uniformly applicable way, an 'ML criterion' based on morpheme frequency is proposed. It states that the ML is the language contributing relatively more morphemes to the conversation, if frequency is considered at a discourse level.

Early Discussions: CS Forms or Borrowings?

While the research question (where in a sentence EL material might appear) was always clear, studies were plagued from the outset by another question: which EL material, in fact, constituted CS material? The issue concerns the status of single-lexeme items. Most early researchers resolved the issue by closing the doors of CS to single-lexeme items and concentrating their attentions on phrases or larger constituents. This tendency is apparent in the earliest studies on constraints, largely dealing with Spanish/English in the American south-west. For example, Reyes (1976: 184) recommends using the term *code-switching* only for Chicano bilingual phenomena when 'The syntactic junctures that divide the Spanish and English components of the sentence are easily discernible, and the

---

[1] In an earlier unpublished paper, Joshi (1981) had used the terms 'host' and 'guest' languages from Sridhar and Sridhar (1980); in a footnote (1985: 203) Joshi credits Sridhar and Sridhar's paper with convincing him of the asymmetry of the system.

English component has its own internal syntactic structure'. He proposes the term *borrowing* for such examples as [1].

[1] Hizo *improve* mucho.
'She's much improved.'

The convention will be followed of listing the ML first when examples are labelled; in regard to data quoted from others, however, ML assignment is tentative, since I can base it only on the information available, typically examples one sentence in length. Linguistic material from the EL will be italicized.

Einar Haugen, a giant in the field of language contact and bilingualism from the 1950s, had earlier been very clear in asserting that single lexemes might be considered CS forms. In an overview of bilingualism and language contact in the United States (1973: 521), he reaffirms his earlier use of the term CS

to refer to the alternate use of two languages including everything from the introduction of a single, unassimilated word up to a complete sentence or more into the context of another language.

But while his definition clearly includes single lexemes, the sticking point is *unassimilated*. Assimilation, of course, was mentioned as a gate-keeper because of the erroneous view that (full) integration of borrowed forms into the recipient language is nearly categorical; therefore, it was believed CS could be distinguished from borrowing by its degree of non-assimilation. The fact that assimilation is rarely so complete (and sometimes hardly existent) is never considered. (An example of a relatively unassimilated borrowing in English from French is *rendez-vous* [rɛnde vu].) Further, why should assimilation be *the* defining criterion separating CS and borrowing, anyway? These issues are discussed in Chapter 6 when CS is compared with borrowing.

Rather than dismiss single lexemes out of hand, some early researchers did attempt to appraise single lexemes as possible CS forms, using assimilation as a criterion. But many either treated assimilation as a holistic phenomenon or, if they recognized different types of assimilation, still proceeded as if each type were an all-or-nothing phenomenon. That is, a form showing *any* phonological integration was considered a borrowed form, even if this integration was only partial.

Several prominent early studies, particularly Pfaff (1979) and Poplack (1980; 1981), seriously consider the CS versus borrowing question. Pfaff does not resolve the issue of separating the two, while Poplack's definition of CS material becomes increasingly narrow, although still not absolute. Her work has been influential in the distinctions many other researchers made between CS and borrowing, especially in the 1980s.

In her 1980 paper, Poplack recognizes three types of integration (assimilation) which EL material might show in relation to the ML (phonological, morphological, and syntactic). Using Spanish/English CS examples, she considers four possible combinations of integration, suggesting that a lexeme may show any of three types of integration and still be considered a bona fide CS form. These are cases showing (1) only syntactic integration, (2) only phonological integration, or (3) no integration at all. The fourth possible type, that showing all three types of integration, constitutes borrowing. In the 1981 paper, however, Poplack seems to reserve the term *codeswitching* for those examples showing no integration of any type. At the same time, she does imply that there is something of a continuum, with complete adaption of EL forms to the ML at one end (i.e. borrowed forms); she goes on to say (1981: 170): 'At the other extreme is the complete lack of adaptation of patterns from one language to the patterns of the other, which I am calling *codeswitching* . . .'. She cites this example:

[2] You didn't have to worry *que* somebody *te iba a tirar con cerveza o una botella* or something like that.
'You didn't have to worry that somebody was going to throw beer or a bottle at you or something like that.'

(Spanish/English; Poplack, 1981: 170)

Note that Poplack's definition of CS does not rule out single-lexeme CS forms, even though it rules out CS forms showing any integration into the ML. And later in the article, she refers to the switching of certain types of single lexeme as also constituting CS, presumably because they show no integration into the recipient language. She writes (p. 171): 'Another type of codeswitching can be characterized by high proportions of what I call *noun switching*: switches of a single noun in an otherwise L1 utterance . . .'.

In more recent work, Poplack seems to qualify further her view of CS. In (1988*b*: 97), she defines 'unambiguous' CS forms as, 'multiword sequences, which remain lexically, syntactically, and morphologically unadapted to recipient language patterns'. This was at the same time as she and her associates introduced the category of 'nonce borrowings' (Poplack, Sankoff, and Miller, 1988). These are single lexemes/bound morphemes which are morphologically and syntactically integrated into the ML, but which show little phonological integration. Also, they do not meet the criteria of frequency (i.e. some recurrence) or acceptability (i.e. recognition by native speakers) typically satisfied by established borrowings. Further, they are always produced by bilinguals, never monolinguals, who often use established borrowings. Removing single lexemes from the CS playing-field simplifies the data to be explained under CS constraints, to be sure. For example, Poplack, Wheeler, and Westwood (1987) set aside (i.e. categorize as nonce borrowings) English nouns with Finnish case markings in discussing a corpus of Finnish/English CS. But, as will be argued in Chapter 6, I reject nonce borrowing as a motivated category and include most items so designated as CS forms.

Up until today, the CS versus borrowing problem has proved a thorny methodological bush, impeding efforts to assess the efficacy of any model of constraints. How does the model being evaluated treat singly occurring EL lexemes which are largely morphologically and syntactically incorporated into the ML? Sometimes this morphosyntactic integration means that such lexemes appear as bound forms, as least as far as the CS utterance is concerned (e.g. *suggest* in the Swahili/English CS utterance *ni-me-suggest* 'I have suggested', with *suggest* treated as a verb stem inflected with Swahili tense/aspect prefixes just as a Swahili-origin verb stem would be inflected).

In the 1970s and far into the 1980s, most researchers accepted the idea that only full constituents (or clauses or sentences) qualify as 'true' CS. Obviously, such structures represent the 'easiest' cases since they (largely) avoid the issue of assimilation/integration. Still, many researchers hedge (when it comes down to actual examples) on categorizing CS versus borrowed forms (e.g. Heath, 1989; Hill and Hill, 1986). Today, however, researchers increasingly reject 'nonce borrowing' as a resting-place out of harm's way for single lexemes which are not clearly established borrowings (e.g. Bokamba, 1988; Eliasson, 1989; 1991; Nortier, 1990; Scotton, 1988*b*; 1988*c*). Still, as recently as 1990, Poplack and her associates have made a case for nonce borrowing (Sankoff, Poplack, and Vanniarajan, 1990).

What makes disagreements as to how to treat singly occurring EL lexemes especially unfortunate is that many researchers, whose arguments seemingly are intended to cover all CS between a given language pair, do not make clear how they are classifying EL single lexemes. Or, they circumvent the issue by employing alternative terminologies: the proposals of some researchers that the term 'code-mixing' (CM) be used, either alongside the term 'codeswitching' or to cover everything called

CS data here, seems so motivated. For example, Kachru (1978) and his associates prefer CM as a term for any intrasentential switching which includes many EL single lexemes, but also seem to use it in some cases for phrases and constitutents. Others also (e.g. Swigart, 1992) use CM to label conversations containing much intrasentential switching. It seems that these researchers are not willing to label as borrowed forms all singly occurring EL forms, so 'code-mixing' becomes a compromise designation. I suggest, however, that the use of both terms, CM *and* CS, only creates unnecessary confusion.[2]

Early Proposals for Structural Constraints

Through the 1970s and into the mid-1980s, one after another, various 'local-solution' constraints were proposed by CS researchers. Most seem to have an inductive motivation; that is, they represent conclusions arising from applying a classificatory discovery procedure to a data set, and they are presented with no suggestion of independent motivations from other sources. Also, their perspective is linear; that is, they apply to an unprincipled set of form classes (e.g. tags can be easily switched, clitic pronouns cannot) or to linear ordering (e.g. juxtaposed ML and EL material must be compatible according to the syntax of both languages). Finally, and perhaps most importantly, the early constraints are descriptive, not theoretical; that is, they stand as descriptive statements unrelated to any larger formulation of linguistic phenomena. Therefore, while they may *account* for a specific data set, in no way do they *explain* it.

Not all constraints will be discussed. Those which have generated the most discussion and which relate to the MLF model are the main ones presented. A few others are mentioned, to give a flavour of the investigation. For a more thorough survey of the literature of the 1970s and 1980s on constraints, see Bokamba (1987) and Clyne (1987).

---

[2] Bokamba (1988: 24) argues : 'The distinction between CM and CS, as Sridhar and Sridhar (1980) correctly point out, is not merely convenient, but *necessary* because the two phenomena make different linguistic and psycholinguistic claims. For example, CS does not require the integration of the rules of the two languages involved in the discourse, whereas CM does.' I can agree with Bokamba that intrasentential CS makes different demands from intersentential CS. But CS, as he defines it, includes intrasentential forms as well as intersentential ones. As he defines them, the difference between CS and CM is that CS also includes full sentences (i.e. intersentential CS) and CM also includes bound morphemes. Otherwise, they cover the same forms. Forms showing bound morphemes require no special treatment under the MLF model (cf. Ch. 4); the ML hypothesis and its two principles must hold, but this is the case for *all* intrasentential CS from my point of view.

Some constraints are very specific. For example, Timm (1975) proposes five constraints on the types of construction or form class which can undergo CS, based on a Spanish/English corpus. She argues that switching does *not* occur between pronominal subjects and the finite verbs to which they belong, between finite verbs and their infinitive complements, between a verb and its auxiliary, between verbs and a negating element, and in most NPs containing nouns and modifying adjectives.

Constraints on pronoun-switching have attracted attention from others. Also arguing from Spanish/English data, several other researchers (Wentz and McClure 1976; Pfaff, 1979) narrow Timm's proposed constraint on switches between pronominals and finite verbs to clitic pronouns. Pfaff's constraint (1979: 303) refers specifically to pronoun objects, claiming that they must be in the same language as the verb to which they are cliticized. Basing his argument on no single language pair, Gumperz (1982: 87) also proposed that switches between a subject NP and its predicate are possible, but unlikely if the subject is a lexical pronoun. The discussion of system morphemes in Chapter 5 will show how non-congruence between pronominals across languages may explain some of the occurrence restrictions noticed by these earlier researchers.

Because of his earlier prominence in studies on the social functions of CS, many later studies addressed themselves to testing Gumperz's claims. Like most researchers of this period, he bases his arguments on the experimental presentation of substitution frames to subjects, as well as on some naturally occurring data. He proposes a number of constraints, some very specific, such as that, while both co-ordinate and subordinate conjoined sentences can be switched, 'the conjunction always goes with the second switched phrase' (1982: 88).

Gumperz was among a number of researchers who suggests that constraints favour longer switches (i.e. the longer the switched stretch of material, the more natural the switch). Shaffer (1977: 268) offers two related constraints: switch boundaries correspond mostly to phrase structure boundaries; and the language of a phrase agrees with its head word. The idea that 'more is better' (at least in regard to promoting CS) is also expressed by Poplack (1981: 177): 'it appears that the higher the syntactic level of constituent, the greater the probability that it will be switched'.

Another constraint, necessarily informally stated, comes up often: the use of an EL word may 'trigger' a longer switched segment (developed e.g. by Clyne in a number of publications from 1967 onwards; also in McClure, 1981). (The Embedded Language Island-Trigger Hypothesis is discussed in Chapter 5; however, while a 'trigger' under that hypothesis also necessitates producing further EL words, the motivation for the claim seems different from that in earlier work.)

An issue, of course, is which EL word will be a trigger and which will not? The Embedded Language-Island Hypothesis makes specific predictions about its triggers. Clyne's conception of triggers is quite different. He suggests (e.g. 1987: 754–5) that triggers are often items of ambiguous affiliation. He has in mind words 'belonging' both to the ML and to the EL, such as words borrowed from one language to the other, bilingual homophones, proper nouns, and compromise forms (e.g. [kən] to cover Dutch [kan] and English [kæn] 'can'). Example [3] shows *is* as belonging to both German and English:

[3] Das is [ɪz] *taken round the coast here.*
'This [a route?] is taken round the coast here.'

(German/English; Clyne, 1982: 107)

Word-Order Equivalence: A Possible Constraint?

Late in the 1970s, four different researchers or research teams (see below) came up with similar proposals for a far-reaching constraint on CS. Three of these proposals were based exclusively on Spanish/English data. In general, the constraint inhibits or prevents CS in contexts with word order conflict between the ML and the EL. This idea has attracted a good deal of attention and many counter-examples in the literature; however, as recently as Poplack (1990), it has still been advanced as tenable.

First in print was Lipski (1977). Following a lengthy discussion of specific constraints for specific combinations and a strong form of a hypothesis calling for total surface syntactic equivalence between participating languages in CS, he concludes with this weaker version (p. 258), based on his Spanish/English data:

whereas the portion of a code-switched utterance that falls before the code-switch may indeed contain syntactically divergent elements, those portions falling after the switch must be essentially identical syntactically.

That is, syntactic differences may exist before the switch to English, but then the syntaxes of the two languages must be the same for the portion switched to English. He cites [4] as an illustration of an acceptable example under the constraint; i.e. the Spanish rendition of *she wanted to take mechanics* would show the same order.

[4] Tonces salio eso que *she wanted to take mechanics.*
'It turned out that she wanted to take mechanics.'

(Spanish/English; Lipski, 1977: 258)

Pfaff (1979) discusses a number of possible specific constraints regarding equivalence, such as this for nouns and adjectives (p. 306): 'Adjective/noun mixes must match the surface word order of both the language of the adjective and the language of the head noun.' And later, in a general summary of a number of constraints, she states (p. 314): 'Surface structures common to both languages are favored for switches . . .'.

About the same time, what was labelled 'the equivalence constraint' was introduced by Poplack and her associates (Poplack, 1980; 1981; Sankoff and Poplack, 1981). The equivalence constraint has this form in Poplack (1980: 586):

Code-switches will tend to occur at points in discourse where juxtaposition of L1 and L2 elements does not violate a syntactic rule of either language, i.e., at points around which the surface structures of the two languages map onto each other. According to this simple constraint, a switch is inhibited from occurring within a constituent generated by a rule from one language which is not shared by another.

Finally, Sridhar and Sridhar (1980: 412) produced their own constraint on linear ordering, restricting the point at which a CS constituent may begin, but allowing for the possibility that a constituent's internal structure differs from that of the 'host' language. Their database is Kannada/English CS. Their Dual-Structure Principle is as follows:

The internal structure of the guest constituent [EL constituent] need not conform to the constituent structure rules of the host language [ML], so long as its placement in the host sentence obeys the rules of the host language.

Counter-Examples Presented

It was the equivalence constraint which received the most attention, probably because it is both general and succinct. And Poplack and her associates should be credited as being very influential in setting standards for CS research, in striving for constraints which are at once general but also stated in such a form that it is clear what would constitute counter-examples to the predictions. They also championed the idea of basing claims on the quantitative analysis of large corpora, rather than on anecdotal examples. Some early research, especially on Spanish/English CS, is marred by limited data bases as well as by its methodology; researchers often relied on acceptability judgements of isolated sentences, not of naturally occurring data sets.

Of course, no matter how dazzling sophisticated statistical analyses of large data sets are, the proof is in the pudding. And a number of counter-examples to the equivalence constraint have been cited, starting with a diverse set of data from languages spoken in Africa. Nartey (1982) provides counter-examples not only to the equivalence constraint but also to its sister, the free-morpheme constraint, discussed below. Nartey uses Adaŋme/English data collected among a group of younger educated Ghanaians. (Adaŋme is a Kwa language spoken in south-eastern Ghana, with such better-known languages as Ewe as close relatives.) Counter-examples to the equivalence constraint include [5] and [6]. Adaŋme morpheme order is followed (SOV), and head-first NP (not English SVO and Adj + N in the NP).

[5] a   ŋe mĩ *help*-e
    3 PL COP me help-PRES PROG
  'They are helping me.'

[6] e   hé   *house red* ò [ɔ]
    he/she PAST tone buy house red ART
  'He/she bought the red house.'

(Adaŋme/English; Nartey, 1982: 185, 187)

(Even earlier, but in an unpublished doctoral dissertation, Forson (1979) cites data which constitute counter-examples from the Akan cluster of languages in Ghana. Some of these appear below and in Chapter 4 where they are cited to support claims of the MLF model.)

The Nairobi corpus of Swahili/English CS, which was introduced in Chapter 1, offers other African counter-examples, as those in [7] and [8]. There is a clash between Swahili and English order within the NP, with Swahili calling for a head-first NP and English requiring a head-last NP. In fact, these 'prohibited' examples occur in the Nairobi data corpus.

[7] Unaweza kumpata amevaa nguo   nyingine *bright* . . .
                              clothes other   bright
  'You can find her wearing other bright clothes . . .'

(Swahili/English, No. 17)[3]

---

[3] Numbers in citations such as these refer to conversations from the Nairobi corpus. This corpus will be described more fully in Ch. 3.

[8] Anaonekana kama ni   mtu   *innocent.*
             COP person innocent
'He looks like [he] is an innocent person.'

(Swahili/English, No. 11)

Bentahila and Davies (1983), who cite such examples as [9] from their Moroccan Arabic/French corpus, also provide many counter-examples. In Arabic, adjectives must follow their nouns; while this is true of most French adjectives, there are some others which must precede their nouns. The equivalence constraint would predict that a switch is only possible where an adjective follows a noun, since this is the only order common to both languages. Yet examples, such as [9] occur:

[9] j'ai vu un ancien *tilmid djali*
                    student of mine
'I saw an old student of mine.'

(French/Moroccan Arabic; Bentahila and Davies, 1983: 319)

Berk-Seligson (1986) also presents many violations of the equivalence constraint in a Spanish/Hebrew corpus of data both from immigrants to Israel and from persons born there. In both Spanish and Hebrew, the adjective usually follows the noun. However, Spanish *otro* 'another' is an exception, preceding the noun it modifies. Yet Berk-Seligson's corpus includes switching examples in the face of this non-equivalence (e.g. a Spanish noun followed by the Hebrew lexeme for 'another', *gwenga axeret* (language another) 'another language' (1986: 332)). This example violates Spanish constraints.

Numerous other counter-examples are cited in the recent literature (e.g. Bokamba, 1988 on Lingala/French and Swahili/English; Scotton, 1988*b* on Swahili/English). There are some dramatic examples, such as [10], which shows a noun and a modifying adjective following Swahili order for such NPs, not English order—even though in [10] both N and ADJ are English. Admittedly, however, there are only a handful of NPs following Swahili order when both elements are from English; still, they are not isolated cases, either.

[10] nikapata chakula nyingine iko *grey* ni- ka-   i-   *-taste* nikaona
                                          1S CONSEC OBJ CL 9

i-na   *taste lousy* sana
it with taste lousy very
'And I got some other food [that] was grey and I tasted it and I thought it had [was with] a very lousy taste.'

(Swahili/English, No. 16; also Scotton, 1988*b*: 74)

Example [11] shows a switch at the boundary between an English V′ (V + NP (primary) object) and a Hindi postpositional phrase (PP) which receives from the V the thematic role of beneficiary. The PP, of course, violates English syntax.

[11] *John gave a book* ek larakii ko
                        a   girl   to
'John gave a book to a girl.'

(Hindi/English; Pandit, 1990: 45)

The Free-Morpheme Constraint

Another constraint which has generated a good deal of discussion was also presented in Poplack (1980). Labelled the free-morpheme constraint, it takes this form:

> Codes may be switched after any constituent provided that constituent is not a bound morpheme. (Poplack, 1980: 585)

This constraint predicts that such forms as *burn* in [12] and *rub* in [13] would not occur as CS forms; as an alternative, the constraint assigns *burn* in [12] and *rub* in [13] to the category of borrowings (whether nonce or established).

[12] Hapa *flame* hiyo inaenda juu—haiwezi ku- -ku- *-burn*.
                                          INFIN 2S OBJ
'The flame is going upwards, it can't burn you.'

(Swahili/English, No. 19)

[13] . . . Nikaisafisha na maji moto, ni- -ka-   -i-   *-rub* na kitambaa.
                                      1S CONSEC CL 9 OBJ rub
'And I washed it with hot water and then I rubbed it with a cloth.'

(Swahili/English, No. 39)

Note: The convention will be followed of presenting what would be free-form morphemes in English as bound morphemes when they occur in CS utterances and are inflected with bound affixes (e.g. *-burn* and *-rub* above). That is, they will be presented preceded by a hyphen. Also, any inflectional prefixes which are preceded by another prefix will be presented with hyphens on either side.

Effectively, the free-morpheme constraint disallows as CS forms *any* morphemes which are morphologically integrated into the ML. Many researchers in the 1980s, especially those more concerned with language contact phenomena in general than with the issue of CS constraints in particular, have accepted the constraint. That is, they reserve the designation of CS for passages entirely in the EL material ('EL islands' in my terminology); EL material occurring with bound forms from the ML is grouped with borrowings. A reason for accepting the free-morpheme constraint is that far fewer counter-examples to it have been cited in the CS literature than is the case with the equivalence constraint. For example, while Berk-Seligson (1986) reports many violations of the equivalence constraint in her data (Spanish/Hebrew), she finds only one or two counter-examples to the free-morpheme constraint. The same is the case with Bentahila and Davies (1983) for their Moroccan Arabic/French corpus. However, in Bentahila and Davies (1992) they report a number of counter-examples consisting of French verb stems inflected with Arabic affixes (cf. [15] below).

That there are few violations means that there are few instances in their corpora of lexical items consisting of morphemes from both the ML and the EL. In other data sets, however, such counter-examples to the free-morpheme constraint are not hard to find.

It happens that many of these counter-examples showing intraword switches come from agglutinative languages. Researchers on Bantu languages especially have come forward with counter-examples (e.g. Bokamba, 1988; Scotton, 1988*b*; Myers-Scotton, 1989; Kamwangamalu, 1989*b*). In addition, Eliasson (1989), who also argues against the free-morpheme constraint, uses data from Maori/English, and Maori is an agglutinative language as well.

In fact, it does seem to be the case that agglutinative languages are better suited to generating new words than other languages (Levelt, 1989). Hankamer (1989) makes this argument for Turkish, another agglutinative language, speaking against various Full-Listing Hypotheses from language production researchers. Basically, such hypotheses claim that a lexical entry includes representations of morphological structure so that affixed forms of the entry are accessed via the entry for the root. Of course in certain agglutinative languages, words consist of roots plus many affixes.

Hankamer's point is that the enormous number of 'new' words which can be formed from one Turkish root and a stock of affixes points to the necessary independence of affixes from the root in the language's mental lexicon. He reports (p. 403) that, when Turkish morphotactics are incorporated into a generator programme which counts all forms generated from one root in accord with morphotactics, results show that a single Turkish noun root can appear in more than 9 million different forms. This figure even discounts recursions—that is, patterns produced by reapplications of a rule. And even though most of the forms are never used, they will be recognized as words.

This state of affairs suggests to Levelt (1989) that different types of languages may have different types of lexical entry in a mental lexicon. He hypothesizes that affixes have a separate lexical entry from stems for the Turkish speaker. 'The stored forms in his mental lexicon will probably consist of all stems (such as *ev* for "house"), all possible affixes, and a certain number of frequently used multimorphemic words' (pp. 185–6). In contrast, Levelt suggests, English is at the other extreme. English speakers use words they have probably used before, and these are stored in their mental lexicon as full words (i.e. not as stems and affixes). Of course the same would hold for other typologically similar languages, such as German or French.[4]

If the mental lexicon for a speaker of an agglutinative language consists of stems and affixes, it is an easy step to argue that speakers with such representations have the potential to combine a stem from one language with an affix from another. That is, a CS form might be 'just another word' for such speakers. After all, what is a lexical item consisting of morphemes from both the ML and the EL which also meets the usual requirements of a CS form (i.e. shows no 'recurrence value', spoken by a bilingual) if not a new word? And such CS forms are reported relatively frequently for CS corpora from agglutinative languages. (For example, there are 91 instances (all tokens) of inflected verb forms showing inflectional morphemes from the ML (Swahili) and a verb stem from the EL (English) in the Nairobi corpus discussed in more detail in Chapter 4. Clearly, these are not so few that they can be dismissed as aberrant, even in a variationist-sociolinguist's net.

How Important Are Typological Factors?

This state of affairs has led some researchers to attempt to salvage the free-morpheme constraint by suggesting that it still holds, but only for languages with certain typological features (i.e. non-agglutinative ones). But this suggestion is misguided: a fuller examination of the CS literature reveals numerous counter-examples in non-agglutinative languages. For example, the Ghanaian language, Adaŋme, cited above, is highly analytic, if not isolating, in its typology; yet [5] (showing Adaŋme/English CS) constitutes a violation of the free-morpheme constraint. There are also

---

[4] I thank Georges Lüdi for this observation.

counter-examples in the literature from pairs including inflectional languages (e.g. Petersen, 1988 on English/Danish; Enninger, 1980 on Pennsylvania German/English; and various languages from the Indian subcontinent), as well as relatively analytic languages such as the language in [18] from the Akan cluster in Ghana. A number of counter-examples follow, with only one, [17], involving an agglutinative language, Chiluba, a Bantu language of Zaïre.

[14*a*] I'm *lav*-ing *pandekege*-s
'I'm having pancakes.'

[14*b*] *bor*-s 'live-s' (verb + PRES)

[14*c*] *vask*-ing 'washing' (verb + PART)

(English/Danish; Petersen, 1988: 481, 483)

[15] . . . hija lli ta- t-   *sécréter*-na   *les hormones* . . .[5]
                   DUR -3SF/SUBJ-secrete-1PLF/OBJ
'. . . it's that which secretes for us the hormones . . .'

(Moroccan Arabic/French; Bentahila and Davies, 1992: 450)

[16] Ellaam   *confused*-aa   irundadu
     everything confused-ADV COP PAST
'Everything was confused.'

(Tamil/English; Annamalai, 1989: 50)

[17] Ba-aka-*rendr*-agan-a   *visites* ya bungi *quand elle était ici.*
     3PL-HABIT-return-RECIPR-INDIC
'They visited each other a lot when she was here.'

(Chiluba/French; Kamwangamalu 1989*b*: 166)

[18] wó- -rè- [-sɔ spɛ nd] no sɛ́   w--ǎ- -ỳɛ dɛ́ǹ
     2S PROG suspend   3OBJ COMP 3S PERF do what
'Why are you suspending him?'

(Akuapem/English; Forson, 1979: 158)

Poplack formulated the free-morpheme constraint based on Spanish/English CS data. But even Spanish/English counter-examples, with the same configurations as Poplack's original example of a prohibited form under the free-morpheme constraint, appear in naturally occurring conversations. Poplack (1980: 586) cites (19) as starred:

[19] **eat*-iendo
'eating'

---

[5] Note that the French verb is in its infinitival form, *sécrét-er*. This is evidence (albeit only suggestive) that French verbs may be entered in the mental lexicon with the infinitival suffix.

But Walters (1989), who has been working on Spanish/English CS, finds such sentences as [20*a*],

[20*a*] El agua está *boil*-ando.
'The water is boiling.'

He also notes acceptable variants of [20*a*]:

[20*b*] The *water* está *boil*-ando.
[20*b*] La *water* está *boil*-ando.

As I will argue in later chapters, the key to acceptability is not whether a switch of languages may follow a bound morpheme (as the free-morpheme constraint proposes) but rather the *source* of the bound morpheme in question. As I will suggest, what I refer to as system morphemes (i.e. mainly inflections and function words) must come from the ML when they occur in constituents consisting of morphemes from both the ML and the EL. That is, EL bound morphemes, such as -*ait* 'third person past' in [17], occur in CS utterances only in a permissible EL island, a constituent entirely in the EL. (Recall from [17] *quand elle était ici* 'when she was here'.) Also, *the water* in [20*b*] is an EL island: it contains the determiner *the*, which is a system morpheme.

These examples mean that both the bound: free distinction and typological distinctions are basically irrelevant for permissible intraword switching sites.

Summary of Earlier Constraints

A review of data presented in current CS literature shows that there are good reasons to reject all the earlier constraints noted above as generally applicable. Some of the more specific constraints may be supported for specific language pairs (e.g. no switching between clitic pronominal subjects and the finite verbs to which they belong).

If the claim is that the constraints are general (and this is certainly implied even when it is not explicitly stated), they must be rejected for two reasons. First, the counter-examples are not so few that they can be attributed to part of the natural variation inherent in any speech community. Second, because they come from such typologically diverse languages, the counter-examples cannot be ascribed to typological differences among languages, at least those differences based on word composition. In Chapters 4 and 5 I discuss more fully why the equivalence constraint (and therefore also the Dual-Structure Principle, its weaker version) as well as the free-morpheme constraint appear to be too powerful, and why principles derived from the MLF model predict CS data more accurately and are better motivated. However, I also discuss how the MLF model's principles clearly build on the earlier constraints. That is, most of the ideas incorporated in the MLF model were stated in one form or another in earlier studies, whether as actual constraints or just observations. But they were never organized to produce a principled, independently motivated model.

Proposals for Non-Local Constraints

More recently, at least three types of proposals from a different perspective have received attention. They depart from earlier works in not focusing their attention on the point of transition between the ML and EL.

The first group has these new features: it attaches importance to an asymmetry between the two languages involved in CS, and it views production and processing as the key to structure. Such ideas were first systematically stated by Joshi (1985), who took Garrett's (1975) analysis of speech errors as his motivation for suggesting that 'closed-class items' (approximating system morphemes) come only from the ML. Joshi also emphasized a left-to-right organization in CS.

The MLF model developed in Chapters 4 and 5 starts with the same premiss regarding differential accessing of morphemes. Both the MLF model (including its antecedent, the Frame-Process Model of Myers-Scotton and Azuma, 1990, and also Azuma, 1991*a*; 1991*b*) follow Joshi in applying Garrett's (1975) ideas about how language production is organized to how the different participating languages are accessed in CS production.

Recognizing Asymmetry

Joshi offers two insights. First, he suggests that CS is characterized by a basic asymmetry regarding the participation of the languages involved. He bases this idea on the observation that

> speakers and hearers generally agree on which language the mixed sentence is 'coming from'. We can call this language the *matrix language* and the other language the *embedded language*. (1985: 190–1)

Joshi then makes his idea of asymmetry more specific by arguing that the *direction* of switching is asymmetrical; that is, 'switching a category of the matrix grammar to a category of the embedded grammar is permitted, but not vice versa' (p. 192).

Note that this 'asymmetry rule' implies that constituents are first formulated or even accessed in the matrix language and then somehow switched to the embedded language. At the same time, Joshi also states that the two language systems are simultaneously active (p. 190). While I support the notion of asymmetry between the ML and EL, I conceptualize it differently. First, there is no switching of categories at all in the MLF model, but rather a switching of procedures from those of the ML to the EL. This happens only when EL islands are formed. Second, there is no obvious motivation to restrict the *direction* of inhibition and activation of procedures. It will turn out that there are restrictions, but based on more abstract, grammatical principles than 'direction'. They are contained in the EL Island Trigger Hypothesis (discussed in Chapter 5). And third, the MLF model assumes that the two language systems are *not* equally active at the same time; in fact, EL islands only result when the ML system is inhibited.

Joshi's second major insight is to suggest that, while all major categories such as N can be switched, closed class items cannot. His final statement of this constraint is as follows:

> Closed class items (e.g. *determiners, quantifiers, prepositions, possessive, Aux, Tense, helping verbs*, etc.) cannot be switched.   (1985: 194)

In formulating this constraint, Joshi notes evidence from psycholinguistic and neurolinguistic studies. These studies show the differential behaviour of closed-class and open-class items in some speech errors, and the absence of closed-class items in certain types of aphasia. Although Joshi gives no details and makes no further comment, he concludes:

> I believe, however, investigating this relationship may give some clues concerning the organization of the grammar and the lexicon, and the nature of the interface between the two language systems.   (p. 191)

As will become clear, the MLF model relies especially heavily for its motivation on psycholinguistic studies dealing with the relation between speech errors and language production; these matters will be discussed in detail below.

Joshi's perceptiveness regarding asymmetry between the role of the ML and the EL, as well as that between open- and closed-class items, is very striking. Few other researchers explicitly notice these related differences, even today, and no others did at all until several more years passed.

However, in a paper presented in 1986 (published in 1988), Petersen arrives at the conclusion that one language is more dominant than the other in supplying all grammatical morphemes. Writing only about word-internal CS, she notes that, in contrast to the non-dominant language, 'grammatical morphemes of the dominant language may cooccur with lexical morphemes of either the dominant or the nondominant language' (p. 486). Petersen apparently had no knowledge of either Garrett's or Joshi's work.

While Joshi's general insights seem correct, their application to his Marathi/English data is sketchy. He says nothing about the exact membership of closed-class items. He makes a number of unmotivated statements about other restrictions (e.g. 'It is also not possible to switch the entire VP' (1985: 194)) which are not supported by other data sets. Also, a number of his other claims receive no support from other data sets (e.g. that complementizers are closed-class items and therefore cannot be switched at all; they *are* closed-class (i.e. system) morphemes, but they may head EL islands for some language pairs, showing they can be switched).[6] While the notion of differentiating ML and EL is crucial for Joshi, he achieves this differentiation only by relying on speakers' judgements about where the sentence is 'coming from'. He does not consider all types of CS, dealing only with constituents with both ML and EL material and ignoring 'islands' of either ML or EL material. Also, there is a curious early claim in his paper, which is not further developed, to the effect that the 'Root node [Sm] cannot be switched' (1985: 193; [Sm] seems to stand for 'sentence' in the matrix language), also noted and criticized by Pandit (1990: 48). Exactly what is intended is hard to fathom, since certainly an entire S can appear in the EL (as an EL island). Finally, the claim about asymmetrical directionality mentioned above is not supported.

Pandit (1990: 50–1) also gives a number of counter-examples to Joshi's claim that closed-class items cannot be switched. However, I will argue in Chapter 5 that most (perhaps all) of Pandit's counter-examples may be explained in terms of claims about system versus content morphemes and congruency between the languages involved in CS. Further, I will claim that the same categories are not necessarily system morphemes across

---

[6] e.g. Bokamba (1987: 39) points out that the Romance languages' complementizer *que* can occur in Kinshasa Lingala in structures where either the main or the subordinate clause is either in French or Lingala. Note that, at least for Lingala/French CS, *que* may be considered a borrowed form in Lingala, as I will argue in Ch. 6. See also the discussion in Ch. 5 of complementizers in general.

languages, and that the informally defined class 'closed-class items' is not entirely isomorphic to system morphemes. Also, some of Pandit's examples may represent a type of marked choice for a special effect and, therefore, may not be true counter-examples.

A Model Derived from Joshi's Claims

In a related paper, Doron (1983) makes some similar suggestions to those of Joshi, referring frequently to an unpublished paper (Joshi, 1981). But Doron emphasizes aspects of Joshi's claims other than those I develop in the MLF model. She is more interested in parsing, arguing for further development of what she calls 'the Left-Corner Constraint'. Rather than state restrictions on switching in terms of such generalizable hierarchical relationships as open-class/closed-class items, she makes an argument based on left-to-right parsing.

Her relevant generalization ('switches are not allowed on leftmost daughter nodes' (1983: 43)) is presumably intended to prevent specifiers (as closed-class items) from switching. But the generalization fails because Specifier is not fixed in position with respect to head direction. In head-first languages, the closed-class items will not necessarily be in the leftmost daughter node. (And even for head-last languages with Specifier to the left, the reason switches are not allowed on the leftmost daughter nodes, I will argue, is not because they are leftmost, but for reasons more generally stated by the Morpheme-Order and the System Morpheme Principles of the MFL model.) Another parsing strategy Doron discusses, the Early Determination Strategy ('the parser seeks to determine as early as possible the language of the major constituent it is currently parsing', 1983: 46), has no predictability, as she states it. But at the same time the discussion accompanying this strategy implies that Doron has in mind a 'setting of the frame' regarding morpheme choice (between closed- and open-class items) similar to that in the MLF model.

Subcategorization Restrictions: A Solution?

While Doron's ideas regarding left-to-right processing seem to lack support, she is to be credited with recognizing that clashes in subcategorization may underlie inadmissible switches. Such arguments are contained in a second group of studies offering a non-linear approach to CS constraints. Doron writes (1983: 50):

I am suggesting that what blocks switches such as (22b) [i.e. *seven *chiquitas* houses 'seven small houses', English/Spanish] are not considerations about differences of the order of constituents . . . but considerations about agreement. The fact that word-order is not the only thing that distinguishes grammars of different languages seem to be neglected . . .

About the same time as Doron was writing, Bentahila and Davies (1983: 329) also raised the subcategorization issue, concluding their discussion of Moroccan Arabic/French CS by stating that 'all items must be used in such a way as to satisfy the [language-particular] subcategorisation restrictions imposed on them'. In many ways, Bentahila and Davies were ahead of their time in the insights expressed in this paper. That is, they were among the first researchers to recognize (in print) problems with the Equivalence Constraint, and they saw at least 'some fairly clear tendencies for the two languages to fulfil rather different functions within structures exhibiting switching' (p. 326). However, one of their major conclusions ('switching is freely permitted at all boundaries above that of the word, subject only to the condition that it entails no violation of the subcategorisation restrictions on particular lexical items of either language', p. 329) cannot be supported by other data sets. As will be shown, there is extensive evidence that the frame set by the ML for ML + EL constituents imposes definite restrictions on switchability.

Much more recently, suggestions that lexically based subcategorization rules explain why some switches are not permitted also figure prominently in Muysken (1990; 1991) and Azuma (1991*b*). For example, Azuma (1991*b*: 7) suggests that 'the subcategorization of the main verb is always preserved', going on to state that 'the main verb provides a planning frame . . . content word insertion must be done within the specifications of the planning frame'.

Muysken (1991: 266) suggests that the equivalence constraint can be saved if it is combined with the notion of 'categorical equivalence' in a government-based theory. He does not elaborate, so it is not clear what he has in mind; however, his notion seems somewhat similar to the congruence-based constraints proposed in the MLF model (Myers-Scotton, 1991*a*; 1991*b*; and this volume). Further, while he points out examples of what would be considered 'problem-areas in categorial equivalence' for language pairs involved in CS, he does not seem to see any factor or factors *unifying* constraints in CS data. The 'problem-areas' he mentions are: full pronouns versus clitics, auxiliaries versus main verbs, predicate adjectives versus stative verbs, clauses versus nominalizations, and cases versus adpositions. He takes a typological approach, citing the language groups for which these contrasts would cause problems, but offering no details (p. 266).

The MLF model explains similar problems with constraints which are more specific than reference only to 'subcategorization' or 'equivalence', but which are more general than reference to the requirements of any specific category, such as the main verb. Also, the MLF model is able to relate constraints based on subcategorization to other constraints holding in the CS utterance, but with a different basis. The model does this by locating the solution to the constraints question in three types of congruence between the ML and the EL, most prominently congruence in regard to thematic role-assigning and in the related system/content morpheme distinction. This matter is discussed in more detail in Chapter 5, when the Blocking Hypothesis is discussed.

Do Government and Binding Principles Explain CS?

The third group of studies offering a non-linear approach to CS constraints includes Woolford (1983), DiSciullo, Muysken, and Singh (1986), and Pandit (1990). They seek to explain CS phenomena in relation to constituent structures licensed under the syntactic theory of government and binding (GB). While each proposal accounts for the example sentences it cites, and has the attraction of relating CS constraints to a larger theory of language, all are ultimately unsuccessful because many counter-examples immediately present themselves.

Woolford's proposal is couched in terms of GB, but, in fact, her main claim is essentially the same as that of the equivalence constraint. When there is an overlap in syntactic structural specifications between the two languages, speakers may draw lexical items freely from either language. But when a phrase structure rule unique to language x is in place, then only language-x lexical items may fill the terminal nodes; the same applies when a rule from language y is in force. That is, Woolford claims that, in areas other than overlap, the language to which the phrase structure is unique is the only one from which lexical items may be drawn.

She claims that the model of Spanish/English CS she develops supports two assumptions of Chomsky's 1981 formulation of GB, the constituent structure of NPs under X-bar theory,[7] and lexical projection of portions of the constituent structure under VP.

---

[7] X-bar theory, of course, seeks to capture what is common between the structure of different phrases by specifying that all phrases are headed by a lexical head. The layered notational scheme of this theory links nodes in the same hierarchical projection of a lexical head with the symbol X (where X can equal N or V, etc.) followed by other Xs with progressively fewer numbers of 'bars', with the topmost node having the most bars.

In regard to NPs, Woolford states that there is empirical evidence that no switching occurs in Spanish/English CS between a noun and a following modifying adjective; that is, both noun and adjective must be in Spanish. Woolford argues that GB theory would predict no switching between a noun and a following, modifying adjective since they are elements under N'. However, DET is in another node in the NP, according to GB; and since the phrase-structure rule that expands an NP into a determiner + N' is common to both languages, she claims DET can be filled from either lexicon. (Since DET is a closed class-item, or a system morpheme in my terminology, I will argue in Chapter 4 against this claim that either language can fill this node, as part of my discussion of the System Morpheme Principle.) She also argues that, since Spanish alone has the rule N' → N A, the nodes this rule creates can only be filled from the Spanish lexicon. (This rule means that the node headed by N (noun) can be rewritten as N followed by A (adjective); such an order for nouns and adjectives is generally not possible in English, of course.) Thus, this is a restriction on lexical insertion in non-branching nodes compatible with GB theory, Woolford argues. Counter-examples to this claim are discussed below.

She also proposes to explain the inadmissibility of a clitic object pronoun in English with a Spanish verb, while accounting for the possible presence of an English adverb in an otherwise Spanish utterance. She argues the VP node is expanded by a general X-bar-type phrase-structure rule common to both languages, thus allowing a node in the sentence structure, such as that for an adverbial phrase, to be filled from either language. However, the necessity of having only Spanish for a pre-verbal object pronoun clitic can be explained by claiming it results from a subcategorization frame unique to Spanish (i.e. the lexically projected construction could be a verb and an associated clitic). This latter argument is more theoretically interesting and better supported by empirical evidence than her other claims. It is similar in spirit to the position of those scholars mentioned above who are seeking to base constraints on subcategorization clashes.

Overall, however, there are a number of problems with Woolford's analysis. First is her claim about the possibility of filling nodes created on the basis of a shared phrase-structure rule with items from either lexicon. It has no independent motivation, and there are many counter-examples from other data sets on a number of grounds. My discussion of constraints on system-morpheme assignment in Chapter 4 is a strong argument against such 'freedom of lexical choice'.

Second, the claim that an expansion rule which is unique to one of the languages must be filled from that language's lexicon simply does not hold. See the examples above cited as counter-examples to the equivalence constraint, in which a head-first language accommodates an adjectival modifier from a head-last language (e.g. [6] from Adaŋme/English and [7] and [8] from Swahili/English). Pandit (1990) cites another excellent example from Hindi/English CS. He notes that the verb governs to the left in Hindi and to the right in English. Still, CS can take place in the VP and in the PP. He gives this example, showing CS in the VP (the English NP *traditional Indian women* plus the Hindi Suffix for accusative case are governed by the Hindi verb):

[21] *Some Englishmen traditional Indian women*-ko   passand karaten hain.
                                        ACCUS like   do   are
'Some Englishmen like traditional Indian women.'

(Hindi/English; Pandit, 1990: 44)

No CS Within a Maximal Projection?

DiSciullo, Muysken, and Singh (1986) make a more principled argument, claiming that the process of intrasentential switching is constrained by the government relation holding between sentence constituents; Pandit (1990) makes a similar claim. (Note that DiSciullo *et al.* refer to intrasentential switching as code-mixing.)

The key claim in this model is that, within a maximal projection, no switch is allowed. (A maximal projection, of course, is the highest projection of a category, such as N or V, meaning that such a projection constitutes a full projection—e.g. a full NP or VP.) However, DiSciullo *et al.* begin by arguing against the equivalence constraint, especially for its theoretical inadequacies. Also, they point out that it 'over-predicts' in the case of French/Italian CS in Montreal and 'under-predicts' for Hindi/English CS. They also note that Woolford's main proposal basically resembles that of the equivalence constraint.

Instead, they claim, constraints on CS can be handled parsimoniously under a government principle, or at least that, among constraints, it is 'the only universally applicable one' (1986: 4). They claim that a government principle will account for the data. They base this on their data showing (*a*) possible switching between verbs and subjects, but none between verbs and objects, and (*b*) differences in behaviour of complementizers (which may be in a different language from their sister S) and conjunctions (which must be in the same language as the constituent they conjoin to something else).

DiSciullo *et al.* redefine government, but in a rather non-controversial way: *X* governs *Y* if the first node dominating *X* also dominates *Y*, where *X* is a major category N, V, A, P and no maximal boundary intervenes between *X* and *Y*. Basically what they argue is this: 'if *X* has language index *q* and if it governs *Y*, *Y* must have language index *q* also' (1986: 5). (Their definition is not particularly clear, since it is formulated to prevent switches between V and Det of NP; however, Det is dominated by NP, a maximal projection, which intervenes.)

Their claim is that the lexical governor and a governed maximal projection must be in the same language. They go on to say, 'Whenever the syntagmatic coherence principle of government does not hold, the lexical elements may be drawn from different lexicons' (1986: 7–8).

The problem is that there are many counter-examples to this claim. For example, on the basis of Panjabi/English data, Romaine argues that switching between V and its NP constituent is possible. She discusses at length compound-verb constructions containing a Panjabi 'operator verb' (*kərna* 'to do', for example). Another example Romaine cites to support her argument is [22], with the 'operator verb' *honda*.

[22] *Parents* te *depend* honda   [ε]
            on   be/become AUX
'It depends on the parents.'

(Panjabi/English; Romaine, 1989: 124)

She writes (p. 130):

it appears that we must recognize that the boundary between V and NP is a permissible site for code-switching. Constructions such as *time waste kərna* and *exams pass kərna* do not have any special syntactic or semantic status in bilingual discourse. Assuming, too, that there are ordering restrictions governing the internal constituency of X under V, if we allowed *exams pass* to function as a unit, it would violate English word order. If we allow it to serve as the preceding object complement, Panjabi word order constraints are preserved.

Pandit (1990: 52) also argues against the proposal of DiSciullo *et al.* He cites examples of switching between V and NP, such as [21], and also within a PP, such as [23].

[23] *Of all the places John has hidden* kuch *books bathroom* men
                                       some   in
'Of all the places, John has hidden some books in the bathroom.'

(Hindi/English; Pandit, 1990: 53)

Pandit points out that both the specifier of the object NP *kuch books* as well as the postposition of the subcategorized PP *bathroom men* are in Hindi, while the governing verb is in English. *Kuch books* should have been all in English, according to DiSciullo *et al.*, but not necessarily *bathroom men*. *Bathroom* should have been in Hindi, since its postposition is in Hindi, and the postposition should govern its complement in that maximal projection, according to their analysis.

The Nairobi Swahili/English corpus also offers numerous counter-examples to the constraint against switches between a governor and its governed nodes. For example, even if likely borrowings are eliminated there are still approximately 100 examples of NP complements in English in a Swahili VP; in fact, this clearly is the most common site for CS forms. Two examples follow. In [24] the NP *a lot of nonsense* has as its governor the Swahili verb *ulikuwa ukiongea* 'you were speaking'. And in [25] the English noun *jokes* is governed by the Swahili infinitive *kuleta* 'to bring'.

[24] Wewe ulikuwa mlevi sana jana. Karibu mkosane na kila mtu. Ulikuwa ukiongea *a lot of nonsense*.
'You were very drunk yesterday. That you should almost make a fool of yourself with every person. You were talking a lot of nonsense.'

[23] Kwetu sisi mtu hawezi kuleta *jokes* kama hizo . . .
'At our place, a person can't bring jokes like these ones . . .'

(Swahili/English; Nairobi corpus, Nos. 21, 24)

Another GB-Based Approach

While Pandit (1990) provides telling criticisms of earlier proposals, from the idea of 'nonce borrowings' to the proposals of DiSciullo *et al.* (1986), he himself says little about an alternative. He does offer this proposal (p. 43):

Code switching must not violate the grammar of the head of the maximal projection within which it takes place.

Pandit claims this follows from the more general principle that 'the grammar of the head of a maximal projection obtains in a maximal projection'. Exactly what is intended about CS is not clear. As I will argue in Chapters 4 and 5, CS within a maximal projection is certainly possible, as long as it meets ML specifications of morpheme order and also system morpheme assignment.

Why GB Theory Alone Does Not Explain CS

The problem with these proposals based on GB theory is that they are operating at a level which is too 'purely syntactic', or too close to the surface. All approach permissible arrangements of items using a level of analysis where relatively low-order phrase structure is involved. I will argue that CS constraints come into play at a much more abstract level, which is presyntactic in that it involves such issues as form class membership and the specific subcategorization constraints this membership entails, not just 'subcategorization' in some general sense. Clues about possible constraints come from looking at models of how language is accessed and retrieved *before* it takes its final surface form. These models of language production will be discussed in the next chapter.

Conclusion

If the constraints question were put in 'language production' jargon, it would be: what mechanisms support the retrieval, directed by lemmas in the speaker's mental lexicon, of some morphemes from the ML, but some from the EL during normal, continuous speech? It has been shown that the earliest theories concerning constraints on CS were based on examination of the juxtaposition of ML and EL elements or the susceptibility of specific form classes to CS. Later, others tried to reach the answer by placing CS under constraints similar to those which GB syntactic theory posits for monolingual syntactic structures.

A review of the major proposals shows that they do not answer the question, as posed, very successfully. The proposal which comes the closest to succeeding (Joshi, 1985) starts from a quite different perspective, by sketching a hypothesis from the standpoint of the production process. This line is also pursued by my associate, Shoji Azuma, and myself in formulating a CS model; Azuma's model, however, takes a somewhat different tack from the MLF model. My version of such a model will be presented in Chapters 4 and 5 as the MLF model.

3
Background for the Matrix Language-Frame Model: Production Models and Identifying the Matrix Language

Introduction

This chapter has two purposes. First, it develops independent motivation for the major arguments of the Matrix Language-Frame model to be presented in Chapters 4 and 5. Such motivation comes from psycholinguistic research on several fronts, but especially from research on speech errors as it relates to language production models. Additional motivation comes from studies of patients with certain types of aphasia. Both these sources show a difference in the way closed-class and open-class morphemes (i.e. system versus content morphemes) are accessed in monolingual speech production. Finally, other psycholinguistic studies on bilingual speech offer further motivation for the MLF model.

Second, the chapter contains another preliminary to the MLF model: the identification of the matrix language (ML) as opposed to the embedded language (EL) in CS utterances is discussed. The sociolinguistic and dynamic nature of the ML is also addressed.

Independent Motivations for the MLF model

Psycholinguistic models of language production, as well as neurolinguistic studies of brain-damaged patients, support the major claims of the MLF model. This support comes in four areas: (1) the pre-eminence of one language over the other during language processing by bilinguals; (2) the distinction between the behavior of system and content morphemes in speech errors; (3) other distinctions regarding these morphemes in patients with Broca's aphasia; and (4) the possibility of each language having its own direct access to a common conceptual store during CS production.

Differential Activation of Two Languages

First, research by Grosjean and his associates provides motivation for the overall premise of the MLF model that two (or more) languages are being accessed at the same time, but with the formulator having access to linguistic information from the different languages in non-identical ways. A number of experiments (e.g. Grosjean, 1988; Burki-Cohen, Grosjean, and Miller, 1989) have studied language processing in speakers of both French and English. Grosjean (1988) considers how 'guest words' (CS forms and borrowed (B) forms from the EL) are processed by such listeners. English words were embedded in French sentences, with the goal of studying the bilinguals' recognition processes. Of interest here is the 'base language effect' (i.e. the first reaction of subjects is to think that the language of the word is the context (base) language, or what is called the ML here). For example, Grosjean's subjects rarely proposed an English candidate correctly at the onset of the word when the base was French.

This base language effect . . . could explain why many studies have found some delay in the recognition of code-switched words as opposed to base language words (see, e.g. Soares and Grosjean, 1984). In the case of code-switches, the listener may at first search the wrong lexicon, whereas in the case of base-language words they immediately search the correct lexicon. (Grosjean, 1988: 262)

I am even more interested in one of Grosjean's conclusions in the same study (p. 270):

Both networks are activated but the base language network is more strongly activated (this accounts for the base language effect). The resting activation level of the language not being used as the base language (the guest language network) can be increased or decreased depending on the amount of mixed language (code-switching, borrowing) that occurs during the interaction.

The idea that both languages are not equally activated all the time is a motivation for the ML hypothesis and the stronger role it claims for the ML. It also motivates the hypothesis that there will be fewer EL islands than ML islands (i.e. constituents all in the EL or all in the ML within a sentence containing CS). At the same time, however, Grosjean's conclusions that what one might call the 'participation' of the guest language (the EL) is *open to increase or decrease* supports the notion of EL islands occurring with any frequency.

Relevant Ideas in Language Production Models

Second, on the basis of speech error data, some psycholinguists argue for a two-step (monolingual) production model which, in turn, suggests an explanation for the distribution of system versus content morphemes, according to languages, in CS. In a series of papers, Garrett (e.g. 1975; 1988; 1990) states that what he calls closed-class items are retrieved in a different manner, or at a different stage in production, from open-class items. His argument is largely based on speech error data showing that these two types of morpheme do not pattern together when errors occur.

Recall that 'closed class' more or less equals 'system morpheme' and 'open class' more or less equals 'content morpheme' in the MLF model. Differences in the referents of these terms will be discussed in Chapter 4. From now on, only the terms 'system morpheme' and 'content morph-eme'[1] will be used, except in direct quotations.

Garrett argues that the same data also provide evidence for a two-step retrieval hypothesis, i.e. that lexical retrievals occur in two steps: first at the functional level, involving interactions between what I will call lemmas (to be defined below) and grammatical procedures, and then at the production level, where words receive their phonological features and are fitted into surface syntactic slots in the frame which was built at the functional level. The initial formulation of the two-step hypothesis is identified with Fromkin's (1971) speech error analysis.

For many psycholinguists studying language production, two ideas figure prominently. The first is similar to, if not synonymous with, Garrett's two-step retrieval hypothesis. That is, most psycholinguists hypothesize that language production involves *several steps* (or levels), characterized by some modularity (some levels are impermeable, others possibly not).

Modularity is a crucial concept in Azuma's (1991*a*) model of CS. On the basis of a thorough discussion of psycholinguistic theories and findings, he argues for a 'serial model of organization' for CS. Also, his experi-mental studies of CS data (specifically for constituents with morphemes from both languages) support a hypothesis of 'the non-interaction of the frame-building and content-word insertion stages' (1991*b*: 94).

---

[1] The term *'system morpheme'* is borrowed from Bolinger (1968), who uses it to describe both inflectional morphemes and function words.

A second engaging idea is that relatively abstract lexically based information is a major organizing force: although lower-level syntactic processes actually fabricate surface structures, the lexicon is more of a gatekeeper on possible configurations than most current syntactic theories in linguistics acknowledge. The idea that representations of syntax are mediated through entries in a mental lexicon and what they entail is attractive. Levelt (1989), whose discussion of language production I largely follow, prefers a lexically based grammatical theory; the one he uses is along the lines of Bresnan (1978; 1982). My comments also are influenced by Levelt's interpretation of Kempen and Hoenkamp's model (1987), Garrett (1975; 1988; 1990), Bock (1987; 1989; 1991), and Bock and Loebel (1990).

What Directs Morphosyntactic Procedures?

Lemma information (or *lemma*, for short) is defined by Levelt (1989: 6) as the 'nonphonological part of an item's lexical information' including semantic, syntactic, and sometimes aspects of morphological information. Put another way, the premiss is that there are syntactic directions originating in the lexicon which shape the end-product through the entire production process. These syntactic directions come from lemmas.[2]

Levelt argues (p. 162) that 'lemmas are the driving force behind the speaker's construction of the surface structure. It is in the lemmas of the mental lexicon that conceptual information is linked to grammatical function.' Among other things, lemmas include lexical pointers which indicate an address in the mental lexicon where the corresponding word-form information is stored for all content and function words. Thus, it is clear that, while syntactic principles shape surface configurations, they are not necessarily alone at centre stage, at least at certain important stages in production.

Limits on This Discussion

I will not attempt here to give anything resembling a full discussion of the literature on language production models, but will mainly deal with those aspects of models relevant to the MLF model of CS to be discussed in the next two chapters.

For example, I will not involve myself in the argument between those

---

[2] I thank Michael Montgomery for pointing out to me that *lemma* has been in use for some time as a lexicographer's term. Ledislav (1971: 249) states: 'The entry consists of two parts: in the first part (which is frequently called the lemma), the lexical unit itself is indicated; the second part contains all the other information.'

who see production as more meaning-mapping or more form-mapping. Some of the psycholinguists I cite much prefer a form-based view, and Bock (1989), and Bock and Loebel (1990) present experimental evidence supporting the view that sentence frames are comparatively independent syntactic representations. I do not think that subscribing to the view that a frame is set in sentence production necessitates the view that such a frame is primarily syntactic 'all the way up'. That is, more abstract syntactic procedures may be directed by more functional considerations than are those procedures which have been studied experimentally so far. Certainly, some discourse-based approaches to syntax within linguistics (e.g. Hopper and Thompson, 1984) remain attractive. And, as I will argue in the concluding chapter, it seems as if the functionally based possibility of making marked choices may exist 'all the way down' to the surface. These choices may be in terms either of linguistic varieties or of specific syntactic structures.

This means that I see lemmas as endowing their lexical items with pragmatic information as well as giving them directions for the syntactic procedures which they may undergo. This suggestion is raised again in Chapter 8.

What is Relevant

I identify and discuss below seven aspects of production theories which are of most relevance to the MLF model. The last of these, a consideration of the implications of speech errors for more general models of language production, is examined in considerable detail.

1. That language production involves the setting of a frame is an assumption found in virtually all accounts of language production, as Bock and Loebel (1990: 1) note. This view gives rise to a theory that variations in surface structure are a result of (a number of?) different procedures specified by the frame. This idea means that certain aspects of sentence production are set long before surface syntactic rules (i.e. phrase-structure rules) apply.

At one point, Levelt (1989: 252) speaks of a *call hierarchy* and a *des-tination hierarchy*, pointing out that the former does the *inspecting* and the latter does the *ordering* tasks in sentence construction. (That is, the call hierarchy is not involved in ordering the output of the procedures it has called.) 'The difference is also reminiscent of the distinction made by rather diverse linguistic theories between *deep structure* and *surface struc-ture*', Levelt remarks. But it seems to me that *several* deep (i.e. abstract) structure levels are now implicated. As will be discussed below, Garrett, for example, argues for a retrieval process for closed-class words (= system morphemes) different from that for open-class words (= content morphemes).

2. Almost all researchers treat grammatical encoding as a set of processes occupying a level autonomous from phonological form, producing surface structures unspecified for their phonological form. That is, at a minimum, production is a two-step lexical retrieval process.

3. Virtually everyone stresses that production is a rapid, multi-valued, incremental processing. The computer science-based model of Kempen and Hoenkamp (1987) highlights the incremental aspect of processing. This means a processing component will be triggered by 'any fragment of characteristic input', and that such a fragment 'can be processed without much lookahead' (Levelt, 1989: 24). In turn, all components can work in parallel, but they all work on different parts of the utterance under construction. Again, as Levelt notes (p. 25), 'in order to make incremental processing possible . . . lookahead should, for each processor, be quite limited. This puts interesting restrictions on the kind of algorithm that is allowable for each component.' What is of special interest in a CS model is the idea that, without much lookahead, fragments being assembled at any given moment do not depend on what comes later. If this hypothesis is supported, the appropriateness of a linear model for CS, which is surface-based, seems remote; decisions must have more abstract origins.

4. Parallel processing is likely. Most psycholinguists would argue that there are important links at various levels. First, most would agree that processing (comprehension) is closely linked to the input (i.e. the production), and that processing involves some parallel procedures. And there must also be links during production. For example, Garrett (1990: 157) writes:

it must be stressed that the evidence . . . requires mechanisms that project constraints at several levels of analysis simultaneously. It is difficult to see how the very rapid resolution of lexical and structural ambiguities could otherwise be achieved.

5. Garrett's outline of the major divisions in a speech-production model seems non-controversial. There are three major units: the conceptualizer (having to do with the non-linguistic preverbal message), the formulator (which transforms this message into a linguistic message), and the articulator (which produces actual speech).

Within the formulator there are two main levels: the function level, having to do with meaning and grammatical relations (including lemma information), and the positional level, having to do with phonological form and surface word order. Parallel processing between these levels seems necessary to explain fluency.

6. Drawing upon the model from Kempen and Hoenkamp (1987), Levelt (1989) fleshes out the discussion of what the formulator might contain. Basically, what is involved is a set of 'procedural packages' of what the major categories (nouns, verbs, adjectives, and prepositions) require of their syntactic environment. These packages are the 'specialists' that take the necessary procedural knowledge supplied by major category lemmas and construct constituents around them (i.e. S, NP, AP, and PP constituents), according to Levelt.

In my model, however, lemmas are abstractions which do not actually occur in constituents, but rather 'call' lexemes. That is, lemmas are in the mental lexicon and lexemes occur in constituents. Categorial procedures provide building instructions for the phrasal category in which the lexeme can function as a head. A categorial procedure interacts with functional procedures for handling all the complements, specifiers, and parameter values it has found.

7. The analysis of speech errors has been the source of many hypotheses about the production model. The implications of some of these errors are primary motivators for the MLF model, as will become clear. Therefore speech errors deserve extensive attention here.

'Trouble in the Works'

The forms taken by speech errors have many implications for a general production model of language. The most striking characteristic of speech errors is that the forms they take are rather few; that is, errors are not a case of 'anything goes'. Just as speech errors must be the product of psycholinguistic stress, but also turn out to be orderly, so with CS. Of course, the psycholinguistic stress in the case of CS seems to be of a different kind (i.e. the stress is not over how to deal with mis-accessed phones or morphemes, but rather over how to avoid mis-accessing while still successfully dealing with two or more linguistic systems 'at once'). It is no accident that insights from the study of speech errors seem very relevant to a model which attempts to explain structure in CS. Current research on speech errors owes much to earlier work by Fromkin (1971), Bierwisch (1971), and Garrett (1975).

Two general observations are in order: speech errors support hypotheses predicting a separation of the functional level (meaning and grammar) from the positional level (phonological form and surface word order). They also largely support a different 'address' (or different procedures) within the mental architecture for system morphemes from that for content morphemes. Further, they also suggest that there may be differences among system morphemes regarding links with their heads.

Types of Speech Errors

The two main issues about speech errors are the error types and whether the morphosyntactic context in which the error occurs accommodates to the error.

Some phonological errors and all lexical errors are germane to this discussion. Of the types of sound error, sound mislocations are relevant to CS. The other types—sound blends (e.g. *stougher* for *stiffer* and *tougher* (Fromkin, 1973, quoted by Levelt, 1989: 216) and sound substitutions (e.g. *vesk* for *desk* in *Sue keeps food in her vesk* (Garrett, 1990: 159)—do not seem relevant and will not be discussed further. Lexical errors fall into three classes, blends, substitutions, and exchanges; all will be discussed and illustrated. Of the most interest to CS modelling are word exchanges which 'strand' affixes (i.e. closed-class items or system morphemes).

Sound Mislocations. These errors involve the misplacement of a sound, such as in (1) and (2):

[1] an *anguage lacquisition* device
(target: a language acquisition device)
[2] even the best *team losts*
(target: even the best teams lost)
(Garrett, 1990: 162)

Note, of course, that the error in [2] also involves a mislocation of a morpheme.

What is of interest here is that the phonological representation seems to be fixed *after* the mislocation. That is, the realization of the morphemes for the indefinite article (*a/an*) and for noun plural/third person singular (*z/s*) is fixed *after* the morpheme is misordered; therefore, this is evidence that regular morphological and phonological processes apply *after* the syntactic frame is fixed. I return to this evidence below.

Garrett (1988: 75) remarks that such errors are 'one of the clearest indications that multiple levels of processing intervene between M [Message] and articulatory control'. Garrett continues, 'Such evidence

dictates a separation of the processing level(s) that fix(es) detailed phonetic representation from that representing abstract segmental and lexical
structure.'

Word blends. Blends are two words fused as one; two lemmas are
retrieved which each call a lexeme for the same syntactic slot. There are
two kinds of blend, words of similar meanings and what Levelt calls
distractions, which are produced supposedly when the speaker has an
intruding thought (a group including so-called Freudian slips). An example of the first kind is shown in [3]. Blends are relevant because they
implicate competing processes in language production.

[3] Irvine is quite *clear.*
(target: . . . close/near)

(Fromkin, 1973, quoted by Levelt, 1989: 216)

Word substitutions. These are of various types, but the most frequent
seem to be antonyms, such as

[4] Don't burn your *toes*
(target: . . . fingers)

(Fromkin, 1973, quoted by Levelt, 1989: 218)

Levelt (1989: 219) asserts that the associative relationship creates the
problem resulting in the error. For example, *fingers* activates the lemma
'fingers', which has 'toes' as an associate, which it activates. 'For some
reason, the activation of *toes* reaches threshold before *finger* "fires" and the
accident is created.'

Simple word exchanges. Word exchanges seem to result from competing directions for the same slot.

[5] Well you can cut *rain* in the *trees*
(target: . . . cut trees in the rain)

(Garrett, 1982, quoted by Levelt, 1989: 222)

Levelt (1989: 222) comments,

Word exchanges are the clearest evidence available for parallelness of . . . the
simultaneous accessing of different lemmas by different fragments of the message.
Such parallel processing probably contributes to the speech and fluency of speech;
it apparently also creates some accident-proneness.

Significance of These Speech Errors for Production

The errors discussed so far provide information about the 'pointing
activity' of lemmas. The exchanged words are often of the same syntactic

category; they are often both heads of phrases, and tend to express similar thematic arguments. 'This is what one would expect if the insertion of the lemma in the developing surface structure were to require a fitting syntactic category', Levelt (1989: 222) also notes.

I would argue that it is an easy step to claim that, if the formulator can make an error in activating related lemmas from their addresses in the same language, the same formulator has the flexibility to call up alternative lexical realizations from different languages, as long as they meet the specifications of a lemma of the ML. This is how CS must work with content morphemes in CS constitutents with morphemes from both languages (ML + EL constituents), as will become clearer in Chapter 4.

Comparing Word and Sound Errors

Researchers posit that the processor operates on different sizes of linguistic units at different stages in production. This is because word exchanges and sound-movement errors contrast sharply in several ways.

Word exchanges are predominantly between phrases and, in a significant number of cases, between clauses, according to Garrett. Further, they occur almost exclusively for words of the same grammatical category; this suggests what is called the form class law (cf. Bock and Loebell, 1990: 2). Also, words involved in errors appear in the appropriate positions for their form class. Bock and Loebel (1990: 2) comment: 'Evidently the processes that put words into place within utterances operate in terms of these grammatical categories, suggesting that both the words and the places carry form-class codes.' These observations and hypotheses are motivations for the stance the MLF model takes regarding content morpheme insertion. That is, in Chapters 4 and 5 it will be argued that, once the frame for CS constituents consisting of morphemes from both languages is set by the ML, then content morphemes from either language may be inserted in these frames, as long as the EL content morphemes are congruent with their ML content morpheme counterparts.

Separation of Sound and Meaning

Garrett (1990: 160) makes another point about the relations of sound substitutions and word exchange errors. They show complementarity of an interesting type:

Those with a clear meaning relation show few similarities of form, and those with a strong form relation show few similarities of meanings. Errors that display both meaning and form similarity do occur . . . but they are not a dominant error type.

This separation of sound and meaning suggests that representations of form and meaning are separate in the production model. This led Garrett to argue for what he calls the *two-step lexical retrieval* hypothesis mentioned above. Again, this has relevance for a model of CS: if the form and meaning of lemmas remains distinct until a level very near the surface, it is easier to see how lemmas from the two languages participating in CS which have similar meanings might be perceived by the formulator as very 'close' to each other (in bilingual 'lemma-land', whatever its architecture), even though their forms are very different. This closeness on the lemma level would facilitate the insertion of an EL content morpheme in a slot prepared by an ML lemma. And, certainly, virtually all psycholinguists studying bilingualism agree that the two languages of a bilingual are always 'turned on', even though the two are not necessarily equally activated at any given point in time.

Differences Between Content and System Morphemes

The survey of types of speech error ends with those types of error which, taken together, give rise to a claim which is crucial in the MLF model of CS. These are illustrated below under 'Exchanges stranding inflection' and 'System morpheme exchanges'. (Example [2] above also illustrates a system morpheme exchange.) What will be hypothesized is this: a difference in the retrieval of content versus system morphemes is a major structuring force in CS utterances. In contrast, it will turn out that such surface differences as whether a morpheme is bound or free are irrelevant to constraints on its participation in CS utterances. (Note that *bound* is not a particularly clear distinction; for example, even in a language such as English, verbs may be free or bound, depending on their syntagmatic contexts.) Also, even nouns in English are inflected for plural and possessive; does this acceptance of a suffix make them bound forms?

Stranding exchanges. In such errors, content morphemes 'move', but leave their affixes behind. That is, affixes (primarily inflectional ones) are 'stranded' (Garrett, 1988: 76).

> [6] That's why they sell the cheaps drink
> (target: . . . sell the drinks cheap)
>
> [7] Make it so the apple has more trees
> (target: . . . so the tree has more apples)
>
> [8] How many pies does it take to make an apple?
> (target: . . . apples . . . to make a pie)
>
> (Garrett, 1988: 76)

[9] We'll sit around the song and sing fire*s*
(target: . . . sit around the fire and sing songs)

(Garrett, 1990: 159)

[10] The flood was road*ed*
(target: . . . road was flooded)

(Stemberger, 1985: 162)

When there is a speech error in which the stranding of an inflectional affix is possible (i.e. a stem taking an inflection has been exchanged), then stranding is the rule. Stemberger (1985: 162) points out that, in his corpus of 135 such errors, affix stranding occurs in 120 cases (88.9 per cent), more often than expected by chance.

Further, when there are content morpheme exchanges with a morpheme coming from the lexicon (i.e. not an exchange within the target utterance itself), inflectional morphemes are also stranded.

[11] . . . and Joe had never *worn* one—driven one before.
(target: . . . never driven one before)

(Stemberger, 1985: 162)

Stemberger reports that, of 165 errors of this type, stranding occurs in 152 (92.1 per cent), again a statistically significant result. Later he comments: 'Stranding of inflections supports the notion that syntactic constraints are stronger on inflections' (p. 164), but what he means by 'stronger' is left unspecified.

System morpheme exchanges. Garrett (1988: 77) calls these exchanges 'non-phonological shift errors'. The elements which move in these errors are just those which are stranded in other error types—function words and inflectional affixes.

[12] Mermaid moves their legs together
(target: mermaids move their legs together)

[13] What that add up*s* to
(target: what that adds up to)

[14] you hafta do come
(target: you do hafta come)

Garrett (1990: 165) interprets these shift errors as 'single element mislocations that arise in the process of mapping features of the frames into sites in the terminal string'.

Note that errors such as those above are not true exchanges, but rather misplacements of system morphemes. However, Stemberger (1985: 163) points out that, while errors involving the actual exchange of inflections are rare (only five are attested), they do occur. Still, he states that he has only one good example in which two affixes are fully exchanged:

> [15] They're just clouds that are *been diverting*
> (target: . . . that are being diverted from the north)

He refers to his other four errors as 'involving a "shift" of an affix (or inflectional category) and accommodation of the words involved to their proper morphological shapes' (p. 163):

> [16] I *wind* up *rewroting* twelve pages.
> (target: I wound up rewriting . . .)

What Exchange Errors Tell Psycholinguists

Most psycholinguists studying errors reach the same conclusion. Stemberger (1985: 163) puts it this way:

> Stranding implies that lexical items and inflectional categories are accessed separately and in parallel. Any failure on one of these two aspects of lexical access is usually not accompanied by failure on the other.

Garrett, who is especially prominent in proposing hypotheses differentiating the behaviour of content and system morphemes, points out that system morphemes, whether bound or free, differ in several ways from content morphemes. They rarely participate in sound-exchange errors. And, as noted, they are stranded in word-movement exchanges. This evidence leads Garrett (1990: 165) to argue:

> Closed class elements are not on the lexical list and are instead assumed to be features of the frames. If exchange arises as a function of misassignment of list members, or segmental features of list members, to planning frames of F [functional level] or P [positional level], elements of the planning frames should not exchange—and this is an empirical observation.

Implications for the MLF Model

On the basis of such evidence as that provided by [6]–[16], what Garrett is hypothesizing is that the status of system morphemes in any 'frame' which structures sentences during production must be different from the status of content morphemes. While both types of morpheme may be 'in the lemma lexicon', system morphemes respond to different (earlier?) calls from content morphemes; this establishes the system morphemes in their slots in the frame before content morphemes are fully specified, although their word classes must be known (i.e. case-markers go on nouns, etc.). Note this does not mean that system morphemes must be fully specified in terms of phonological form and surface structure details.

To continue the argument, if errors occur in which system morphemes are the only ones participating, such errors must be adjustments at a different point in the framing procedure, or in response to a different set of call procedures than those of content morphemes. And indeed, Garrett goes on to state that 'on this hypothesis, the closed and open class elements have a different retrieval history' (1990: 165).

What make the speech error data and hypotheses derived from them of interest in any model of CS is that they promote the claim that system morphemes would be expected to participate in CS in a different way from content morphemes because they are accessed with the frame, not with specific content items. This gives rise to the prediction that, in CS utterances, nouns from an EL language may appear in slots which, for example, are case-marked according to ML specification, or show ML specifiers. And, indeed, this type of CS is found.

Areas of Disagreement

Not all psycholinguists follow all of Garrett's interpretation, nor do all agree with his conception of a production model. Bock (1987) offers a survey of current views, identifying one area of contention as Garrett's statement that there is no feedback between the functional and positional levels, while maintaining that the two levels may show parallel processing. The 'generic' production model sketched below is based somewhat more on the Kempen–Hoenkamp (1987) model, as interpreted by Levelt (1989); feedback seems a possibility under that model. Also, Stemberger (1985) argues explicitly for a model based on parallel processing, with interaction possible at all levels. The two–level aspect of Garrett's model separates out phonological procedures from uninterpreted syntactic representation: 'On the two-step hypothesis, the calculation of a meaning description leads to the recovery of a specific record that does not itself contain information about word form . . . Word form information must be retrieved in a separate step' (Garrett, 1990: 161). Bock's (1989) experimental findings, which contrast the effects of semantic and phonological priming on sentence production, support the double-retrieval hypothesis.

On the specific subject of the distinction between content and system morphemes, others disagree with Garrett on two fronts. First, not everyone agrees with Garrett that inflectional morpheme-stranding errors share two characteristics with sound exchanges (i.e. 'spoonerisms' such as *hissed all the mystery lectures* in which the initial sounds /h/ and /m/ are exchanged). In contrast with other types of word error, both inflectional morpheme-stranding errors and sound exchanges are more likely to violate form-class constraints but occur within the same phrase. This claim has been cited as evidence that system morphemes are somehow to be especially identified with the positional level.[3] But Stemberger, who looked only at stranded inflectional affixes, found no difference between word exchanges and stranding exchanges in regard to the form-class constraint. Stemberger (1985: 169–70) and Bock (1987: 365) offer fuller discussions of this point; and Bock (1991) cites Dell (1990) regarding disagreement about whether the phonological interpretation of system morphemes is different from content morphemes.

However, as indicated above when examples [1] and [2] were discussed, the phonological shape of a system morpheme does not seem to be fixed until the positional level. This is often referred to as an 'accommodation' error. That is, the system morpheme accommodates phonologically to the erroneous element placed in the 'right' slot. Recall example [1]. In this example, the English indefinite article takes the form [æn] rather than [ə] because it now precedes the erroneous element *anguage* in *an anguage lacquisition device*. Certainly, that such accommodations occur implies that the shape of the system morpheme is not yet fixed at the time of the error.

Second, not everyone accepts the idea of differential retrieval of system versus content morphemes. Bock (1989: 4) interprets results of experiments on 'syntactic priming' as suggesting that 'free-standing closed-class morphemes are not inherent components of the structural frames of English sentences'. Bock hypothesized that if closed-class items (system morphemes) are part of sentence frames, then subjects should be more likely to produce prepositional *to* dative sentences (e.g. *The secretary is taking a cake to her boss*) after having been primed with prepositional *to* dative sentences than after other primes, such as prepositional *for* dative sentences (e.g. *The secretary is baking a cake for her boss*). Bock's results showed that subjects did indeed produce more prepositional *to* sentences after such priming; however, it turned out that prepositional *for* dative priming also

---

[3] Butterworth (1989: 114) points out that Cutler and Isard (1980) found that system morpheme words often take their accent with them in exchange errors. That is, a speaker says, *Can I turn* OFF *this?* when the target is *Can I turn this* OFF?. What does this mean? A suggested hypothesis is that system morphemes and certain suprasegmental features are assigned at the same time, whether at the lemma level or elsewhere (at the positional level?).

produced more prepositional *to* dative sentences than it did double-object *for* dative sentences (e.g. *The secretary was baking her boss a cake*). In effect, then, subjects produced configurations similar to the priming sentences, but not necessarily with the same preposition. Bock concludes (1989: 181): 'This suggests that the specific form of a preposition can be dissociated from the structural frame in which it appears, and so cannot be identified with it.'

But there are other ways to interpret these results. First, the prosody of the priming sentence might have been more salient to the subjects in this experiment than the syntactic frame. Both *to* and *for* dative sentences have the same prosody. That is, possibly the prosody, not the syntax, is the structure which subjects transferred when they produced their own sentences. Second, both *to* and *for* datives show the same order in argument structure (patient + goal/beneficiary), while double-object sentences reverse this order (goal/beneficiary + patient). Presumably, argument structure is an even more 'immanent' part of the structural frame than the specific system morphemes which appear in the frame. Thus, Bock's results do not have a single interpretation. Azuma (1991*a*: 73–4) makes similar observations.

In addition, others hypothesize that there is no separability of affixes and stems during production: that words are selected as wholes (Butterworth, 1983; 1989). Also, the Kempen–Hoenkamp (1987) model questions the independent status of affixes in the mental lexicon. True, this model hypothesizes that part of the lemma entry for a lexical item will be the lexical pointers to various features which will affect the word form retrieved, such as number, case, tense, pitch, and accent. At the same time, however, the model hypothesizes that not all lexical items have *individual* lemma entries.

Relevant here is the issue already raised in Chapter 2 as to whether inflectional affixes are part of the same lexical entry as their heads. The question of the 'location' of inflectional affixes is especially relevant to a structural-constraints model for CS, since in a number of language pairs, CS forms show 'double morphology'. 'Double morphology' means that a single head (from the EL, not the ML) has affixes from both the ML and the EL marking a feature.

Is Plurality 'Listed' Separately in the Lexicon?

Double morphology in CS data is examined below. Its relationship to the psycholinguistic evidence is discussed here. Most commonly, double morphology appears to mark plurality. In the Shona/English corpus from Zimbabwe, for example, such forms as *ma-day-s* 'days' occur (*ma-* is the marker for Shona noun class 6 and conveys information both about class and about plurality).

There are various indications that the plural morpheme, at least in English, may be part of the same lexical entry as its head. Stemberger (1985: 165) comments that 'it is plurality that is the greatest exception to stranding'. That is, other inflectional affixes are typically stranded in the slots where they 'belong' rather than moving with their heads to an 'erroneous' slot; but plurality often makes the move with its head.

Stemberger offers an observation at the conclusion of a discussion about syntactic constraints on inflections which may be relevant. He notes (1985: 165) that 'the inflection with the fewest syntactic constraints is plural, since it can occur in almost any noun phrase regardless of position in the clause'.

Levelt's hypothesis (1989: 183) about plural morphemes is that they are at the same lexical address as a singular form (e.g. *dog* and *dogs* at the same address). And, at least for some languages, inflections of a verb belong to the same lemma entry, according to the model he presents.

But recall Hankamer's (1989) claim on this subject under the discussion about the Free-Morpheme Constraint in Chapter 2. Based on Turkish, his argument is against the hypothesis that words are listed in the mental lexicon as full words and therefore that no parsing of affixes is required. At the least, the evidence cited by Hankamer indicates that not all languages necessarily make the same divisions in terms of whether inflections are separate lexical entries. It was noted how agglutinative languages seem to access their bound morphemes to create new words.

The Strength of Attachments to Heads

It is also possible that, while some system morphemes show strong attachments to their heads, others may not. This suggests the possibility of differential treatment of different system morphemes within the production frame. Here, CS data showing double morphology provides evidence of how production must be organized.[4]

---

[4] Petersen (1988: 488) gives an example of another inflection which seems to be accessed with its head, at least in early language acquisition. She reports that her daughter, at about age 1; 6, produced such utterances such as 'the *pige-n*' ('the girl'—the + girl + the) and 'the *navle-n*' ('the navel'—the + navel + the). The daughter's ML was English, and so the English system morpheme *the* would be predicted. Still, she also accesses the Danish suffix -*n*, the Danish realization of the definite article for these cases. Petersen remarks, 'This would seem to indicate that . . . she believed the Danish word for 'girl' to be *pigen* rather than *pige*.' As will be noted in Chs. 4 and 5, Bokamba (1988) also remarks on the doubling of infinitival affixes in Lingala/French CS.

The fact that the most common instance of double morphology from CS data (involving English or French as the EL) is for plurality supports the suggestion above that plurality is at the same lemma address as its head, at least in these languages. A hypothesized scenario for the production of double plural markings on CS forms appears in Chapter 5. The scenario operates on the premiss that plurality is part of the lexical entry for nouns in English, but this does not imply the same case for *all* inflections or *all* languages.

'Fixtures' in the Frame

In contrast to plurality, another system morpheme, that carrying case assignment, seems very separable from its head, but not from the syntactic frame, according to speech error evidence. This separability offers support for claims the MLF model will make about how utterances are structured during CS.

There seems to be room for at least two interpretations of the relevant data. Levelt (1989: 249) interprets the fact that case, number, and other inflections have a strong tendency to be stranded as 'supportive of the notion that the corresponding diacritical features are assigned *after* the lemma is inserted into its grammatical slot'. As I see it, the stranding of these system morphemes is not really evidence of *when* they are assigned; that these forms are stranded could just as well indicate that they are fixed *early* and do not move for this reason.

Under either interpretation, however, stranding can be considered as evidence that at least certain system morphemes are accessed separately from their heads. Separate accessing would be indicated if, for example, when errors occur involving case, inflections show case requirements of the *slot* in which the error occurs rather than accommodating to the erroneous element itself. Put another way, if case marking comes with the frame, this is evidence that these system morphemes are not accessed with their lexical heads.

Limited evidence on another type of 'accommodation error' indicates that this prediction is correct. Evidence shows that the specification of one system morpheme rather than another for a given slot (e.g. case or gender assignment) is fixed by the frame and does not accommodate to a speech error. For example, the specification that a certain slot requires the nominative case is not modified if, by an exchange error, a pronoun which would have been in the objective case in the target sentence finds itself in the nominative slot. That is, the pronoun in the nominative slot must show nominative morphology.

There are few examples from English, since only pronouns show case, but consider [17]:

[17] If *I* was done to that
(target: if that was done to *me*)

(Fay, 1980, quoted by Levelt, 1989: 248)

The evidence from German, which of course has a more extensive case-marking system, is somewhat mixed. But an extensive study by Berg (1987) shows that, as a rule, the erroneous element must make do with the case-marking which comes with the slot in which it finds itself in error. Consider [18]: the erroneous element, *sagt*, requires the indirect object *mir*, but appears with *mich* (objective case), which is required by the target verb, *fragen*:

[18] Wer *mich* nicht *sagt*, dem kann ich auch nichts *sagen*
(target: wer mich nicht fragt)
'If one doesn't ask me, then I can't give an answer.'

(Berg, 1987: 284)

Berg also found that German articles did not generally accommodate to an erroneously placed noun. Out of 36 errors requiring adjustment, the 'original' article is retained in 31 cases. For example, if the target was *das Licht* 'the light' (with an appropriately marked neuter article), but the noun *Welt* 'world' erroneously appears in the target's slot, it appears with *das* (as *das Welt* 'the world'), not with the feminine article *die* which *Welt* requires in accusative case.

Note that these examples show separability at some level between the noun and the inflections it 'controls'. For some psycholinguists (such as Garrett), these data support a two-step retrieval process, with certain morphosyntactic aspects fixed at the first step.

For some, these data also support the hypothesis that system morphemes are either present in the frame before content morphemes or are assigned by a procedure not applicable to content morphemes. For example, Bock (1987: 365) concludes a lengthy discussion by stating, 'It appears that these elements [closed-class items or system morphemes] are specified prior to the open-class words, so the syntactic features of the planning frame seem to be set before other words are inserted.' Such conclusions offer strong independent motivation for the claims of the MLF model to be discussed in the following chapters.

Motivations from Neurolinguistic Studies

The claim that there is a distinction in how system and content morphemes are 'addressed' and/or accessed also receives support from studies
of brain-damaged persons. Of specific interest are individuals with dam-
age to the left frontal lobe of the brain who show a condition called
Broca's aphasia. Although such persons typically show good speech comprehension, they produce little speech, with obvious effort. Of relevance
here is that their speech is 'agrammatic'. As Zurif (1990: 178) writes,

grammatical categories, bound and free—items, that is, of the closed class of
minor lexical categories (determiners, auxiliaries, and other function words)—tend
to be omitted; and there is a corresponding reliance on 'open' class items—mostly
on nouns, and to a lesser extent on verbs.

Experimental studies of comprehension (e.g. Rosenberg *et al.*, 1985;
Swinney, Zurif, and Cutler, 1980) support the view that these aphasics
process open- and closed-class words differently.

Access to the Common Conceptual Store

Finally, the MLF model receives motivation from evidence that the two
(or more) languages involved in bilingual speech production both have
'direct routes' to a common conceptual store. Hypotheses to this effect
(e.g. Paradis, 1978) have been followed by more recent experimental
evidence. For example, a study by Schwanenflugel and Rey (1986) supports a model of bilingual semantic representation where concepts are
represented in a language-neutral conceptual system, with neither language
acting as a mediator for the other. And Green (1986) and Grosjean and
Soares (1986) make it clear that they interpret experimental evidence,
gathered by a variety of techniques, as indicating that both languages are
active in normal bilinguals. Reporting on their own research, Grosjean
and Soares state that bilinguals took longer to access codeswitched words
(i.e. words from a second language) in the bilingual speech mode than
they did base-language words in the monolingual speech mode. They
suggest several related explanations, concluding (p. 170) that they 'prefer
an explanation that involves delay rather than one that requires a search
of the base language lexicon first'.

As will become clear in Chapter 6, where EL islands are discussed, it
is important for the possibility to exist that the EL has direct access to a

common conceptual store via its own lemmas so that EL islands can be constructed. In constituents consisting of morphemes from both languages (ML + EL constituents), EL content morphemes are accessed via ML lemmas, but ML lemmas direct frame building. The Blocking Hypothesis introduced in Chapter 5 is also relevant here.

Thus empirical evidence and hypotheses from psycholinguistics and neurolinguistics about the operation of the brain during language production offer independent motivation for what will be important claims in the MLF model. The idea of a morphosyntactic frame as a separate level in language production is motivated by psycholinguistic studies, especially those of speech errors. These same studies, along with neurolinguistic studies of patients with aphasia, also indicate differences in accessing between system and content morphemes. In addition, there is evidence that, while a bilingual's two languages are both turned 'on' during language processing, one language is the 'base' language. Finally, there is some evidence that both a bilingual's languages have direct access to a common conceptual store. All these ideas will figure in the MLF model.

Identifying the Matrix Language

Importance of the Matrix Language

Because the MLF model argues that the specialized syntactic procedures of the formulator which set the frame must come from the matrix language (ML), the ML's identification is obviously crucial. That is, ML assignment has major structural consequences for CS utterances. Therefore, to avoid circularity, the ML must be defined independently of this structural role which it plays. This means, for example, that the suggested definition (e.g. Klavans, 1983; Treffers-Daller, 1991*a*) of the ML as the language of the main verb stem or of the GB theoretical category INFL (inflection) in a sentence showing CS, is not acceptable. Further, it is entirely possible, even if unusual, for INFL to appear in an EL island; in such a case it would not accurately identify the ML. (Note that Nortier (1990: 158–9) indicates that the prediction that the language of the finite verb is the ML is not supported by her Moroccan Arabic/ Dutch CS data.)

Towards a Definition

Psycholinguistic and sociolinguistic criteria, used together, do point towards a definition. The single definition which best achieves empirical verification, however, is based on the relative frequency of morphemes from the ML and the EL in the interaction type which includes the CS data under study.

Relative proficiency is the psycholinguistic criterion which may be considered. However, because finding a unitary and valid method of measuring proficiency remains an open issue, this criterion is obviously of limited value, and only becomes useful when combined with socio-linguistic data. Generally, of course, the speaker has more proficiency in his/her first language. And a survey of the CS literature shows that the speaker's first language (L1) is almost always the language which can be identified as the ML by the morpheme frequency criterion (e.g. Spanish for Hispanics in the American south-west, at least in the 1970s, as in Pfaff, 1979; French for Canadian francophones in Quebec and Ontario in Poplack, Sankoff, and Miller, 1988; Cantonese for Hong Kong university students in Gibbons, 1987).

But it does not follow that the speaker's L1 will necessarily be the ML in his/her CS patterns. First, it is not always one of the participants in CS; therefore, second languages also may be MLs (e.g. Swahili for non-native Swahili speakers in several Nairobi data sets in Myers-Scotton, 1989; Lingala for some speakers in Lingala/French CS in Zaïre in Bokamba, 1988). Second, there are communities where it is difficult to establish which language of two is the first language (perhaps between French and Alsatian in Strasburg in Gardner-Chloros, 1985; 1991). There are also communities where proficiency in a second language (L2) is greater than in the L1, at least for the topics discussed in the utterances in question. Third, while CS is certainly a feature of 'stable' bilingual communities, it is very often a prominent feature in communities in the process of language shift. In such cases, it is especially difficult to identify the speaker's 'better' language.

Sociolinguistic criteria have a clearer, objective basis, but still result in some vagueness. Beginning with the least precise criterion, I argue that the ML is the more dominant language, across the community, in terms of the *number* of types of interaction in which it is the more socially unmarked choice. More specifically, the ML is the language more un-marked for the specific *type* of interaction in which the CS utterances occur. (See Scotton, 1988*a* or Myers-Scotton, 1993 for lengthy discus-sions of the 'markedness model' as applied to CS. In brief, the model claims that in any community there is a code choice which is more unmarked than other potential choices for each interaction type. 'Un-marked' is synonymous with 'expected', given the situational factors.

That one choice is more unmarked than others for a specific interaction can be demonstrated empirically: an unmarked choice has greater frequency than marked choices.)

Of course, in interactions where CS *itself* is the unmarked choice, one cannot claim that either language is 'more unmarked'. When CS is the unmarked choice, there is a great deal of switching between the two languages; it is the overall pattern of switching which is unmarked, not the choice of either language singly. (Again, see Scotton, 1988*a* or Myers-Scotton, 1993 for an extended discussion of 'CS itself as the unmarked choice'.) But in such cases (as well as all others) a criterion of relative frequency for morphemes, not instances of one language versus the other, will distinguish the ML.

A Frequency-Based Criterion

The following 'ML Criterion' is proposed:

> The ML is the language of more morphemes in interaction types including intrasentential CS.

There are two riders:

> 1. Frequency counts must be based on a *discourse* sample; they offer no reliable evidence if they are performed on single sentences. That is, if a sentence is analysed in isolation and, for example, its main clause is in one language and a dependent clause is in another language, there is no way to identify the ML. The ML can only be identified in sentences containing CS material if such sentences are considered as part of a larger corpus. How large is 'large enough' is an unresolved issue; but certainly a *discourse sample* must mean *more than one sentence*.
> 2. Cultural borrowings from the EL for new objects and concepts are excluded from the count (i.e. not counted as part of the EL total). Such borrowings may be very numerous in discussions of a technical nature, and their inclusion distorts the comparison.[5]

Even in interactions with a great deal of switching, a considerable difference is predicted between the two languages regarding frequency of morphemes for those concepts and objects encoded by indigenous means (or established loan words) in both languages. The operation of this

---

[5] Lüdi (personal communication) points out that neologisms are sometimes difficult to separate from borrowings. Lüdi (1983) discusses the French and German literature on this problem.

criterion, of course, is empirically demonstrable. Note that in some data sets counting words offers a more valid test of the hypothesis than counting morphemes; if one of the languages is agglutinative, it is almost certain to show more morphemes just because of its typology.

Researchers oriented toward formalism in linguistics may have preferred a categorically based criterion for the ML; that is, an either/or distinction. True, it would be neater; but I do not think the distinction has a structural basis. The reason for this claim is that the designation of the ML may change across time, and even within a conversation; that is, the EL may become the ML. This dynamic nature of the ML will be discussed shortly and in more detail in Chapter 7. However, as long as the ML/EL distinction can be verified objectively, there is no justification to discount it. Further, there is too much empirical evidence that the participation of the two languages in CS is different (as will be shown shortly) for us to conclude that the distinction does not exist. It is hard to see how these data can be accounted for and explained more parsimoniously than with the ML/EL division.

Because the criterion involving morpheme frequency is objective, it is open to quantitatively based, empirical testing. In a pilot test, the number of words (counting noun and verb stems as words) in English and Swahili were compared for the conversation (No. 16) showing the most CS utterances in the Nairobi corpus. The hypothesis being tested is that Swahili is the ML in this corpus. In the first two pages of transcript there were 185 Swahili forms against 35 in English. If the two pages which appear to have the most English forms are purposely selected, the figures are 70 Swahili words or stems and 24 English ones. Also, Backus (1990), who studied Turkish/Dutch CS, reports statistics for part of his data which indicate, following my criterion, that Turkish is the ML (Turkish words: 116; Dutch: 33; Turkish/Dutch: 87).

There may be corpora which show an approximate 50/50 split between languages in morpheme frequency for CS discourse. Such data would lead to the hypothesis that a 'turnover' in ML assignment is in progress in a diachronic sense. I would still claim that, even in such communities, a discourse sample will establish a single language as the ML—but only for that sample.

Supporting evidence that *all* sentences have a ML is that CS material in all data sets examined can be classified as one of the three types of CS constituent detailed at the outset of Chapter 4. That is, there are no CS utterances with 'helter-skelter' constituents, at least among those reported in the literature to date.

Experimental Support for the Reality of the ML

Kamwangamalu and Li (1991) tested the hypothesis that bilingual speakers can intuitively identify the ML. They refer to the ML (p. 247) as the language 'that licenses the "mixability" of linguistic elements of the other language, the embedded language'. They presented ten sentences showing Mandarin Chinese/English CS utterances to 59 Chinese–English bilinguals in Singapore. In the oral version, subjects heard a sentence and were then asked to write either E (for English) or C (for Chinese) to indicate if they felt the sentence was English-based or Chinese-based.

Results showed that subjects could make an assignment with little difficulty. For five sentences, the consensus was 80 per cent or more, and it was over 70 per cent for all sentences but one. For example, 71 per cent labelled [19] Chinese-based.

[19] *You mean to say* zai xizao ye   shi na   *handbag* qu, qu *toilet* ye   shi
                       at bath also COP take   go, go   also COP
na   *handbag* qu?
take   go
'You mean to say one takes the handbag along when going for a bath or to the toilet?'

(Chinese/English; Kwangamalu and Li, 1991: 253)

The Possibility of a Turnover in the ML

Any discussion of the nature of the ML is complicated by the fact that ML assignment is dynamic. That is, in CS between two (or more) languages in a given community, one language need not be the ML permanently. The identity of the ML can change either synchronically or diachronically. Synchronically, a change within the same conversation is possible; an extreme case would be a change within the same sentence. Diachronically, a change may occur when the socio-political factors in the community promote some type of shift to an L2. Support for the claim that the linguistic systems involved in CS are not in a static symmetry, even synchronically, but rather in a dynamic 'competition', comes from an assessment of experimental results on bilingual alternation in speech by a psycholinguist: 'Selection is partially a matter of increasing the activation of L1 but, principally, it is a matter of suppressing the activation of L2 words so that words from that system do not get produced' (Green, 1986: 216).

A change in ML assignment may be unusual in some communities; certainly, in the Nairobi corpus there is no change. Recall that the speakers in this corpus are not among the highly educated Kenyans who tend to have even more facility in English and, more important, more of an affinity for the identities indexed by tipping the CS balance in favour of English.

In another Nairobi data corpus of interviews including more highly educated white-collar individuals, there are many more examples of intersentential CS than there are in the main Nairobi corpus.[6] Consider [20a] and [20b] from an interview of a Luo man about his job. While there is much intersentential CS throughout the interview, there is no 'turnover' in ML + EL constituents. That is, Swahili is always the ML in these constituents. Further, such intrasentential constituents are relatively few, compared with the intersentential switches. The interviewee, who is a supervisor of counter personnel at the Nairobi post office, is in his late 30s and has a secondary-school education. The interviewer, who is a Luyia man, asks him (sometimes in English, sometimes in Swahili) about his job and life in Nairobi. The interviewee responds with a good deal of intersentential CS (one sentence in Swahili, one in English). Consider the following exchange.

[20a] INTERVIEWER (English). Now tell me how do you find Nairobi? Do you think of going to work in your own home area—say Kisumu?
INTERVIEWEE. I seem to like Nairobi very much. Hii   ni kwa sababu mama
                                              This is because   mother
watoto   ana   *business* y-ake   hapa *and our children go to school here.* Miaka
children she has business CL 9-her here
mingi siendi Nyanza. *Even my parents stay here.*
'I seem to like Nairobi very much. This is because my wife [*lit.* 'mother (of) children'] has her business here. Many years I don't go to Nyanza [*his home area*]. Even my parents stay here.'

Note that in the sentence *Hii ni kwa sababu mama watoto ana business yake hapa and our children go to school here*, the first independent clause is

---

[6] These data may be at odds with the views expressed by some researchers that intrasentential CS is the more 'skilled' CS. As will become clear from the claims of the MLF model, I see intrasentential CS as the rather 'simple' insertion of allowable EL content morphemes into an ML morphosyntactic frame, or as the production of EL islands according to unconsciously 'known' constraints. In contrast, intersentential CS would seem to involve the more skilled production, since the speaker must produce entire, well-formed sentences. After all, in order to produce full sentences in either language, the speaker's command of both languages must be more extensive, I suggest, than to engage in simply inserting EL content morphemes in an ML frame.

analysed as an ML + EL constituent (with Swahili as the ML), evidenced
by Swahili morpheme order in the NP *business yake* 'business her', Swahili
system morphemes (e.g. *yake* 'her'), and the Swahili construction *mama
watoto*, literally 'mother children'. Such constituents are thoroughly described in Chapter 4.

> [20*b*] INTERVIEWER (Swahili). Bwana O—, niambie kuhusu mpango wa posta
> wa *save as you earn*.
> 'Mr O—, tell me about the postal plan of "save as you earn." '
> INTERVIEWEE. Mpango huu ni *the customer fills forms and surrenders* kiasi
>   plan   this is   amount
> fulani ch-a   pesa   say like 200 shillings every month for two years. The
> some CL 7-of money
> interest paid is good and the customer can collect it after the expiration of the
> agreed period. Tuna   *customers* we-ngi   sana kwa mpango huu.
>   we have   CL 2-many very in   plan   this
> 'This plan is [that] the customer fills forms and surrenders some amount of
> money, say like 200 shillings every month for two years. The interest paid is
> good and the customer can collect it after the expiration of the agreed period.
> We have very many customers in this plan.'

According to the MLF model, *the customer fills forms and surrenders* is
an EL island, as are *say like 200 shillings*, *every month*, and *for two years*.
Tuna customers wengi sana . . . 'we have customers many very . . .' is an
ML + EL constituent.

It is true that Mr O— is more of a 'Nairobi person' (i.e. without rural
roots) than most of the subjects in the Nairobi corpus. This, plus the fact
that he is being interviewed by an interviewer who sometimes uses English, no doubt promotes his switching pattern. And of course the topic is
sometimes his job, a place where the languages he uses daily are both
Swahili and English.

No doubt there is an association between which language is the ML (or
turnovers in ML) and positive or negative attitudes toward the identities
associated with one language rather than another. While ML assignment
has structural consequences (detailed in Chapters 4 and 5), it also co-
incides with functionally oriented specifications. Specifically, empirical
evidence indicates that the ML is often the unmarked choice of solidarity-
oriented activities for the speakers involved; not surprisingly, therefore, it
is often an L1. This means that evaluations of the relative socio-economic
prestige of the languages involved have little to do with ML assignment.

ML alternation within the same conversation may be common under
three conditions:

1. The community as a whole is shifting from the current ML to an EL as its new main language for many or all purposes. The relation between CS and language shift will be discussed further in Chapter 7. There is a language shift in progress in many immigrant communities, and these are also locales for what will be called ML 'turnovers'. For example, Nishimura (1986), in writing about Japanese–Americans in Canada and the United States, claims that Japanese is the ML of some sentences she cites, but English the ML of others.

2. With a change in topic or other situational factors, the speaker perceives that the unmarked medium (i.e. the ML) should be what has been the EL up to this point. A situationally motivated shift in the ML is a typical phenomenon in 'stable' bilingual communities; I have referred to it elsewhere (e.g. Scotton, 1988a; Myers-Scotton, 1993) as CS as a sequence of unmarked choices, and it is what Blom and Gumperz (1972) call situational switching.

Alternation of the ML, with relatively minor situational motivations (e.g. participants stay the same, but the topic shifts), is also very frequent in certain communities. For example, it is reported in Spanish/English CS among Hispanics in Texas (Walters, 1989). And bilinguals with some sophistication about their own CS patterns report that they perceive themselves as changing the ML within some conversations (Kite (1990) reports this for Japanese/English CS with other Japanese living in the United States.) Also, in discussing a corpus of interviews of Swiss citizens originally from the German-speaking part of Switzerland, but now living in Neuchâtel, Lüdi (1986) reports that in the same interview there can be alternation from Swiss German as the ML to French as the ML.

3. Or, when CS itself is the unmarked choice, the speaker perceives that the balance has shifted in regard to the persona or the Rights and Obligations (RO) set he/she wishes to index.[7] If this is more associated with the EL, the speaker therefore also shifts the balance in CS to the former EL. It is worth stressing that the possibility/frequency of changes in ML assignment across conversations, as well as within a conversation, varies with the *sociolinguistic* norms of the specific community, not to mention the dynamics of the specific interaction studied. That is, ML assignment has structural consequences, but ML assignment itself is the consequence of sociolinguistic factors. For example, as noted, changes

---

[7] Under the markedness model (cf. Myers-Scotton, 1993), an RO set is an abstract construct for the relationships holding between participants in an interaction. It is derived from features salient in the specific interaction type, such as relative statuses of participants, and from certain situational factors, such as topic.

in the ML seem nonexistent in the (main) Nairobi corpus of Swahili/ English CS. But in yet another Nairobi data set, interviews between a man from the Luyia ethnic group and a number of Luyias living in Nairobi, the ML in their Swahili/Luyia/English CS changes frequently (from their shared L1 to Swahili). The reason for this change may be the fact that the interviewer was instructed to conduct the interview largely in Luyia, which seems to run counter to the norm of making Swahili the ML.

4
Regulating Two at Once, I:
The Matrix Language-Frame Model

Preliminaries

This chapter and the following one present my current version of a frame-based model of CS. It is called the Matrix Language-Frame (MLF) model. This name highlights its two crucial aspects: (1) CS is envisioned as taking place within the constraints of a conceptual frame; (2) the frame is largely set by semantic and morphosyntactic procedures dictated by only one of the two (or more) languages participating in CS, the Matrix Language (ML). The other language is called the Embedded Language (EL). In some interactions in some communities, CS may involve more than two languages; while there may be more than one EL in such cases, there is always only one ML.

How the frame of ML + EL constituents is structured is the main topic of this chapter. A detailed treatment is offered of what is called the ML Hypothesis and its two principles, the Morpheme-Order Principle and the System Morpheme Principle. These principles provide structural descriptions of ML + EL constituents. However, this discussion will not be entirely completed until Chapter 5.

The Goals of the MLF Model

The MLF model has two main goals. First, it seeks to predict the form of CS utterances. There are two complementary predictions:

It predicts which utterances containing CS forms will be considered well-formed (and which, therefore, are predicted to be possible occurrences).

It predicts which such utterances are not well-formed and therefore will not occur, unless they are stylistically marked (in order to serve some socio-pragmatic purpose, such as emphasis). Such possibilities are discussed briefly in Chapter 8.

Presentations of the specific claims of the model and examples supporting the claims are followed by examples of the types of utterances which would falsify the model.

Second, the model offers an explanation of the differential appearance of ML and EL morphemes in intrasentential CS by fitting CS into a larger theoretical model of language production. This task is begun in this chapter, but will not be finished until the discussion of the Blocking Hypothesis in Chapter 5.

Note that accounting for the diachronic effects of the EL on the ML (or vice versa) is *not* a goal of the MLF model; that is, the role of CS in morphosyntactic convergence is not considered. However, some CS data from convergence situations are discussed briefly at the conclusion of Chapter 5. Also, suggestions are made in Chapter 7 as to how CS influences outcomes in cases of language shift or language death.

The Premisses of the MLF Model

The MLF model takes its cue from psycholinguistic models of monolingual language production and processing, as indicated in Chapter 3. Although these models offer few details, their basic premiss is that production proceeds by accessing various grammatical procedures to build a sentence frame. A second premiss is that a sentence is assembled incrementally, but with different procedures operating simultaneously. Taken together, these two premisses imply that, while parallel processing is posited for the procedures, there are, nevertheless, likely hierarchies which direct the procedures, hierarchies which are evident in the makeup of the sentence frame.

The basic premisses of the MLF model are motivated by these views of language production. Its premisses are: (1) In bilingual speech production, a frame also is built. (2) Key hierarchies in the way frame-building procedures apply have the effect of constraining selections of the *languages* of CS utterances.

The terms of these premisses need clarification. 'Frame' refers to a pre-S structure configuration (i.e. prior to surface realization) such that a frame consists of (*a*) specifications for morpheme order and (*b*) directions for the realization of system morphemes. The 'key hierarchies' applying to CS are (*a*) those between content and system morphemes and (*b*) between the ML and the EL as participants in frame-building. (The distinction between content and system morphemes was introduced in Chapter 1; a more thorough discussion follows shortly.)

As indicated in Chapter 3, a motivation for the model is Garrett's (1990) contention that system morphemes are retrieved in a different step from that relating to content morphemes in the monolingual language production process, with the system morphemes part of a frame prepared for content morpheme insertion. However, the MLF model takes Garrett's hypothesis in a different direction. If system and content morphemes can be accessed separately in monolingual production, they can be further separated in bilingual production, so that it is possible to have constituents with a frame of system morphemes from just one of the participating languages, but content morphemes from both the languages. This idea underlies the hypothesis offered by the MLF model to account for constituents with morphemes from both languages, ML + EL constituents.

Frame-Building

When the frame of ML + EL constituents is being built, all basic linguistic procedures specify selecting the ML; that is, it is the ML which sets the morpheme order and also supplies the syntactically relevant system morphemes. (What is meant by 'syntactically relevant' will be discussed below.) Even though EL content morphemes may be inserted into these ML frames, only an EL content morpheme congruent with the morphosyntactic specifications of an ML lemma is allowed. (Recall from Chapter 3 that a lemma is an entry in the mental lexicon; it contains all the non-phonological part of an item's lexical information.) Thus, EL lemmas may 'call' EL content morphemes for ML + EL constituents, but only direct grammatical procedures for EL islands.

Types of Data

The MLF model makes a distinction in CS data not found in other models; that is, it views intrasentential CS as involved in three types of constituent. While they are different, they are interrelated through the constraints governing them. These constituents are first described and then exemplified below.

1. ML + EL constituents. These typically consist of morphemes from both the ML and the EL. The prototypical ML + EL constituent contains a singly occurring EL lexeme in a frame of any number of ML morphemes. Example [1] below illustrates two such constituents, *leo si-ku-come* 'today I didn't come' and *na books z-angu* 'with my books'.

In some of these constituents, phrases of more than one EL morpheme occur together (e.g. modifier + noun); an example is *job small* in [3] below. But there are few such cases in the Nairobi corpus.

ML + EL constituents are differentiated from the other two types of CS constituents in that they conform to the structural specifications of the ML Hypothesis to be discussed below.

2. ML islands. These are constituents consisting entirely of ML morphemes. They must be well-formed constituents according to the ML grammar, and must show internal structural-dependency relations. In example [2] below, *nimemaliza kutengeneza vitanda* 'I have finished fixing the beds' is an ML island. There are numerous other examples, such as *ilikuwa kwa gazeti* 'it was in the newspapers' in [4] below.

3. EL islands. These islands parallel ML islands. They also must be well-formed constituents, but according to the EL grammar; they also must show internal structural dependency relations. In [2], *all the clothing* is an EL island; example [4] illustrates two EL islands, including *last year*. Note that *job small* in [3] cannot constitute an EL island because it is not well-formed according to English word-order.

Examples

As indicated in Chapter 1, many examples will come from the Swahili corpus of 40 naturally occurring conversations which include Swahili/English CS. Swahili is the ML in all conversations; recall that the identification of the ML is discussed at length in Chapter 3. In brief, the ML is identified as the language of more morphemes in the discourse sample in question; it is also the more 'unmarked' language in the interaction type from which the sample is drawn. Examples [1]–[5] illustrate types of CS utterance; however, only such examples as [1]–[4] are considered under the MLF model, since they alone show intrasentential CS. Example [5] is included only to illustrate intersentential CS.

Example [1] is a sentence showing not only intrasentential CS but specifically 'intraword' CS in *si-ku-come* [si-ku-kam] 'I didn't come'. This VP is an ML + EL constituent. A tree structure for this sentence is presented in Fig. 4.1. For illustrative purposes only, the tree is within the GB (Government and Binding) framework. GB designations will be used at times in discussing the MLF model; this is only for descriptive purposes, since the GB theory of syntax is particularly well studied and therefore more familiar to most readers than other current syntactic theories. This should not be taken to imply that the MLF model is more compatible

(Leo) [si-ku-*come* na *books* z-angu]
S′
'(Today) I didn't come with my books'

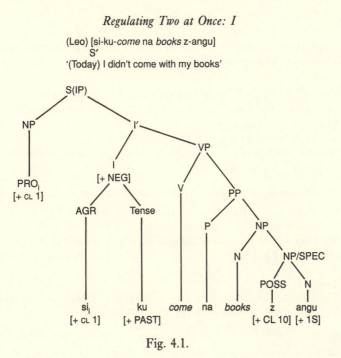

Fig. 4.1.

with GB theory than with other syntactic theories. In fact (as I hope will become clear) it is *more* compatible with a more lexically based theoretical approach. Further, the MLF model implies that syntactic theories such as GB would require revision to incorporate some of the distinctions made by the MLF model (e.g. differential accessing of content and system morphemes).

Note that, in Fig. 4.1, the nodes for INFL (inflection) are filled by ML morphemes but an EL morpheme fills the V node of VP (which moves into INFL to be inflected for tense and agreement). Also in the PP (prepositional phrase), N″ (i.e. the NP under PP in the figure) is composed of an EL morpheme in the N node and an ML morpheme in the Modifier (i.e. Specifier) position. The IP at the top of the tree diagram in Fig. 4.1 stands for 'INFL phrase'. INFL refers to verbal inflections such as tense and aspect. IP is synonymous with S; it allows for INFL and VP to be more closely related to each other at the I′ ('I bar') level than to the subject.

[1] Two pre-teen children with ethnically mixed parentage (mother is a Luyia and father is a Luo) are chatting about their school work in the Buru area of Nairobi. Swahili is probably their main home language and Swahili/English

is their unmarked choice in casual conversation, observation indicates. English is italicized. The convention will be followed of so marking the EL in all examples.

Leo si-   -ku-   *-come* na *books* z-angu.[1] James a-li-end-a
today 1s/NEG PAST/NEG   with   CL 10 my   3s-PAST-went-INDIC[2]
na-zo   mpaka kesho.
with-CL 10 them until   tomorrow.
'Today I didn't come with my books. James went with them until tomorrow.'
(Swahili/English No. 20)[3]

[2] A housewife, who is also a schoolteacher, is berating her house servant.

Ni-me-maliz-a   ku-tengenez-a vi-tanda ni- -ka-   *-wash all the clothing*
1s-PERF-finish-INDIC INFIN-fix-INDIC CL 8-beds 1s CONSEC
na wewe bado   maliza na *kitchen.* Ni nini   u-na-fany-i-a
and you   still [to] finish   with   [it] is what 2s-PROG-do-APPL-INDIC
huko?
there
'I have finished making the beds and I washed all the clothing and you haven't yet finished with the kitchen. What are you doing there?'
(Swahili/English No. 39)

[3] A discussion takes place among three young men about someone who was arrested.

Wa-ju-a   yeye hu-wa   jamaa w-a   *job small—small* hivi
2s/PRES-know-INDIC he   HABIT-COP person CL 1-of   thus
'You know he was a small-time thief—just that, small.'

(Swahili/English No. 16)

[1] Notations such as 'CL 10' refer to the class of the noun in question. Bantu languages have a large number of noun classes (up to 22); Swahili has about 15 (more or fewer depending on the basis of the count). Bantuists have numbered the classes in order to compare them across languages. Noun-class prefixes signal number as well as governing class agreements (i.e. prefixes on specifiers and adjectives and the shape of subject and object clitics in the verbal assembly).
   The NP *books zangu* represents the type of CS form showing double morphology which will be the subject of discussion later in this chapter. The noun itself has been 'placed' in Bantu noun class 10, as is evident from the agreement it controls on the possessive adjectival stem *-angu* 'my'; that is, z- is a class 10 prefix. For nouns, this prefix may be a zero allomorph. It is argued that the English suffix -s is being analysed (by the speaker) as part of the nominal stem, not as an affix.
   [2] INDIC (indicative) will be used to refer to the final vowel -a in a Swahili verbal assembly. Although it is the main final vowel when indicative mood is signalled, in fact, other vowels also appear with the indicative mood, depending on what other relationships are being signalled in the verbal assembly. And, to complicate matters further, -a also appears as the final vowel when the imperative mood is signalled and there is no object prefix. (See Ashton, 1944 for further information.)
   [3] As indicated in a note in Ch. 2, the numbers in these citations (1–40) refer to the source of the example as a conversation in the Nairobi corpus.

Note that *jamaa wa job small*, literally '[a] person of job small', is an ML + EL constituent.

[4] Several form 4 leavers (who have completed the equivalent of high school) are talking about job opportunities in the government.

Ah si-vyo,   kawaida hu-wa   kwa gazeti.   Kama *last year*
ah NEG-MANN usually HABIT-COP in   paper[s]   as
i-li-ku-w-a   gazeti   *under Public Service Commission.*
CL 9-PAST-INFIN-COP-INDIC   paper[s]
Ma-jina   i-li-to-lew-a   tu hapo   na   mahali p-a
CL 6-*name* CL 9-PAST-place-PASS-INDIC just there   and place   CL 16-of
ku-fanya *interview*
to-do

'Ah, no, usually it's published in the papers. For example, last year it was in the papers under Public Service Commission. The names are just released [of persons to be interviewed] and the place of doing [the] interview.'

(Swahili/English No. 9)

Example [4] shows two EL islands (*last year* and *under Public Service Commission*) as well as many ML islands. *Mahali pa kufanya interview* 'place of to do interview' is an ML + EL constituent.

Example [5] illustrates intersentential CS. In this type of switching, of course, all nodes under S are filled by morphemes from the same language.

[5] Three young women (a Kikuyu, a Kamba, and a Luo), who have all completed Form 4, are chatting in the home of one of them. Swahili/English is their unmarked choice for casual inter-ethnic conversation, observation indicates.

It [Kisumu] is half that of Nairobi's population. Mombasa and Kisumu ought to be given different city status. Hata Wakikuyu wamesambaa huko—nini—huko, huko Kisumu.
'. . . Even the Kikuyu are spread about there—you know—there, there [in] Kisumu.'

(Swahili/English No. 6)

Comparing the MLF Model with Earlier Work

One of the reasons some earlier researchers even questioned whether structural constraints on CS exist, and later researchers fell short of producing constraints to which there are few real counter-examples, may be they assumed that the key to CS lay in classifying its surface configurations. They did not consider that more abstract procedures and principles are behind CS. Many who did look beyond surface linear ordering still consider CS as basically a syntactic phenomenon; thus, they see constraints on CS as flowing from the same constraints on sentence structure already posited for monolingual surface structures (e.g. those attempting to use the GB theory of syntax, such as Woolford, 1983; DiSciullo, Muysken, and Singh, 1986; and Pandit, 1990). In contrast, the MLF model calls on a suprasyntactic level to motivate its constraints.

Many earlier researchers indicate that they are aware of many of the phenomena which the MLF model recognizes in its major claims.[4] Some remark on the differential appearance of ML and EL system morphemes.[5] A number of researchers make some type of distinction between the languages participating in CS, mentioning a base or matrix language (e.g. Ewing, 1984; Kamwangamalu, 1989*a*; 1989*b*; Eid, 1992; Treffers-Daller, 1991*a*; 1991*b*). And Joshi (1985), discussed at length in Chapter 3 and Petersen (1988) actually relate what Joshi calls closed-class items (i.e. system morphemes) to the matrix language. Therefore, it would be a mistake to claim that the observations of the MLF model are unique. But how it interprets these observations *is* quite different. Also, conceptions of categories do not necessarily coincide across models. An important difference is that the category of 'closed-class items', as used by Joshi (1985) and Azuma (1991*a*; 1991*b*), following psychologists writing about language-production models, is not exactly the same as the MLF model's category of 'system morphemes'.

The ML Hypothesis

The ML hypothesis is proposed to account for the differential activation of ML or EL morphosyntactic procedures during the production of ML + EL constituents.

> The ML Hypothesis: As an early step in constructing ML + EL constituents, the ML provides the morphosyntactic frame of ML + EL constituents.

[4] The model benefits from earlier collaborative research with Shoji Azuma, resulting in Myers-Scotton and Azuma (1990), which presents an earlier model called the Frame-Based Process Model. Azuma's own current model (1991*a*; 1991*b*) takes a form related to the MLF model, but differing in a number of ways.

[5] e.g. Gibbons (1987: 57) clearly recognizes that the EL (English in his Hong Kong data set) does not have the same role as the ML (Cantonese): 'The English elements found in MIX are mostly of one or two words in length, and are usually "content" or "open class" rather than "structure" or "closed class" . . . The items are mostly English nouns, verbs and adjectives, with the occasional adverb. It can be seen from the description given . . . that such words can fit into the surrounding Cantonese phrase fairly easily . . .'

Put another way, the ML hypothesis states that those grammatical procedures in the formulator (the central structure in the language production system) which account for the surface structure of ML + EL constituents are only ML-based procedures. Further, the hypothesis is intended to imply that frame-building precedes content morpheme insertion.

Two testable hypotheses about the nature of the frame follow from the general hypothesis. They are stated as principles:

The Morpheme-Order Principle: In ML + EL constituents consisting of singly-occurring EL lexemes and any number of ML morphemes, surface morpheme order (reflecting surface syntactic relations) will be that of the ML.

The System Morpheme Principle: In ML + EL constituents, all system morphemes which have grammatical relations external to their head constituent (i.e. which participate in the sentence's thematic role grid) will come from the ML. System morphemes will be defined below when this principle is explicated.

Morpheme Order from the ML

Evidence indicates that the Morpheme-Order Principle holds categorically when a single-lexeme CS form (from the EL) is present. Examples [6]–[17] below show how, across typologically diverse languages, whenever there is a clash between morpheme order of the ML and the EL in ML + EL constituents, ML order prevails. Hypothetical examples, which would constitute counter-examples to the principle, follow. The Nairobi corpus provides strong empirical support for this principle; out of 374 CS tokens occurring in ML + EL constituents, only one case is a counter-example to this principle. This example is discussed in the concluding chapter as an instance of a structurally marked choice for socio-pragmatic effect.

A limit on the Morpheme-Order Principle is that it does not apply automatically when two or more EL morphemes appear. When two or more EL morphemes appear, they may be either part of an ML + EL constituent or of an EL island. When the constituent in question consists entirely of EL morphemes and is well formed according to EL grammatical criteria, not ML criteria, the result is an EL island, *not* an ML + EL constituent. At least in the Nairobi corpus, such cases of two EL lexemes forming EL islands often include a quantifier and a noun (e.g. *next weekend, any letter*). These cases are accounted for under the EL Island Trigger Hypothesis, which requires a constituent to be entirely in the EL when it includes an EL system morpheme (as is the case with quantifiers).

Much rarer are cases of two EL morphemes which are not EL islands, but rather parts of ML + EL constituents. They are so identified by the fact that they follow ML morpheme order (see [3] and [9]). They all consist of an EL noun and EL descriptive adjective (e.g. *timing proper*) in the Nairobi corpus, where there are only five such examples.

Nouns and descriptive adjectives, one from the ML and the other from the EL, are prototypical parts of ML + EL constituents involving nouns and their modifiers. An example showing an ML head and a modifier from the EL is *mambo mengi new*, literally 'things many new', as in [6] below. An example showing an EL head with an ML modifier is *balance nzuri*, literally 'balance good'.

Why modifiers which are descriptive adjectives may come from the EL in ML + EL constituents has to do with the fact that descriptive adjectives are content morphemes. The EL modifiers which are quantifiers occur only in EL islands; this is related to their status as system morphemes. This and other aspects of the content/system morpheme distinction are discussed below.

There are many examples of ML + EL constituents consisting of heads and modifiers in the Nairobi corpus. A common constituent consists of an EL noun with an ML modifier, showing ML morpheme order (= Swahili order). (With most modifiers, Swahili morpheme order is head-first and in clear contrast with English's head-last order for NPs.) For example, there are 17 instances alone of EL nouns with ML descriptive adjectives in ML order (e.g. *problem kubwa* 'problem big'). And there are many more EL nouns with ML possessive adjectives or quantifiers (e.g. *books z-ako* 'books your'; *story ny-ingi* 'story many'). There are also examples of ML adverbs modifying EL adjectives; the ML adverbs follow their heads according to Swahili, not English, order (e.g. *huyu mtu ni sly sana*, literally 'this person is sly very').

There also are 91 cases of English verb stems inflected with Swahili tense/aspect prefixes, resulting in verbs which follow Swahili, not English, morpheme order.

To introduce what counts as evidence for the Morpheme-Order Principle, examples [6]–[10], which come from the Nairobi corpus, are discussed in detail. (Generally, a morpheme-by-morpheme translation is given only for the relevant constituent.) The other examples are largely left to speak for themselves. For even more examples, see the counter-examples to the equivalence constraint given in Chapter 2.

Codeswitching in NPs

[6] The conversation takes place among an ethnically mixed group of young men; first football is discussed at length and then other topics, such as religion.

Mungu anaweza yote muamini ataweza kubadilisha na utakuwa na

                                                 with

ma-mbo   m-engi   *new*—ma-pya   katika ma-isha y-ako.
CL 6-things CL 6-many new—CL 6-new in   CL 6-life CL 6-your

'God is able to do all [if] you believe he will change you and you will have many new things—new in your life.'

(Swahili/English No. 19)

This example is especially interesting on a number of grounds. Of primary interest here, of course, is the NP *mambo mengi new* (things-many-new); the English lexeme *new* follows its head, according to Swahili syntactic restrictions but in opposition to those of English. Thus, the example supports the hypothesis that the ML is the source of morpheme order in such an ML + EL constituent. But also consider two other points illustrated here.

First, there is the matter of agreement and the differential behaviour of Swahili and English adjectives. The Swahili noun *mambo* 'things', 'affairs' is a class 6 noun, with the class prefix *ma-*, which indicates both class membership and plurality. The adjective following it, *mengi* 'many', consists of the adjectival stem *-ingi* plus the class 6 prefix *ma-*.[6] But the English adjective *new* lacks the agreement prefix (*ma-*); such examples are to be recalled later when 'bare forms' are discussed. Second, circumstantial evidence that *new* is not a borrowed form is provided by the fact that the Swahili adjective for 'new' occurs after a moment (*ma-pya*); so clearly the English lexeme *new* has not replaced its Swahili equivalent. Further, if the entire Nairobi corpus of 40 conversations is examined, it turns out that this is the only instance of *new* occurring as a singly occurring EL lexeme.

It is also of interest to any discussion about modularity that the Swahili adjectival stem (*-pya*) does take the class 6 prefix, according to Swahili

---

[6] The morphophonemic rule of [a] + [i] > [e] applies in Swahili at a morpheme boundary; hence *mengi* from *ma-* + *-ingi*.

rules of well-formedness, even though the uninflected *new* intervenes. That is, it appears that the ML system morpheme procedure is first activated for *mengi*, then inhibited for *new*, and then activated again for *mapya*.

[7] Three young women are talking about job opportunities, and the conversation shifts to the way students coming from a certain area behaved at their boarding secondary school.

Hata *midterm*, wakipewa hawaendi ma-*home*. Wanakaa tu. Wanakaa huko wakisoze[7] tu. Akikosa mlo[8] siku moja anakuja kudai siku ya pili-

a-na-ku-l-a   *plate* m-bili   z-a   murram[9]

3S-PRES-INFIN-eat-INDIC plate CL 10-two CL 10-of maize

a-ki-kos-a   moja. Hawa wanapenda kula kweli kweli.

3S-CONDIT-miss-INDIC one

'Even at mid-term, when they are given [breaks] they don't go home. They stay [at school]. They stay in order to eat. When a student misses a meal one day he/she comes to claim [it] on the second day. He eats two plates of maize if he missed one. These people really like to eat.'

(Swahili/English No. 6)

Of relevance here, of course, is the NP which is a VP complement, *plate mbili za murram* 'plates two of maize'. Note that the head-first order of Swahili is followed here, even though the noun is English. The intended plurality of *plate* is indicated by the possessive agreement marker *z-a*, which shows the prefix (*z-*) of noun class 10, a plural class. Indigenous nouns in class 10 may show a zero allomorph for the noun prefix to mark the class (and plurality); in fact, before voiceless consonants it is the rule. Therefore, *plate* fits the Swahili pattern for class 10 nouns. (The lexeme *plate* occurs in only one other conversation, or twice altogether in the corpus.)

[8] An inter-ethnic group of young men, with educational levels between form 2 and form 6, are conversing about a dance held last night.

Wewe katika hiyo *party* nzima hukuona msichana kasoro Rose tu? Wewe ulikuwa umejikunja kwa *corner* u-na-m-*time* tu. Unamuangalia *movements*   y-ake

                                                        movements CL 9-her

---

[7] Note the verb stem -*soze*. This is a slang word in urban varieties of Swahili in East Africa, apparently coming from the English word *sauce*.

[8] The lexeme *mlo* is relatively common as slang for 'meal'; in fact, it is so common it has been integrated into the noun-class system, placed in class 3 (so that its plural occurs as *mi-lo*).

[9] The lexeme *murram* seems to be the English word (British East African usage) for a type of gravel. It occurs in the OED with a primary meaning of 'a type of marsh grass' and a secondary meaning of 'a type of sand'. I heard this word often in East Africa in reference to a certain type of road surface. Here, it is used to refer to maize, which may well resemble pieces of gravel (when taken off the cob).

z-ote . . .
CL 10-all
'In that whole party you didn't see another girl, just Rose [isn't that right]?
You just put yourself in a corner and 'timed' her. You were watching all her
movements . . .'
(Swahili/English No. 16)

The interest is in *movements yake zote* 'all her movements'. In this NP,
the head-first word order of Swahili, not the head-last order of English,
is followed. Just as important, note that the Swahili modifiers follow
Swahili modifier order, with the possessive (*y-ake* 'her') preceding the
quantifer (*z-ote* 'all'). *Movements* may be considered to be morphosyntactically integrated into Swahili as a class 10 noun, since its modifier *zote*
'all' shows the class 10 prefix (*z-*). The Swahili modifier *y-ake* shows non-
standard agreement, since it has the prefix of noun class 9 (which pairs as
the singular of class 10), *y-* rather than *z-*. The lexeme *movements* occurs
only in this example in the entire corpus. Of the other English lexemes in
the example, *party* is a borrowed form, since it occurs in other conversations (and is in effect a cultural loan, anyway). The use of *time* as a verb
indicates it is a CS form, since it does not occur as a verb elsewhere.

[9] Three young men from different ethnic groups, two who are students at
a commercial college and one who is in form 5 (beyond four-year secondary
school), are talking about burglaries and the police.

LUO MAN. Ndio, sijui tutawashikaje.
'Yes, I don't know how we are going to catch them.'
KAMBA MAN. Hao   wanataka *timing proper*.
         those they want
'Those [people] want proper timing.'
(Swahili/English No. 8)

As already noted, such NPs as *timing proper* (N + modifier, both from the
EL, but not constituting an EL island) are unusual.

Codeswitching and VPs

[10] Two school-age children (ages about 8 and 9), brother and sister, are
talking about school. Their parents come from two different ethnic groups.

Hiyo ni uwongo. Labda yeye hana vitabu vyake *father*
a-li-m-*buy*-i-a   vi-tabu   a-ka-potez-a   vy-ote.
3S-PAST-IO-buy-APPL-INDIC CL 8-book 3S-CONSEC-lose-INDIC CL 8-all

'That's a lie. Maybe he doesn't have his books [which] [his] father bought for him and he lost them all.'

(Swahili/English No. 20)

Of interest here is the verb form. Its morphemes follow Swahili order for parts of the VP. Literally, *a-li-m-buy-i-a* is (*he/she*-past-*for him/her-buy*-applied suffix-final vowel). Obviously, the morpheme order is quite different from that in English. This verb form, showing an object prefix, an 'extended' suffix, and the final vowel indicating (mainly) indicative mood, is quite unusual among those verbal assemblies including English verb stems in the Nairobi corpus.

EL Verb Stems in ML + EL Constituents

Altogether there are 91 inflected verb forms and 31 infinitive forms with an English verb stem and Swahili prefixation. (There are 6 English infinitive forms with no Swahili prefix.) (Recall also *si-ku-come* 'I didn't come' in [1] and *ni-ka-wash* 'and I washed' in [2].)

There are only a total of three English verb stems taking extended suffixes (two take the applied/prepositional suffix, the suffix shown in [10]; one takes the passive suffix). These forms with extended suffixes are also the only CS verb forms taking a final vowel, even though the phonotactics of Swahili require open syllables and all indigenous Swahili verbs take a final vowel. That is, these English verb stems with extended suffixes are the only ones showing real phonological integration into Swahili. In contrast, in the Shona/English CS data set, a final vowel appears on many English verb stems, and many verb stems also take a number of extended suffixes.

To take an object prefix (for DO) is not so unusual; there are 15 examples of CS verb forms taking an object prefix (13 finite verbs and 2 infinitives). For example, *wa-na-m-rob* (*they*-non-past-obj. prefix-*rob*) 'they rob him' (No. 17) or *ni-ka-i-rub* (*I*-consec.-obj. prefix-*rub*) 'and I rubbed it' (No. 39). These objective prefixes signal mainly direct objects (either animate or inanimate), but some signal other objects. The single example in the corpus with a prefix for the manner complementizer appears in [25] in support of the System Morpheme Principle. None of the CS finite verb forms shows an English tense suffix; this follows the prediction of the System Morpheme Principle introduced below.

Putting an English verb stem in the verbal assembly does not frequently trigger English material after the verb. Only 13 per cent (12) of the finite-verb CS forms were followed by English material, and 4 of these may be considered phrasal verbs (e.g. *a-na-make sure*).

Note that *father* is a borrowed form, with occurrences in more than three conversations (either as /faða/ or /faðee/).

Further Support for the Morpheme-Order Principle

Examples [11]–[17] come from the data sets of other researchers. They are included as evidence that the Morpheme-Order Principle has general applicability.

[11] *Idea* bubua de gale asi woa?
   idea another
'Do you have another idea?'

(Ewe/English; Dzameshie, 1989: 2)

Note that Ewe is the ML, and the modifier follows the noun in accordance with Ewe structure.

[12] *Idea* bura: nahi:hai.
   idea bad
'It's not a bad idea.'

(Hindi/English; Vaid, 1980: 39)

Note that, again, morpheme order for the modifier is that of the ML, which is Hindi in this case.

[13] Noch schlimmer, wenne de *client recalé* wurd am permis . . .
[*Note*: recale wurd = Fr. est recalé
         failed is   is failed]
'Even worse, when the learner is failed in the test . . .'
(discussion about drivers who have taken a course)

(Alsatian/French; Gardner-Chloros, 1985: 216)

Of interest here is the fact that the French verb stem *recalé* precedes the Alsatian auxiliary *wurd* in accordance with Alsatian syntactic specifications, with Alsatian as the ML.

[14] na:Du *les privés*
   arose   the private practitioners
'The private practitioners arose'

(Moroccan Arabic/French; Bentahila and Davies, 1983: 319)

Note that Arabic is the ML here and the exhibited VSO order is possible in Arabic, but not in French (the EL here), which usually requires the subject to precede the verb.[10]

[15] *The Sports Centre*? hóuchìh haih tìngyaht   *close* [kləus]
               seems   is   tomorrow
'The Sports Centre. It seems [to me] it is closed tomorrow.'

(Cantonese/English; Gibbons, 1987: 145)

The interest here is that the main verb *close* follows Cantonese order by appearing in sentence-final position, with Cantonese as the ML.

[16] *Building*-cyā samor   ubhā   rahā
     building of   in front stand keep
'Stand in front of the building.'

(Marathi/English; Pandharipande, 1990: 18)

Note that the order in the PP which includes *building* is that of Marathi, the ML, not English. Marathi has postpositions.

[17a] *Dan* mi sa   *leg* yu   moro betre *uit*
      then I FUT lay you more better out
'Then I'll explain things better.'

(Sranan/Dutch; Seuren, 1990)

[17b] Dan zal ik [het] je   beter uitleggen
      then FUT I [it] you better out-lay

(Dutch; Seuren, 1990)

[17c] Ik leg het je   beter uit.
      I lay it you better out.
'I explain it better to you.'

(Dutch; Seuren, 1990)

Seuren points out that what would be a one-word infinitive form in final position in Dutch, as illustrated in [17b], turns up as two separate words in Sranan/Dutch CS [17a].[11] He recognizes that [17a] does look very much like [17c], which follows the Dutch rule of separating the two verbal elements when the verb stem is a finite form. Still, he argues that Sranan's

---

[10] Georges Lüdi (pers. comm.) observes that VSO does exist as a marked order in French declarative sentences, e.g. *Viendra le jour ou tu te souviendras de moi* 'Will come the day when you will think of me'.

[11] Sranan is a creole spoken in the Republic of Surinam. Dutch has been an important lexifier.

own syntactic processes are equally influential, and that *uit* functions as a serial verb in [17*a*].[12] Note that in this example, as would be the case with other data on creoles, it is difficult to draw the line between material from a lexifier language (Dutch in this case) which has been incorporated into the creole (i.e. borrowed forms) and CS forms. However, since both borrowing and CS forms are predicted to be subject to ML morpheme-order constraints (with the ML as the creole, at least in this case and many others), such data constitute valid examples.

What Would Counter-Examples Look Like?

The [*a*] examples in [18]–[20] contrast with the [*b*] examples. Nothing similar to the [*a*] examples occurs in the Nairobi Corpus, or in the CS literature in general.

[18*a*] *Ni-ka- -wa-on-a   sana wa-nene *workers*.
1S-CONSEC-OBJ-see very CL 2-fat
'And I saw [some] very fat workers.'
[18*b*] Ni-ka-wa-ona *workers* wa-nene sana.
'And I saw [some] very fat workers.'

Note that in [18*a*] the adverb *sana* 'very' and the adjective *wa-nene* 'fat' follow English morpheme order, while in [18*b*] they follow Swahili order. Both the [*a*] and [*b*] examples are hypothetical, but examples structurally identical to [18*b*] are found in the Nairobi corpus. Examples such as [18*a*] cannot be uncovered. Just as important, similar sentences (i.e. showing EL morpheme order when a single CS form occurs) are not found in other CS corpora.

[19*a*] *U-ta-on-a   *ma-new/new*   mambo [mengi].
2S-FUT-see-INDIC CL 6-new/new things   many
'You will see [many] new things.'
[19*b*] U-ta-ona mambo [mengi] *new*.
'You will see many new things.'

[19*a*] illustrates the inadmissibility of an English adjective as a modifier of a Swahili noun if it precedes the noun. [19*b*] actually occurs in the Nairobi corpus; with one exception (discussed in Chapter 8), no examples such as [19*a*] are present.

[12] As an analogy, Seuren gives the following example of a serial verb in Sranan (*gwe*) and the equivalent Dutch sentence: *I no mus seni a man gwe*/you not must send the man go away/'You mustn't send the man away'; *je moet de man niet wegzenden* you must the man not away-send.

[20*a*] *Ni-li-on-a   him last week.
1S-PAST-see-INDIC
'I saw him last week.'

[20*b*] Ni-li-mw-on-a   last week.
1S-PAST-OBJ-see-INDIC
'I saw him last week.'

[20*c*] Ni-li-m-*grab   last week.
1S-PAST-OBJ-grab
'I grabbed him last week.'

[20*a*] shows that object complements of the verb, which are prefixes in the verbal assembly in the ML (Swahili), cannot occur as CS forms following the verb stem in CS utterances. There is only one possible counter-example similar to this which actually does occur; it is discussed in Chapter 5. In contrast, there are many cases of ML + EL constituents showing Swahili ordering of both tense/aspect and object prefixes in a verbal assembly which includes an English verb stem. As long as the prefixes of the verbal assembly are maintained in their Swahili order (and of course are realized in Swahili, not the EL, a necessity which will become evident in the discussion of system morphemes below), sentences such as [20*c*] are possible. Note that in either [20*b*] or [20*c*] the PP *last week* is a permissible EL island. Again, evidence from other data sets for other language pairs also do not show examples violating such a ML constraint on order.

Three Ways to Preserve the Morpheme-Order Principle

There are three possible strategies found in data sets which all maintain the Morpheme-Order Principle. Under one strategy, alternate ML syntactic procedures apply (the case of marked morpheme order); in another, full ML lexical insertion procedures are inhibited (the case of 'bare forms'). In all cases, however, the variations in syntax do not violate ML morpheme order. The three strategies are:

1. The procedure for unmarked ML morpheme order is specified, no matter how different it is from the EL order.

2. A procedure calling up what is an optional (marked) morpheme order in the ML, but an unmarked one in the EL, is specified.

3. The activation of some EL lemmas may cause blocking of ML syntactic procedures which would ordinarily call up subroutines providing specifiers and certain inflections. (Such procedures are building instructions for phrases in which the EL lexeme functions as a head, in

the Kemp–Hoenkamp model sketched in Levelt, 1989.) That is, some EL lexemes (necessarily content morphemes) may be sufficiently congruent with ML counterparts to be accessed when content morpheme insertion occurs in the production process. But, for reasons not entirely clear, their congruence is not complete. The result is that the EL lexemes appear as 'bare forms', content morphemes standing on their own.

Strategy 1 has already been discussed and illustrated in [6]–[17].

Strategy 2, using a marked, but permissible ML order, is also a possibility compatible with the production model being followed. The formulator (at the production level where morphosyntactic procedures apply) simply blocks the more unmarked ML procedures and activates the more marked ones when those marked ones happen to coincide with unmarked ones in the EL. This may well be the way syntactic convergence begins in some cases.

For example, strategy 2 seems to be at work in the Swahili corpus in reference to N + Demonstrative (DEM) constructions. Although the standard prescriptive grammars of Swahili (e.g. Ashton, 1944: 57, 181) do not specify unambiguously a preferred morpheme order for such constituents, my educated guess (I have studied Swahili structures for thirty years) is that the head-first order is more unmarked for the demonstratives in two of the three demonstrative paradigms (the *h*- and the *-le* ones, as in *hu-yu* 'this' and *yu-le* 'that'), but perhaps not for the third one (*-o*, as in *hu-yo* 'this aforementioned one'); but what quantified evidence there is remains inconclusive.[13] Still, the N + DEM order is definitely the unmarked order for other modifiers in the head-first NPs.

At any rate, in the Nairobi corpus, all instances of demonstrative constituents were studied, whether entirely in Swahili or including EL lexemes as CS forms. The comparison is between such forms as *watu hawa*

---

[13] Swahili demonstratives (and those in Bantu languages in general) need a new analysis. They are currently very poorly understood by grammarians. Some argue that the DEM + N construction is used to highlight the particularity of the noun (i.e. 'this particular one'). Another argument is that the N + DEM construction garners more attention for the noun itself (Leonard, 1982). But which order is more unmarked in any general sense is very open to question. Leonard (p. 18) counted demonstratives in 3 chapters of a modern novel by a Zanzibari author. He found more instances of the N + DEM order (22 in total, with similar numbers for each of the 3 demonstrative forms). But he also found 17 instances of the DEM + N order; fully 16 of these were the *-le* demonstrative. On the basis of reading Swahili grammars, I would have expected more instances of the *-o* demonstrative in the Demonstrative-first construction, because it is supposed to be the one carrying the meaning of 'this, the aforementioned one'. However, the statistics for the Nairobi corpus (n.17 below) reinforce Leonard's finding: the *-le* demonstrative accounts for 52% of the forms in this head-last construction.

(people these) 'these people', *area hii* (area this) 'this area', and *wale wachezaji* (those players) 'those players' and *ile green* (that green) 'that green [one]'. The great majority were NP complements of the VP (N = 162), not subject NPs (N = 17). Classified according to morpheme order, only 42 per cent (75) show the 'classic' head-first order (N + DEM), with 58 per cent (104) showing the presumably more marked head-final order (DEM + N).[14] Are my intuitions wrong? At first blush, the answer is 'yes'. But if one considers the distribution of those which are entirely in Swahili (SS)—i.e. (Swahili N + Swahili DEM) or (Swahili DEM + Swahili N) as against those which are mixed, i.e. (ES) or (SE), (English N + Swahili DEM) and (Swahili DEM + English N), another interpretation is possible.

First, all-Swahili configurations predominate in the head-first order; 85 per cent (63) are SS and only 15 per cent (11) are ES. But of those with head-last order, the scale is almost balanced; there are slightly more SE forms than SS forms (52 per cent or 54 out of 104 versus 48 per cent or 50).

Second, grouping those ES and SE forms which are clearly B forms, not CS forms, with SS forms produces an even more telling statistic. (That is, any forms which are either cultural loans or which occur across at least three different conversations are counted as borrowed forms; e.g. *ile betri* 'that battery' or *Omo ile ndogo* 'that little [box of] Omo [detergent]'.) This operation leaves only 5 CS forms in the head-first configuration (ES), but still 20 CS forms in the head-last configuration (SE).

This means that, of the 25 N + DEM forms showing CS, 80 per cent (20) are head-last constructions: they are SE forms, such as *zile trips* 'those trips' or *ile scale ya chini* 'that lower scale').[15] Recall that this is the (apparently) more marked construction for Swahili. Clearly, the data, while not overwhelming in number, allow us to argue that the strategy of

[14] It is true that of the 66 head-first SS constructions, only 3 nouns account for 70% of the data (N = 44): *saa* 'hour', *siku* 'day', and *namna* 'way' (in the sense of 'manner') plus a DEM make up most of this group (e.g. *saa hii* 'this hour' or *siku hizi* 'these days').

[15] If all DEM tokens in the Nairobi corpus are added together (i.e. including indigenous Swahili nouns, borrowed nouns, and CS nouns), there is not a great difference between the raw count for the 3 different types of demonstrative. There are 61 of the '*ile* type', 52 of the '*hii* type', and 48 of the '*hiyo* type'. But most of the *ile* type occur in the head-last construction (47), where they account for 52% of the total. Most of the *hii* type occur in the head-first construction, and they account for 51% of such forms. Finally, the *hiyo* type divides itself about equally between the two constructions (28 head-last and 20 head-first).

The statistics are as follows: *Head-last construction (DEM + N) (N = 91)*: *ile* type, 52% (47); *hii* type, 17.5% (16); *hiyo* type 30.5% (28); *Head-first construction (N + DEM) (N = 70)*: *ile* type, 20% (14); *hii* type, 51% (36); *hiyo* type, 29% (20).

accessing a marked, but acceptable, ML morpheme order, which just happens to be unmarked for the EL, is at work here. Example [21] illustrates such usage.

[21] I-le   *membership* kule kilabu kw-enu   ilikuwa pesa   ngapi?
    CL 9-DEM   there club LOC-yours it is   money how much
'How much is the membership [fee] at your club?'

(Swahili/English No. 9)

A much more universal strategy than selecting marked ML procedures may be allowing for 'bare forms', strategy 3. And in the Nairobi corpus, there are many English nouns which occur as CS forms with no modifiers. Certainly, there are far more bare CS nouns than there are modified CS nouns (i.e. those taking either an adjective, a demonstrative, or a possessive adjective). But in order really to make a case for the bare noun strategy, a comparison should be made with the number of Swahili bare nouns. Unfortunately, that statistic has not been calculated in the current analysis.[16]

Some examples of 'bare nouns' follow. Recall there is a 'bare adjective' (*new*) in [6] above.

[22] Edwin? Ah, nilipoamka sikumuona, niliangalia dirisha   z-ao
                                           window(s) CL 10-their
ni-ka-on-a   *curtain* zi-me-fung-w-a
I-CONSEC-see-INDIC   CL 10-PERF-close-PASS-INDIC
'Edwin? Ah, I didn't see him when I woke up. I checked their windows and saw [the] curtains were closed.'

(Swahili/English No. 17)

This is a particularly telling case because the bare CS form stands in contrast to a preceding Swahili noun which is not bare. Note that *dirisha* has a possessive pronoun (*z-ao*) as a modifier ('their windows'), even though the agreement is non-standard (in standard Swahili, *dirisha* is a class

---

[16] Contini-Morava (1991) has made a study of nouns and their modifiers in novels and plays. Under her coding system, a noun is counted as a bare form if it governs no agreements (subject or object ones) in the verbal assembly, whether it has modifiers or not. Thus, her data are not quite relevant to the issue here since the 'governance' criterion will mean that many more nouns will be declared 'bare forms' than they would under my criteria. Still, Contini-Morava's results for a play are suggestive. Certainly, they do not support the hypothesis that Swahili shows few bare nouns, since 33% (109) of the corpus (N = 331) are bare forms as against 67% (222) showing some modifiers/governance. Still, they do support the claim that bare nouns are more marked than not. She also noted that many of the bare nouns (by her definition) occur as VP complements. This where almost all the single lexeme EL nouns occur in the Nairobi CS corpus, whether bare or modified.

5/6 noun and the standard agreement here would be *ma-dirisha y-ao*).
But *curtain* stands as a 'bare form' with no modifier. (One can assume
curtain itself is a class 10 noun, with a zero allomorph for the class prefix.
Its plurality is indicated by the noun class 10 subject prefix on the verb,
zi-.)

> [23] Mbona hawa *workers* wa East Africa Power and Lighting
> wa-ka-end-a   *strike* hata wengine nasikia washawek-w-a
> 3PL-CONSEC-go-INDIC   even others   I hear 3PL-already-put-PASS-INDIC
> *cell.*
> 'And why did the East African Power and Lighting workers go [on] strike, I
> even heard that some of them have already been put [in] cell[s] [*i.e. jail*].'
> (Swahili/English No.18)

The bare forms here are especially interesting because they are nouns
fulfilling a locative function, and Bantu languages typically require marking of a locative role by affixation. However, Swahili is one of the few
Bantu languages not marking locative with a noun-class prefix. Instead, it
uses one of the following strategies: (*a*) a nominal suffix *-ni*; (*b*) a self-
standing form, either *kwenye*, literally 'the place having' (which does show
the locative prefix *ku-* which becomes *kw-* before the vowel); or (*c*) *katika*
(apparently a defective stative form of the verb *-kata*, meaning 'cut', with
katika taking on the meaning of 'be in' as well as other related meanings).
(This example and similar instances are discussed again in Chapter 5 in
relation to the Blocking Hypothesis and congruence between the ML
morpheme and its EL counterpart in regard to system morpheme status.)

Others also note bare forms. Berk-Seligson (1986) comments that, in
her Hebrew/Spanish data from Israel, some Spanish nouns (with Spanish
presumably the EL) appear with no articles or determiners. While there
is no indefinite article in Hebrew, a definite clitic marker (*ha-*) as a prefix
is obligatory in Hebrew sentences with no copula. Berk-Seligson puzzles
over such data: 'The question as to why the Hebrew definite article is
omitted is difficult to explain, since its presence would not violate Spanish norms' (p. 329).

Backus (1990) finds that bare forms also appear in his Turkish/Dutch
CS data. He cites the following example, noting that Turkish possessive
and accusative markers would have been expected with the Dutch noun
prijs. (This expectation is in line with the System Morpheme Principle
about to be discussed.) Had it occurred in an all-Dutch sentence, there
would have been a Dutch possessive. Instead, there are no function

elements at all, making *prijs* a bare form. Turkish morpheme order is followed.

[24] *Nee*, bun-lar herkes kendi *prijs* soyluyor.
  no this-PL every REfl price name-PRES-3S
  'No, here everybody names price himself.'

(Turkish/Dutch; Backus, 1990: 3)

Nortier (1990) offers an extremely thorough investigation of Dutch nouns which appear as bare forms in her Moroccan Arabic/Dutch CS corpus, but is unable to explain their occurrence in the great majority of cases. Nortier examined 285 Dutch single nouns, which occur in several different syntactic configurations; for example, there are 82 cases in which the definite article is missing from a Dutch noun in contexts requiring a definite article in Arabic (i.e. Arabic is the ML). While I offer an explanation for some bare forms in Chapter 5, when the role of ML system morphemes is discussed, the motivation for other bare forms remains something of a puzzle.

The Morpheme-Order Principle: Summary

Under all three strategies, the morpheme order of the ML is followed. In fact, the only data in the Nairobi corpus, apart from one example, *not* following ML order qualify as EL islands; other data sets show similar distributions. (Recall that to qualify as an EL island requires more than EL morpheme order. The EL material must be well-formed according to EL specifications, showing internal structural dependencies. This means that singly occurring lexemes are excluded.) Recall that the Morpheme-Order Principle only claims to apply categorically to single CS forms.

Following any of three strategies will preserve the Morpheme-Order Principle. The first strategy of following ML order has been illustrated in [6]–[20]. That is, the lemmas activate only ML grammatical procedures, including those for assigning an unmarked ML surface morpheme order. In the second strategy, lemmas activate other surface syntactic procedures which are marked for the ML, but still entirely possible; equally important, these are unmarked for the EL, as in [21]. Finally, in the third strategy (illustrated in [22]–[24]) lemmas send directions for only *some* of the ML grammatical procedures which would be set in motion in mono-lingual ML production; the result is a bare form. At the same time, ML procedures are blocked for marking certain semantic and syntactic relationships which would have been expressed by what will be defined as system morphemes. One explanation for this blocking is lack of congruence between the ML and the EL in regard to expressing these relationships; this is discussed in Chapter 5.

The System Morpheme Principle

This principle contains the hypothesis that if system morphemes are required in ML + EL constituents to signal system relations, they will be ML system morphemes.

This principle does not exclude the appearance of EL system morphemes, such as plural affixes on nouns. But if there are EL system morphemes inflecting a stem, there *also* must be the ML version of the inflection. The existence of some CS forms showing inflections from both the ML and the EL (i.e. showing double morphology) was discussed in Chapter 3.

In such cases, only ML system morphemes may have grammatical relations external to the lexical item (e.g. signal agreement). To date, the only doublet EL system morphemes appearing in data sets are those whose only role could be construed as signalling lexically internal relations (e.g. plurality). Even then, since the doublet ML inflection appears, there is no reason to assume that the EL system morpheme is, in fact, performing any function. Such EL system morphemes in ML + EL constituents are a form of production error, it may be concluded. Such a scenario is suggested in Chapter 5.

Defining System and Content Morphemes

The SM principle embodies a far-reaching hypothesis: the ML and EL are not equally empowered when it comes to system morphemes in ML + EL constituents; only the ML may assign such morphemes.

As noted above, one must credit some earlier researchers with recognizing, if incompletely, that there is support for this hypothesis. For example, in writing about his Akan cluster/English CS data, Forson (1979: 116) notices that EL inflections are not used with Akan stems in what are called ML + EL constituents here.

Indeed extensive switching by the typical Akan with high education may include any grammatical units from the top of the rank scale, the sentence, to the bottom, the morpheme, *except that English bound morphemes are not used with Akan stems.* (my emphasis)

Others notice that there may be restrictions governing singly occurring EL function words (i.e. what might occur outside EL islands). For example, Sridhar and Sridhar (1980: 409) state: 'Grammatical items such as articles, quantifiers, auxiliaries, prepositions and clitics are least likely to be mixed by themselves.' And, of course, Joshi (1985), discussed earlier, argues that closed-class items are from only one of the languages in what the MLF model terms ML + EL constituents. But no earlier treatments were able either to put together the precise details of a warrant to the ML to supply system morphemes for specific types of constituent or to identify system morphemes in any general sense.

This warrant, the Principle, entails this prediction:

> Within ML + EL constituents, *all* active system morphemes are from only one of the languages participating in CS, the ML.

What Is a System Morpheme?

The issue of actually defining what I am referring to as system morphemes is hardly ever raised. Linguists would generally agree that closed-class items (a grouping similar, but not identical, to system morphemes) include all inflectional affixes, since their syntactic behaviour is very different from that of content morphemes, such as nouns and verbs. But they also proceed as if the distinction between free-form function words (which are system morphemes) and content words were obvious. True, membership of the function word class is obvious, in that it is relatively closed in contrast to the openness of membership of the content word class. In regard to syntactic behaviour, however, the line becomes blurred between function and content words. This is especially true cross-linguistically, with prepositions and pronouns as the most problematic cases.

Because the distinction between content and system morphemes is so pivotal in the MLF model, universally applicable criteria to define these categories are necessary. In addition, such criteria must be independent of the model itself to avoid circularity. For example, it would be circular to state that any ML morpheme which might be construed as a system morpheme *is*, in fact, a system morpheme, simply by virtue of appearing in test positions in ML + EL constituents.

Jake and Myers-Scotton (1992) identify three properties of content versus system morphemes. They are [+/− Quantification], [+/− Thematic Role-Assigner], and [+/− Thematic Role-Receiver]. We began by recognizing certain functional properties of specific categories of lexical items. These categories possess a general *deictic* function; that is, categories such as determiners 'point to' particular individuals. Next, we saw that certain other morphemes 'select' events in a similar way; for example, tense morphemes select one time-frame rather than another.

From a more formal perspective, this deictic function can be treated as a lexical feature associated with morphemes that are members of particular syntactic categories. This lexical feature is [Quantification], as the term is used in systems of logic. We express this insight in this way: any lexical item belonging to a syntactic category which involves quantification across variables is a system morpheme.

This feature is most evidently a property of those syntactic categories involving quantification across individuals. This includes quantifiers, determiners, and possessive adjectives, or any other category which can be inserted under the specifier position of NP. However, as noted above, [Quantification] is seen as a property of other categories, such as tense and aspect, which involve quantification across events. That is, we are proposing that not just quantifiers (e.g. *all*, *any*, *no*), but any category which behaves quantificationally in a model-theoretic semantic sense, is also subcategorized by the feature [+ Quantification].[17] The assumption, therefore, is that any lexical item or affix which is a member of a syntactic category specified as plus for [Quantification] is a system morpheme.

Any categories which are [−Quantification] are potential content morphemes. Those which are, in fact, content morphemes have plus readings on one of the two features relating thematic roles to the predicate-argument structure of a constituent, [Thematic Role-Assigner] and [Thematic Role-Receiver]. (As indicated earlier, 'thematic [or 'theta'] role' refers to the more specific semantic relationships between verbs (and some prepositions) and their arguments. For example, the verb *beat* takes two arguments to which it assigns thematic roles: the role 'agent' is assigned to the subject argument and the role 'patient' is assigned to the object argument.) Verbs are the prototypical example of a category having the feature [+ Thematic Role-Assigner]. Most prepositions also qualify. Similarly, nouns are the prototypical example of a category showing the feature [+ Thematic Role-Receiver]. Any lexical item with a negative setting for either of these two features is a system morpheme. Among verbs, this will include the copula and *do* verbs, for example. See Fig. 4.2 for a schematic representation of content and system morpheme categories. (For brevity, θ-role is here used to denote 'thematic-role'.)

---

[17] Treating tense within a Montague framework, Dowty (1979) proposes that tense and time adverbs pick out individual events or subsets out of sets of possible events.

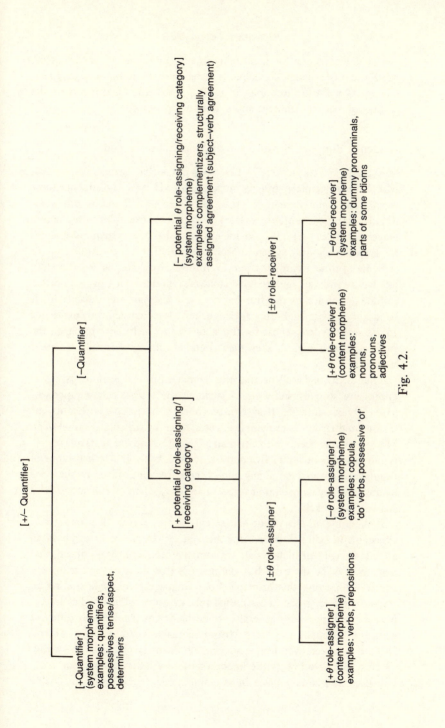

Fig. 4.2.

Using the criteria for identifying system morphemes just discussed, the System Morpheme Principle is tested across a number of data sets. Chapter 5 will offer examples of more problematic cases involving the distinction between content and system morphemes.

Evidence Supporting the System Morpheme Principle

In the Nairobi corpus of 374 CS types not in EL islands, the System Morpheme Principle is strongly supported for ML + EL constituents; there is only one counter-example. Also, the general CS literature offers additional empirical support, with no clear counter-examples to my knowledge. Examples [25]–[39] provide evidence that ML system morphemes are typically the only system morphemes in ML + EL constituents.

Some of these examples come from the Nairobi corpus and therefore involve Swahili, an agglutinative language. As noted in Chapter 2 when counter-examples to the free-morpheme constraint were discussed, it seems likely that agglutinative languages may have lemma entries for affixes separate from those for the stems with which they appear on the surface. In this regard, they may contrast with typologically different languages.

That is, it may well be that the lemma entries of agglutinative languages are so constructed as to facilitate the typical configurations of ML + EL constituents. If system morphemes have separate lemma entries from their heads in these languages, then the CS configuration of an ML system morpheme with either an ML or EL head (content) morpheme is not hard to imagine. In contrast, it is possible that other types of languages may include stems and certain frequent affixes in the *same* lemma entry, making combinations of an ML system morpheme with an EL head less likely.

If these hypotheses about lemma entries are correct, then one would expect many examples supporting the System Morpheme Principle when a CS language pair includes an agglutinative language. And, indeed, that does seem to be the case. But the point is that there *also* are many examples supporting this principle from language pairs *not* including an agglutinative language. This means that evidence supports the System Morpheme Principle as generally applicable across typologically different pairs. For example, the West African languages cited in [33], [36], and [37] are as far removed from agglutination as any languages in the world.

This finding supports the hypothesis that a 'cafeteria line' construction does in fact take place in assembling ML + EL constituents. The formulator's directions for these constituents are to the effect: 'you must get in this line for your system morphemes, and then wider choices are open to you for the content morphemes'.

[25] Three young women are considering the effects of taking a job in a remote area of Kenya.

Lakini uzuri ni huu tu—Lake Bokoria. Ukikaa huko Baringo,
u-na-*change*,   mazee. Unafikiri kama watu wa huko, jo! Ukija huku
2S-NON-PAST-change
watu wanashangaa. U-na-anza   Ku-*behave* kama watu   wa
        2S-NON-PAST-begin-INDIC INFIN-   as   people of
huko wa-na-vyo-   -*behave*.
there 3PL-NON-PAST-MANNER behave
'But the attraction is only this—of Lake Bokoria. If you live there in Baringo, you change, my friend. You think as people from there! If you come here people will be amazed. You will begin to behave as people from there behave.'

(Swahili/English No. 6)

Such verb forms as *ku-behave* 'to behave' and even *wa-na-vyo-behave* 'as they behave' are not rare in the Nairobi corpus, as already noted above. Recall there are 91 finite verbs with English stems, all with the full set of requisite Swahili prefixes (even if they lack an obligatory, but more functionally peripheral, suffix).

[26] Five children, all of whom come from ethnically mixed marriages, are exchanging information about a fire they saw in Maringo Estate. The first speaker is a boy about 12 years old and the second is a girl of about 8.

Na, je, ule aliingianga[18] mpaka ndani ya *hao* ata hakujali *fire*?
                    up to inside of house
'And, say, what about that one who kept going back inside the house even without paying attention to [the] fire?'
Mmathe wa hiyo *hao* alikuwa akilia joo vile vitu zi- -me- -spoil-i-w-a.
                            they PERF spoil-θ-PASS-INDIC
'The mother of that house was crying oh how things were spoiled [for her].'

The interest here is in the English verb stem *spoil* which is inflected with Swahili System morphemes. I offer the literal translation of *zi-me-spoil-i-w-a* as: 'they were spoiled [for her]'. This verb form shows only one verbal extended suffix, but shows an epenthetic vowel ([i]) before the

---

[18] The *-ng-* suffix on the verb form is borrowed from the speaker's first language. Many of the Kenyan Bantu languages have such a suffix, conveying the meaning of repetitive or habitual action.

suffix (for passive).[19] The speaker gives the verb a non-standard agreement: it should agree with *vitu* (class 8, with *vi-* as a prefix); instead, it shows *zi-*, the subject prefix for class 10 nouns. As has been noted elsewhere by many researchers (e.g. Scotton, 1979), class 9 and 10 inflections tend to be generalized in up-country Swahili to replace those for other classes. It is very interesting that this child gives the borrowed form *mathe* 'mother' the class 1 prefix (*m-*) which standard Swahili requires for (most) singular humans. This is the only example in the Nairobi corpus of this prefix appearing on either a borrowed form or a CS form standing for a person (instead, most are put in class 9, taking advantage of its zero allomorph for the class prefix).

[27] Four people in a Luyia home are discussing the career plans of one of them, a young man who has just finished form 4.

Eh, unalipwa, lakini ile *scale* y-a   chini kabisa . . . nilitoka Eldoret nikaja
                        scale CL 9-of below
Nakuru na *hope* y-a   kufanya *interview.*
                CL 9-of to do
'Yes, you are paid, but the lowest scale completely . . . I went from Eldoret to Nakuru with [the] hope of doing [the] interview.'
(Swahili/English No. 9)

Here there are two instances of the use of the '*a* of association', a possessive stem which is a system morpheme (*scale ya chini* (scale-of-low) and *hope ya ku-fanya* (hope-of-to-do)). It appears in accordance with standard Swahili (i.e. in an N + *a* + N construction in standard Swahili, with the possessor noun in initial position). There are few adjectives in Swahili, and this construction is commonly used to express qualities of a noun, as it is used here, with a CS form in the initial position (*scale* and *hope*). In both cases, the constructions take the system morpheme signalling agreement with class 9 (*y-* + *-a*); this is usual for non-animate singular CS nouns. But one should not assume that *ya* has become a fixed form; other agreements appear in the data, e.g. the plural equivalent of *ya*, which is *za*, as in *plan za Saturday* 'plans of Saturday' (Nairobi corpus No. 8); or even class 11/14 agreement, as in *wimbo wa teacher* 'song of the teacher' (Nairobi corpus No. 39).

---

[19] For some reason, this passive suffix (with the epenthetic vowel) is relatively common with English verb stems in Nairobi; I have heard it often myself, and other linguists in Nairobi comment on its occurrence.

Specific Support for the System Morpheme Principle

Data on the '*a* of association' construction in the Nairobi corpus strongly support the System Morpheme Principle. In the 55 examples of the use of an English noun as a CS form in one of the two noun slots in this construction, there are no examples of the English preposition *of* being used instead of the Swahili system morpheme. This is even the case when the two nouns in the equation are both English borrowed forms (e.g. *charlie ya mine* 'friend of mine'; *course ya typing* 'typing course'). It happens there are no examples in which both members of the English-origin pair of nouns are unambiguously CS forms; but since there are a number of examples with two borrowed forms, this result may just be accidental.

Other tests for the System Morpheme Principle are possessive adjectives and demonstratives, forms which are [+Quantification] and therefore system morphemes under the definitions proposed above. The prediction is that English members of these form-classes will not occur with Swahili heads (i.e. in ML + EL constituents). This hypothesis is supported: possessive adjectives and demonstratives are always in Swahili in these constituents. (There are two cases of EL islands, consisting of an English possessive adjective and an English noun. But the point is that these occur as islands, not ML + EL constituents. They are counted as islands because they meet the definitional criterion of EL islands in showing EL morpheme order, not that for ML + EL constituents.)

What is important to note is the reverse pattern: absolutely no EL system morphemes occur with Swahili nouns. (A counter-example would be *this mtu* or *mtu this* 'this person'; or *mfuko my* or *my mfuko* 'my bag'; instead, one finds *mtu huyu* 'this person' and *bag yangu* literally 'bag my'). The fact some EL descriptive adjectives *do* occur with Swahili nouns, but following ML morpheme order (e.g. *nguo nyingine bright*, literally 'clothes other bright'), strengthens the case for claiming that while content morphemes (for descriptive adjectives) may come from either language, only the ML is licensed in system morpheme specification.

There are only a few instances (N = 6) of an interrogative pronoun in the Nairobi corpus, none occurring with CS forms, but several with borrowed forms (e.g. *uko class gani?* literally 'you are in class which?'). But the point is that interrogatives are always in the ML, as would be expected, given that they have the feature [+Quantification].

[28] Two Meru sisters are conversing with a Luyia man. All are in their twenties.

... *results* zake ha-zi-ku-w-a   nzuri, basi a-ka-*judge* kuwa skuli
       his   NEG-CL 10-PAST-be-INDIC good well 3S-CONSEC COMP school
ni mbaya.
COP bad
'... His results were not good, so he judged that [the] school is bad.'
(Swahili/English No. 10)

The NP r*esults zake* (results his) 'his results' is important to the double-morphology issue in CS, already raised and to be discussed again in Chapter 5. Here, what is relevant is that all the system morphemes are from Swahili, the ML. Note the possessive adjective *zake* 'his', but also the tense/aspect prefixes on the English verb stem *judge* (i.e. *a-ka-judge*).

[29] Three young men of form 4 education are talking.
Si   hiyo ni *early* sana! Z-ile   ma-*time* z-ote   z-engine
NEG DEM COP   early   CL 10-DEM CL 6-   CL 10-all CL 10-other
utafanya nini?
you will do what
'Isn't that very early! What will you do for the rest of the time?
[Note that *z-ile ma-time z-ote z-engine* is literally: 'those time all other'.]
(Swahili/English No. 32)

Note that in the first sentence of this example all the system morphemes (NEG, DEM, COP) are from Swahili, the ML, with an English content morpheme (the adjective, *early*, taking a Swahili (ML) adverb, *sana* 'very'). In the second sentence, an English CS noun (*time*) has been inflected with the class-marker which class 6 takes, but its modifiers show class 10 agreements. This agreement pattern is non-standard, and will be taken up later when modularity is discussed. The point here is to show that the system morphemes modifying the noun (the demonstrative *zile* and the quantifiers *zote zengine*) are Swahili.

Examples from other languages with system morphemes coming from the ML follow. Relevant morphemes will be pointed out.

[30] Tajziw tajdiru dak *la regulation*[20] djal *les naissances* ...
'They come and do that-the limitation of the births ...'
[The Arabic morpheme encoding 'of' *djal* appears in this construction, even though both the possessed and the possessor are from the EL, which is French here.]
(Moroccan Arabic/French; Bentahila and Davies, 1992: 450)

---

[20] Such constituents as *dak la regulation* 'this-the regulation' will be analysed in Ch. 5 as instances of an EL island within an ML + EL constituent.

[31] À moins qu'ils diraient que le *brain* est *completely finished*, pis que toute, toute, toute est fini.
'Unless they say the brain is completely finished, and absolutely everything is finished.'

(French/English; Poplack, 1988*b*: 99)

(Note that, while EL content morphemes (from English) are possible, all the system morphemes which go with them (i.e. the article *le* and the copula *est*) are from French, the ML. Note also that *finished* is interpreted as an adjectival complement of the copula, not as a verb stem inflected with the past-tense suffix.)

[32] *Second group. Second group*-ul ceyil cwohahay.
'Second group. I like [this] second group best.'

(Korean/English; Park, Troike, and Mun, 1989: 9)

Note that a case-marker (*-ul*) from Korean, the ML here, appears with the English content morpheme.

[33] Yɛ- [sɛ̌jest]   -i-i na   wɔ́- [-kɔmfɛː m-] -i- -i
    1PL suggest v-[21] PAST and they confirm   V–PAST
'We suggested [it] and they confirmed [it].'

(Fante/English; Forson, 1979: 170)

While content morphemes from English appear for the verb stems, all inflectional morphology comes from Fante, the ML, including the null object pronominals. As will be argued in Chapter 5, English pronouns are blocked here.

[34] Ben *kamer*-im-i   *opruimen* yap-ar-ken, hepsini geri korum.
     I   room-POSS/1S-ACC tidy   do-AOR-CONV
'When tidying my room, I put them all back.'

(Turkish/Dutch; Boeschoten, 1991: 90)

Of interest here is that all system morphemes are in Turkish, the ML. The free-form emphatic pronoun *ben* 'I' is also from Turkish, but it will be argued in Chapter 5 that such forms are content morphemes, while the co-occurring null pronominal is a system morpheme.

[35] *Some Englishmen* ne *tribal girls* ko phusalaa liyaa.
               NOM   ACC seduce did

---

[21] The abbreviation V in the morpheme-by-morpheme translation here stands for 'extra Asante vowel' (Forson, 1979: 91). Forson notes that it figures prominently in CS in the speech of Asantes in various syntactic positions. It is a mid-vowel agreeing with a preceding high vowel.

'Some Englishmen seduced the tribal girls.'

(Hindi/English; Pandit, 1990: 44)

Here, the case-markers (i.e. *ne* and *ko*) are from the ML, Hindi. *Some Englishmen* and *tribal girls* are EL islands within the larger ML + EL constituents which include the case-markers. Such islands are discussed at the end of Chapter 5.

[36] Dafa ko ko *meuble*-el,   *frisideer   manquer*-wul *gaz manquer*-wul,
     He   IO DO furnish-APPL frigidaire lack -NEG   gas lack-NEG
fotoy manquer-wul, *armoor*, lai, weer   wu nekk *cinquante milles* lay yónne ci
armchair lack-NEG armoire bed month REL be   fifty thousand 3S send to
yaayam
mother-POSS
'He furnished it, there's a refrigerator, there's gas, there's an armchair, an armoire, a bed, and every month he sends fifty thousand [francs] to her mother.'

(Wolof/French; Swigart, 1992: 164)

Obviously, this example shows a number of cultural borrowed forms from French; but the point is that its system morphemes all come from Wolof (e.g. the negative marker *-wul* with the verb *manquer*).

[37] Awon nkan   ti   o *come naturally to me* ni mo *like*
     those things that it   is I   like
'I like those things that come naturally to me.'

(Yoruba/English; Oloruntoba, 1990: 1)

Once again, all system morphemes, including the copula (*ni*) and the pronominals (*o* 'it' and *mo* 'I') come from Yoruba, the ML. Also note that what will be discussed in Chapter 5 as another system morpheme, the complementizer (*ti*), comes from Yoruba. Note that the VP *come naturally to me* is an EL island.

[38] Ta—mbo—*discuss* ne-ma-HPO tione kuti tinga ku-*appreciate* here?
     1P   earlier discuss about-CL 6-HPO
'Earlier we discussed about the HPO [head post office] that we should see if we appreciate [it]?

(Shona/English; Crawhall, 1990)

While English verb stems are possible, all the inflectional morphology comes from Shona, the ML, since these forms are all system morphemes.

[39] Ja   ma *koka*-sin   kahvin.
     and I   cook-PAST coffee
'And I cooked coffee.'

(Finnish/Swedish; Hyltenstam, 1991: 246)

While the content morpheme for 'cook' comes from the EL, Swedish, its subject pronoun and the past-tense marker, as system morphemes, come from Finnish. Example [39] comes from a data corpus drawn from spontaneous speech by Swedish patients with Alzheimer's dementia; they are bilinguals, with Finnish as their first language. Note that Hyltenstam himself (p. 246) refers to morphemes such as *koka* as borrowings because they show morphological and syntactic integration. The interpretation followed here, of course, is that these singly occurring EL lexemes are CS forms; the fact that CS and borrowed forms cannot be distinguished, based on their morphosyntactic integration, is discussed in Chapter 6.

Counter-Examples to the System Morpheme Principle?

If examples occurred in the Nairobi corpus of Swahili or English nouns or verbs inflected with English affixes, or with English specifiers, these would falsify the System Morpheme Principle. These do not occur. Hypothetical counter-examples follow (as the [*a*] examples) along with [*b*] examples which themselves do not occur, but are patterned exactly as configurations actually present in the Nairobi corpus.

[40*a*] *Yule mtu   ni *the boss's* mtoto.
      that person is   child
'That person is the boss's child.'

[40*b*] Yule mtu ni mtoto w-a   *boss*.
                   child CL 1-of
'That person is the boss's child.'

As noted above, all specifiers in the Nairobi corpus in ML + EL constituents are from only one language, Swahili, which is the ML. Also, possessive *of* is always in Swahili.

[41*a*] *Ni-(i)-*suggest*-ed i-le   *plan* wiki jana.
      1s-(OBJ)-   CL 9-DEM   week yesterday
'I suggested that plan last week.'

[41*b*] Ni-li-i-*suggest* i-le *plan* wiki jana.
'I suggested that plan last week.'

As indicated above, there are many cases of English verb stems (finite verbs and infinitives) taking Swahili inflectional prefixes; but there is not a single case of an English verb with English affixes, as in [41*a*]. The Shona/English data set studied also offers categorical evidence that Bantu system morphemes for verbs in ML + EL constituents come from only one language, the ML. The same applies in Zulu/English CS in South Africa as studied by Koopman (1990).

Three Strategies for Maintaining the System Morpheme Principle
Just as three strategies are possible under the Morpheme-Order Prin-
ciple, there are three possible ways one can maintain the System
Morpheme Principle.

1. *ML system morphemes.* The formulator goes only to addresses with
ML morphemes for system morphemes. The many examples just cited
illustrate this strategy. In fact, in all data sets examined there are no
examples of inflectional system morphemes in ML + EL constituents from
any language other than the one defined as the ML (except those showing
double morphology and discussed immediately below).

2. *Simultaneous system morphemes (double morphology).* The formulator
accesses not only ML system morphemes but also those EL system
morphemes which are at the same lemma address as an EL noun or verb
stem (or somehow automatically accessed with the stem). Here, however,
the resemblance between the morphological doublets ends: these EL
system morphemes have no relationships external to their heads; i.e. they
show no interrelations with other items in the sentence, such as
agreement.

3. *EL content morphemes as bare forms.* As with the Morpheme-Order
Principle, the formulator admits EL content morphemes, but blocks the
procedures for the ML system morphemes which would have been assigned to slots alongside those of the surface slots of the EL content
morphemes.

Double Morphology[22]
The System Morpheme Principle allows for 'double morphology', as I
call it in Chapter 3. The phenomenon is discussed here in reference to
this principle, but a scenario explaining how double-morphology forms
are produced is offered in Chapter 5.

Bokamba (1988) was the first to point out in Lingala/French CS what
he called the *double infinitive* and the *double plural*:

[42] *L'heure* ya kala *trois quarts* ya ba-*jeune-s* baza ko-*comprend-re avenir* te *mais*
sik'oyo na *quatre quarts, trois quarts* baza ko-comprend-re *l'avenir* mpe *la plupart*
bakoti *class.*

---

[22] In earlier versions of the frame model, when noun or verb stems showed double
prefixation, the ML affixes were referred to as 'productive' and the EL ones as 'non-
productive'. I have dropped these terms because they are confusing. I note that 'productive'
is normally used in linguistics in reference to derivational affixes, not inflectional ones, in
reference to their ability to combine with new relevant stems.

'In the past three-quarters of the young people did not understand what their future meant, but now out of four-quarters, three-quarters understand what their future means and most of them are in school.'

(Lingala/French; Bokamba, 1988: 37)

Bokamba remarks that ba-jeune-s 'young people' shows both the prefix marking Bantu class 2 (used for plurals referring to humans) and the suffix marking French plural. The noun stem *jeune*, of course, is French. Similarly, the infinitive (*ko-comprend-re* 'to understand') has a Lingala prefix and a French suffix, both making the French verb stem -*comprend*-an infinitive.

Kamwangamalu (1989*b*) gives another example from Lingala/French CS which is even more convincing, because in this case the French plural suffix is followed by a word beginning with a vowel, and therefore the plural suffix is definitely realized in speech:

[43] Ba-*programme-s* oyo ya ba-*chemins de fer* ekoti na mai o bung!
'All the plans for railroads have failed.'

(Lingala/French; Kamwangamalu, 1989*b*: 120)

Double morphology turns up in CS corpora across a number of language pairs. Double-plural affixes are the main exemplars. For example, they occur across all Bantu languages for which CS has been studied (e.g. those in Zaïre, as well as Eastern and Southern African Bantu languages). They present themselves most often on CS forms placed in Bantu noun class 6, as is the case in example [44] from Shona/English CS. And, in at least Swahili/English, they also occur on class 10 nouns.

[44] *But* ma-*day-s*   a-no   a-ya handisi kumuona.
     CL 6 day-PL CL 6 DEM CL 6 DEM
'But these days I don't see him much.'

(Shona/English; Crawhall, 1990)

Some double forms with class 6 prefixes appear in the Nairobi corpus (e.g. *ma-watchmen*) but they are relatively few (N = 3); however, there also are a few established borrowed forms with double plurals.

[45] In an office, a Kalenjin man addresses three secretaries who have been chatting, not working. He jokes with them.

Mnashinaje wamama? Leo inaonekana hamna kazi. Tangu asubuhi ni
                                            since   morning is
kupika ma-*stories* tu.
to cook stories   just

'How are you passing the day, ladies? Today it seems you don't have any work. Since morning there's only "to cook" stories.'

(Swahili/English No. 36)

There are more double plurals in class 10 (e.g. *zile trip-s*) in the Nairobi corpus than in class 6. The nouns govern class 10 agreements elsewhere in the sentence, and therefore assuming the presence of a zero allomorph as a class 10 prefix is justified.

Double plurals are also reported for other language pairs, e.g. Backus (1990: 4) for Turkish/Dutch; Eliasson (1991: 19–20) for Maori/English; and Kamwangamalu (1990: 5) for Lingala and Chiluba/French; Hill and Hill (1986: 165) for Mexicano (Nahuatl). Appel and Muysken (1987: 172–3) point out that in Bolivian Quechua, Spanish plural suffixes are so integrated that they show up in indigenous Quechua nouns as well. Note that the Quechua plural suffix (*-kuna*) is also always present (e.g. *polisiya-s-kuna* 'policemen').

Accessing Bare Forms

Using bare forms, EL morphemes without inflections, or modifying function words from either language, is a common strategy. As noted above, allowing such bare forms (without modifiers which would have to be positioned) may be a strategy to avoid clashes between ML and EL morpheme order.

A full discussion of bare forms necessarily would distinguish between those forms which are bare because they are lacking ML system morphemes and those which would occur with no obligatory system morphemes even in a monolingual EL utterance. Entirely predictable are those which are bare because they are missing EL system morphemes: i.e. the EL requires a system morpheme (e.g. a specifier), but the ML does not. These bare forms could be predicted by a corollary to the System Principle. That is, non-occurrence of 'syntactically relevant' EL system morphemes would be predicted.

In Chapter 5, it will be suggested that there may be a partial explanation for bare forms: lack of congruence in regard to system morpheme status for a given morpheme between the EL and ML.

Here, a widespread case of bare forms will be detailed. This is the use of *do* constructions, consisting of a *do* verb from the ML, carrying any necessary inflections, followed by a bare EL verb stem which provides the semantic content. Such constructions allow EL verb stems to 'avoid' ML inflectional morphemes. These constructions occur in a widely diverse set of language pairs (e.g. Romaine, 1989: 120–30 on Panjabi/English; Azuma,

1991*a* on Japanese/English; Bickmore, 1985 and Madaki, 1983 on Hausa/ English). Many other researchers find these structures in Indian languages, whether they are Indo-Aryan or Dravidian. I add Shona/English in this discussion.

Typically, such EL verbs are entirely uninflected stems, but accompanied by an inflected ML verb which is the equivalent of *do*. In (46) the ML verb is the Panjabi verb *kerna* [kərna] 'to do' and in [47] it is the Shona verb *kuita* 'to do'.

[46] O   apni *own language* nu *look down upon* kərən.
     they their   ACC   do
'They look down upon their own language.'

(Panjabi/English; Romaine, 1989: 129)

[47] Eh, *because* mukadzi unogona kukasika ku-zvi-ita *adjust* kuziva   kuti
                                              to CL 8 OBJ-do to know that
yaa, *I am somebody's wife.*
yes
'Yes, because a woman can easily adjust to know that yes, I am somebody's wife.'

(Shona/English; Crawhall, 1990)

There are variations on what appears as the bare verb form. For example, Annamalai (1989: 50–1) states that, in Tamil/English CS, unbalanced bilinguals (her term) are more likely to use the nominal form of the verb, while balanced bilinguals use the stem or infinitive form:

[48*a*] Avan enne *confuse*-paNNiTTaan
        he   me   did
'He confused me.'

[48*b*] Avan enne *confusion*-paNNiTTaan
'He confused me.'

(Tamil/English; Annamalai, 1989: 51)

And Hausa only accepts a nominalized form of English verbs in such constructions (example [49]). Bickmore (1985: 31–4) argues that the reason for this is that, although Hausa grammar does not require a noun to be of any certain tonal type, Hausa verbs must fit into one of seven tonal grade patterns.

[49] A'a mun san abin da muka   yi *creating* dai
                       REL 1PL PAST do   that is
'No, rather we knew what we created.'

(Hausa/English; Madaki, 1983: 87)

There are no indications in the Nairobi corpus (or in other Swahili data sets studied) that the '*do* construction' will enter Swahili/English CS; however, it is quite common in the Southern Bantu languages, such as Chewa in Malawi (e.g. *ku-chita enjoy*, literally 'to do enjoy' for 'to enjoy') and, of course, Shona, as cited above.

Still, there are a few examples in the Nairobi corpus of English infinitives being used as 'bare forms' (i.e. without the Swahili infinitive-marking for class 15, *ku-*). But there are only 5 such forms, as against 31 with the requisite *ku-*. In 4 of the five cases, the bare infinitive occurs with the auxiliary verb *-weza* as in [50]. (Are these loan translations from English? English, of course, does not require *to* with infinitives following this auxiliary.)

[50] Kwa vile ziko nyingi, si-wez-i   *decide* ile inafaa zaidi.
     1S NEG-can-NEG
'Because there are many, I can't decide the most proper one.'
(Swahili/English No. 15)

A more interesting case for Swahili/English CS is how the few past participles are handled. They are being treated as adjectives, one might argue; but they are also what I have been calling bare forms. That is, they show no prefixes inflecting them for noun class. When they appear, they are typically used to refer to humans. And, while many other class agreements may be 'switched off' in up-country Swahili (or with class 9/10 agreements being used instead for all non-animates, as noted above), agreements for humans (classes 1/2) appear fairly robust, at least for modifiers. An example of a past participle as a bare form appears at the end of [51] as *offered*:[23]

[51] Seven young men from different ethnic groups, all relatively well educated, are talking in an Eastleigh home about a dance the previous night.

G. Huyo jamaa a-li-*marry*   *sistee*.
   3S-PAST
'That guy married [my] sister.'
A. Lakini huyo jamaa nasikia ana *wife* wa-tatu.
'But that guy, I hear, has three wives.'

---

[23] [51] is also remarkable for its verbal prefixes with English verb stems. But of more interest in regard to the discussion of bare forms, especially with lexemes for animate beings, are these points: (*a*) the *lack* of an object prefix in the verbal assembly to signal the animate object (*sistee* 'sister'); and (*b*) the *presence* of class 2 agreements on *-tatu* 'three' so that it agrees with *wife* as an animate plural, even though *wife* itself shows no class 2 prefix.

G. Haukuona a-ki- -ni-buy-i-a   *beer* siku hiyo?
       3S-PROG-IO-buy-APPL-INDIC
'Didn't you see him buying beer for me that day?'
A. A-li-ku-w-a   ha-zi-*buy*   hizo, a-li-ku-w-a
    3S-PAST-INFIN-be-INDIC 3S NEG-CL 10-buy those 3S-PAST-INFIN-be-INDIC
a-na-ku-w-a   *offered* tu.
3S-PROG-INFIN-be-INDIC   just
'He didn't buy those, he was just offered.'
(Swahili/English No. 16)

If the fragment *alikuwa anakuwa offered* 'he was being offered' had been
entirely in Swahili, it probably would also have been rendered by a
compound verb, with a form of *(ku)wa* 'be' as the first member, as it
is here. But rather than have a second form of *(ku)wa*, as is the case
here, a verb such as *-pewa* 'be given/offered' would have been used. The
result would have been: *alikuwa anapewa* 'he was being offered'. In other
words, the idea of 'offered' would be conveyed by a finite verb with full
prefixation. Instead, what appears here is the Swahili verb *(ku) wa*, the
copula, functioning much as an ML *do* verb functions in other CS language pairs; the only difference is that, rather than taking a bare EL verb
stem, a past participle form (i.e. *offered*) appears.

There are only a handful of 'bare' past participles[24] in the Nairobi
corpus; but they do illustrate another way in which verb forms avoid ML
system morphemes.

Summarizing the Argument for the System Morpheme Principle
The System Morpheme Principle is maintained in regard to system
morphemes accompanying any ML lexeme and single-lexeme CS forms
by one of these three strategies:
    1. Only lemmas for/including system morphemes from the ML are
called up.
    2. In addition, when lemmas which are realized by EL content morph-
emes are called, those EL system morphemes included at the same 'address' are also allowed, but they govern no modifiers and show no relations
to other system morphemes in the sentence. All evidence points to the
EL affix's having been analysed as part of the stem, at least by the ML
morphosyntactic procedures which are directing frame construction.

---

[24] There are a number of examples of English past participles in an innovating construction in modern Swahili, the *-ko* construction. It represents a 'new' copula construction.
Examples with CS forms are *tu-ko confused* 'we are confused' and *wa-tu wa-ko trained*
'people are trained'.

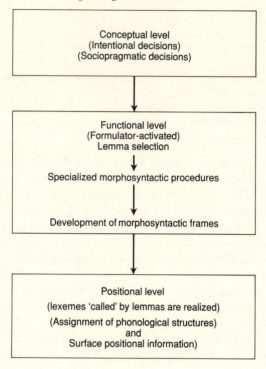

Fig. 4.3

3. Some bare-form EL content morphemes are sanctioned and some special ML procedures are activated to cover the appearance of some EL content morphemes. That is, some ML syntactic procedures are blocked (i.e. those which would have inserted system morphemes to accompany the EL content morphemes).

Setting the Frame in the MLF Model

This chapter has presented the basic ways in which the MLF model hypothesizes that ML + EL constituents are structured. In terms of a production model, this is how such constraints might be described. Fig. 4.3 gives an overall model of a language production processor, and Fig. 4.4 represents a sentence containing CS, after it has passed through the

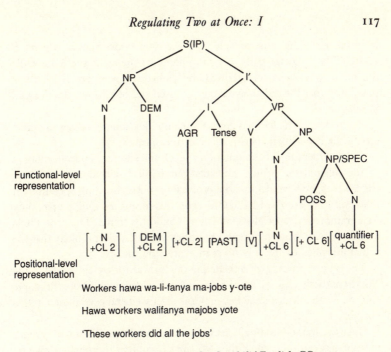

Fig. 4.4. *Functional-level frame for Swahili/English CS sentence.*

formulator in the functional level and is about to go on to the positional level.

Step 1. Speakers decide what they want to convey, and lemmas are selected to meet communicative intentions. This is the message-representation level, and the largely unconscious decisions at this level will involve some socio-pragmatic considerations, which will figure in whether CS or a single linguistic code will result.

Step 2. Language production in general proceeds with the building of a frame into which content morphemes are eventually inserted; the production of CS constituents is no exception. But since two or more languages are involved in CS production, the issue arises: where does the frame come from? The MLF model specifies that, of the two (or more) languages involved in the CS utterance, one language, the ML, is the dominant performer.

Another way of looking at the ML is to define it as the language of 'higher activity or saliency' during CS. The measure of this activity/saliency is the relative frequency of morphemes (across the participating languages) in a discourse sample from the interaction types in which CS occurs. The language of higher morpheme frequency is the ML, while the other language(s) are termed the embedded language (EL). (The possibility that the ML may change is discussed in Chapter 3 and again in Chapter 7.)

At this step, ML lemmas from the mental lexicon are retrieved which satisfy the conceptual specifications of the speaker.

Step 3. Operating at the functional level, the lemmas send information to the 'formulator' which activates grammatical encoding procedures. (Recall that the formulator is the processing centre directing operations at this level.) For an ML + EL constituent, this means the calling up of only ML grammatical 'specialists' which will build the frame. The procedures fix ML specifications for system morphemes, although it is likely that the actual morphemes are only filled in nearer the surface.

The crucial procedures activated in the formulator are embodied in the ML hypothesis and its two principles, the Morpheme-Order Principle and the System Morpheme Principle, as discussed and exemplified in this chapter.

Once the frame-building is set in motion, parallel processing of content morphemes can proceed. Either ML or EL content morphemes may be 'called' by ML or EL lemmas respectively, but they both appear in slots prepared by ML lemmas.

Step 4. Finally, a unified surface structure is produced as output, including phonological representations. This is the positional level-representation.

There is every reason to hypothesize that bilingual production processes are similar to those posited for a single language. The MLF model parallels psycholinguistic models for monolingual speech production by calling for the same two-step procedure these models envision. Bilingual production is more complex, to be sure, because it necessitates the extra 'traffic pattern' regulations entailed by having some lemmas tagged for one language and other lemmas tagged for another language. Recall the suggestion in Chapter 1 that a language is realized as a set of lemmas and the frames and procedures which the lemmas support. The provisions of the MLF model to activate only lemmas tagged for the ML (and to inhibit those tagged for the EL) at the frame-building level supply the basic regulations when ML + EL constituents take shape.

Note that the production of ML + EL constituents, therefore, involves no switching of languages in the frame. Rather, an ML + EL constituent goes through two different major sets of procedures: one sets the frame with morpheme order and system morphemes from the ML, and the other fills in the content morphemes. The overall process, then, is one of ML procedures for both the X-bar (schematic representation of a sentence) and thematic-role templates (or grids—the schematic listings of the particular thematic (or theta) roles which a specific verb (or preposition) assigns), followed by lexical insertion from either language (while maintaining these templates). That is, the claim is that the syntactic components of *both* languages are *not* active in producing these constituents.

When content morphemes are selected, there is no switching of procedures. Rather, either ML or EL lemmas in the mental lexicon are activated, calling up the ML or EL content morphemes associated with them; but among EL lemmas, only those which meet ML thematic grid specifications are selected, as will become clear in Chapter 5.

In Chapter 5, EL islands, the only allowable violations of the ML templates within the frame, will be discussed. EL islands are produced when ML procedures are entirely inhibited by EL procedures. Note that a switching of procedures 'from the top down' (i.e. at the lemma level) is hypothesized in order for EL islands to be constructed, with both system and content morphemes from the EL structures as output.

5
Regulating Two at Once, II:
Congruence in ML + EL Constituents and EL Islands

Preliminaries

This chapter has several goals. First, it will continue the discussion from Chapter 4 of ML + EL constituents by introducing a new constraint on ML + EL constituents, a blocking filter. A Blocking Hypothesis proposes that a filter blocks not only EL system morphemes prohibited under the System Morpheme Principle presented in Chapter 4 but also EL content morphemes which do not show certain specified congruences with ML content morphemes. Second, in a related discussion, this chapter characterizes EL islands; obligatory EL islands are the result of certain noncongruences also involving the Blocking Hypothesis.

The System Morpheme Principle discussed in Chapter 4 makes the prediction that syntactically relevant EL system morphemes will not appear in ML + EL constituents; only syntactically relevant ML system morphemes are allowed. This prediction is supported by all available data; examples in addition to those already discussed will be presented later in this chapter. Clearly, this principle limits the occurrence of EL morphemes in these constituents. However, I now propose the Blocking Hypothesis as a corollary to the SM principle to limit further EL participation by blocking certain EL content morphemes as well.

The Blocking Hypothesis

In ML + EL constituents, a blocking filter blocks any EL content morpheme which is not congruent with the ML with respect to three levels of abstraction regarding subcategorization.

I use 'congruence' in this sense: two entities (linguistic categories in this case) are congruent if they correspond in respect of relevant qualities.

First, even if the EL realizes a given grammatical category as a content morpheme, if it is realized as a system morpheme in the ML, the ML blocks the occurrence of the EL content morpheme. Second, the ML also blocks an EL content morpheme in these constituents if it is not congruent with an ML content morpheme counterpart in terms of thematic role assignment. At a third level, congruence between EL content morphemes and ML content morphemes is in terms of their discourse or pragmatic functions. Discussion of this type is beyond the scope of the current volume. However, this third type of congruence is a topic in Jake and Myers-Scotton (1992), which also especially considers aspects of all types of congruences as a test for current syntactic theories.

This hypothesis strengthens the System Morpheme Principle. It applies to instances in which a syntactic category is a system morpheme in one language but a content morpheme in another. Pronouns, for example, may represent such cases: one language may have pronominal forms which are agreement clitics (system morphemes) while the other language may have free-form pronouns (content morphemes). If, for example, the ML has pronominal clitics, then no EL free pronoun may be substituted for a clitic in CS constituents. Further discussion of this matter follows.

In addition, this hypothesis blocks EL content morphemes on the grounds of their congruency with ML morphemes in regard to subcategorization related to thematic-role assignment. Recall that, in Chapter 2, several other researchers are mentioned who suggest that subcategorization restrictions may explain constraints on CS utterance formation (e.g. Bentahila and Davies, 1983; Muysken, 1990; 1991; Azuma, 1991*b*). Not surprisingly, I find some of these suggestions attractive, since they resemble this part of the Blocking Hypothesis. However, the earlier proposals are not specific enough in important details, including the motivation for subcategorization restrictions. In the case of the Blocking Hypothesis, the motivation is clear. It comes from the dominant role of the ML in CS, not just expressed in regard to subcategorization in some general sense, but specifically in regard to the ML Hypothesis. In language production terms, ML lemmas are the ones activated for ML + EL constituents to provide stipulations for surface realizations. While EL lexemes can be inserted into ML frames, they are only acceptable if they meet ML specifications for these frames.

If the speaker's intentions (at whatever level of consciousness or abstraction) call for EL lexemes such that the congruencies indicated by the Blocking Hypothesis do not obtain, the frame of the ML + EL constituent must be broken. This is how most EL islands are produced.

Recall that the hypothesis suggested is that EL islands result when EL procedures are activated and ML ones are inhibited. This 'call' comes from EL lemmas as heads of constituents. The model assumes that bilinguals have the ability to select lemmas so tagged (for the ML or EL) that the resulting morphosyntax is a feature of one language system rather than another. This assumption that EL lemmas are directing selection in EL islands is supported by the surface configurations in these island constituents. First, they show EL morpheme order (and therefore cannot be ML + EL constituents because this order does not satisfy the Morpheme-Order Principle of the ML Hypothesis). Second, these islands include only syntactically relevant EL system morphemes; once again, they cannot be ML + EL constituents because they do not meet the requirements of the other building blocks of ML + EL constituents, the System Morpheme Principle and the Blocking Hypothesis.

Of course, it is also possible that some EL islands may result from a 'misfiring': an EL system morpheme is accessed in error. Since once an EL system morpheme appears, the constituent must be finished as an EL constituent, such errors may be the triggers which activate EL morphosyntactic procedures for the rest of the constituent.

The System Versus Content Morpheme Distinction: Further Examples

In order to understand the operation of the Blocking Hypothesis, further examples regarding the system/content morpheme distinction are needed.

Prepositions and Congruence

According to the criteria introduced in Chapter 4, some prepositions are content morphemes and some are system morphemes. Also, it is possible that their membership in these categories varies cross-linguistically. To begin with an example showing congruency across languages, consider the English and Swahili NPs, *picture of John* and *picha ya John*. The preposition *of* and its Swahili counterpart, the 'a of association', simply mark *John* as a complement of *picture/picha*. Within the scheme outlined here, both these forms identify *John*. Thus, they have a plus setting for the feature [Quantification] and are system morphemes.[1] Consistent with

---

[1] English, of course, has another preposition *of* which is a content morpheme. Consider *they don't approve of us.* Here, *of* is a thematic role- and case-assigner.

this designation, examples in Chapter 4 show that these genitival markers come from the ML in ML + EL constituents.

Many locative or temporal prepositions are system morphemes, because they show the requisite quantification across individuals. This means they will come only from the ML in a prepositional phrase (PP) which is an ML + EL constituent. This prediction is supported across all data sets in the literature. For example, see *en nineteen seventy-six* 'in 1976' in [3] and the postposition *me* in *merii situation me* (my-situation-in) in [4]:

[3] La organización empezó en *nineteen seventy-six*
'The organization started in 1976'

(Spanish/English; Jacobson 1990: 134)

[4] . . . mai jab   soctii h̶u̶u̶ ke   kitnii aurte   hai jo   merii *situation*
    I   when   think that   how many other women   are who my   situation
me agar ho . . .
in if   are
'. . . when I think that how many other women who are in my situation . . .'

(Urdu/English; Anjum, 1991: 28)

However, some prepositions are content morphemes because they have a plus setting for the feature [Thematic Role Assigner], as well as the feature [−Quantification]. An example of such a preposition is *for* in English. It assigns the thematic role of beneficiary or goal to John in [5]:

[5] I brought the book for John.

However, its content morpheme status in English notwithstanding, *for* does not have congruent status with a Swahili morpheme. In Swahili, the verb assigns the thematic roles of beneficiary or goal. In fact, Swahili has few prepositions. A counterpart for *for* might be the suffix in the verbal assembly, realized as *-i-* or *-e-* (the choice depending on vowel harmony) which is called the 'applied form'. Its presence simply 'spells out' the beneficiary, in much the same way as *of* or *-a* in *picture of John/picha ya John* spells out John as a complement of *picture/picha*. This Swahili suffix is a system morpheme, and therefore is not congruent with English *for*. Note that this suffix occurs in [6], its appearance involving a switch from English to Swahili in accordance with the System Morpheme Principle.

[6] Labda yeye hana vitabu vyake *father* a-li-m-*buy*-i-a akapoteza vyote.
                                    3S-PAST-3S/OBJ-buy-APPL-INDIC
'Maybe he doesn't have his books [which his] father bought for him, and he lost all of them.'

(Swahili/English No. 20)

The lack of congruence of *for* and a Swahili counterpart is implied in the non-occurrence in the Nairobi corpus of a sentence such as [7a], but the occurrence of [7b]:

> [7a] *Nikamwambia anipe ruhusa niende ni-ka-*check*   *for* wewe
>   1s-CONSEC-check for you
> 'And I told him he should give me permission so that I go and check for you.'
>
> [7b] Nikamwambia anipe ruhusa niende ni-ka-*check for you.*
> (Swahili/English No. 38)

That is, *for* occurs when it heads an EL island, but may not occur in place of a Swahili counterpart in an ML + EL constituent.

The predictions of the Blocking Hypothesis also account for the occurrence of two English prepositions in this data set and (presumably) for several examples in Pandit (1990). These are found in [8]–[11]:

> [8] Two middle-aged men, both with secondary school education, and who come from the same rural area are talking at a kiosk about the proposed trip to the home area of one of them. The other wants to send along a letter.
> A. . . .nione kama naweza kuandika barua ukawapelekea.
> '. . . I should see if I can write a letter and you can take [it] to them.'
> B. Sawa tu. Labda *you will have to bring it at my home.* U-let-e   *before*
>   2s-bring-SUBJ
> kesho   jioni.
> tomorrow evening.
> 'Ok. Perhaps you will have to bring it at my home. You should bring [it] before tomorrow evening.'
> (Swahili/English No. 21)

> [9] Two women in their late twenties, with at least two years of secondary school-education, are talking about an accident.
> A. Ile ajali ilifanyika saa ngapi?
> 'At what time did the accident occur?'
> B. Ilikuwa *between* saa mbili na saa tatu asubuhi. Unajua wakati huu tuko na *traffic jam.*
> 'It was between 8 and 9 in the morning. You know that time we were in a traffic jam.'
> (Swahili/English No. 40)

> [10] na to *foreigners* aur na hii *muslims* allowed hain inside tirupatii
>   NEG   and NEG   are   Tirrupati
> baalaaji ke mandir.
> Balaji POSS temple
> 'Neither foreigners nor muslims are allowed inside Tirupati's temple.'
> (Hindi/English; Pandit, 1990: 51)

[11] *life* ko *face* kiijiye *with* himmat *and faith in* apane aap.
　　　　to　　do　　courage　　　　　　self
'Face life with courage and faith in self.'

(Hindi/English; Pandit, 1990: 51)

In [8] and [9], the English prepositions (*before* and *between* with Swahili CS) are content morphemes. They have the feature [+ Thematic Role-Assigner] because they assign thematic roles to the temporal adjuncts in such sentences. There are corresponding Swahili prepositions (*kabla ya* for 'before' and *kati ya* for 'between') which also may be considered content morphemes for the same reasons, and therefore they are congruent with their English counterparts. (In example [8], since verbs do not assign thematic role to temporal adjuncts, the verb -*let*- is not involved in thematic role assignment for *kesho jioni* 'tomorrow evening'; therefore the preposition is the thematic role assigner. In [9] the verb is the copula, which never assigns thematic role, leaving only the preposition for this role.)

Investigating the status in Hindi of the counterparts of *within*, *with*, and *in* (from examples [10] and [11]) is beyond the scope of this discussion. But, consistent with the Blocking Hypothesis and the system content morpheme criteria, the prediction is that the Hindi equivalents are also content morphemes.

Recall that Swahili has very few free-form prepositions available as potential thematic role-assigners. In Swahili both objective and locative cases are usually assigned by verbs. It is surely no accident that English prepositions assigning those relationships do not occur in the Nairobi corpus except in EL islands. That is, the two temporal prepositions cited in [8] and [9] are the only singly occurring English ones in ML + EL constituents in the entire data set.

Sometimes non-congruence between counterparts in the ML and EL can be circumvented—by accessing bare forms. Recall the discussion in Chapter 4 of bare forms—EL lexemes which appear without the system morphemes which the ML would require for a well-formed constituent. An example cited there is partially repeated as [12]:

[12] hata wengine nasikia washawekwa　*cell.*
　　　even others　I heard they were put　cell
'Even others I heard were put [in] cells.'

(Swahili/English No. 18)

Note that the noun *cell* (referring to 'jail') appears with no EL preposition (i.e. *in*) and also without the Swahili suffix -*ni* which would mark it as receiving locative case. That is, *cell* is a bare form. The thematic role of *cell* is assigned by the verb *-wek-* 'put in/on'; this means that the verb is a content morpheme. In English, since the thematic role of goal location is assigned by the verb *put*, and *in* only provides locative specification, *in* has the feature [−Thematic Role-Assigner] and therefore is a system morpheme. For this reason, it is not expected to occur (unless an EL island, such as *in the cell*, were produced, but this would be semantically redundant since the Swahili verb *-wek-* already conveys 'in').

But what makes *cell* a bare form is that it does not take the expected Swahili locative case marking suffix *-ni* (i.e. **cell-(i)ni*). The explanation this analysis suggests is that there is a problem of subcategorization between *-ni* and *in*. It is possible that the problem is that *-ni* picks out its head as a *general* locative noun, while *in* carries more specialized locative content. It is worth mentioning that a number of long-established locative borrowed forms, such as *hospitali* 'hospital', regularly appear similarly, as bare forms, in (monolingual) Swahili discourse with a locative meaning. The only borrowing which almost categorically takes *-ni* is *ofisi-ni* 'office/in the office', and its presence here may be facilitated by the phonological shape of *ofisi*.

Pronouns and Congruence

Nouns, pronouns, and descriptive adjectives are potential content morphemes; that is, since they are dominated by the category NP, they are potential thematic case-receivers. They also, of course, have the feature [−Quantification]. Recall that a plus or minus setting for [Thematic Role-Receiver] is one of the features which distinguishes content from system morphemes. That nouns and descriptive adjectives have a plus setting for [Thematic Role-Receiver] seems non-controversial. As pro-forms for nouns, most free-form pronouns satisfy this requirement and therefore are also content morphemes. However, two groups of pronouns do not so qualify. The first group includes free forms which are dummy pronouns, such as existential *it* and *there* in English. The second group includes clitics; they may be analysed as agreement particles which are co-indexed with a null NP head. Therefore, on the basis of having a minus setting for [Thematic Role-Receiver], pronominals in these two groups are system morphemes.

Without the blocking filter in place, those EL pronouns which are content morphemes (by virtue of having the feature [+Thematic Role-Receiver]) would be predicted to appear in ML+EL constituents.

However, singly-occurring EL pronouns are in fact very rare. This analysis suggests that the reason is this: if their ML counterparts are clitics and therefore system morphemes, the blocking filter prevents the occurrence of the EL pronouns. This claim gives rise to a specific prediction that English pronouns will not occur in these constituents in Swahili/English CS, since Swahili pronouns are clitics (except for the free-form emphatics such as *mimi* 'I', *wao* 'they'). And, except for one counter-example, given in [13], the Nairobi corpus supports the Blocking Hypothesis. That is, all other subject and object pronouns in ML + EL constituents come only from the ML, Swahili.

> [13] A conversation about football players among a group of young men with varying degrees of education. The speaker is among the less educated, not having finished primary school.

> Inataka watu ambao wamejenga sana, mtu   ambaye a-ki-kimbia
>   a person who   3S-PROG-run

> a-na-clear them.
> 3S-NON-PAST-clear them
> 'It [the game] needs people who are strongly built, someone who, when he runs, he clears them.'

> (Swahili/English No. 19)

Two explanations for [13] are possible. (1) One might argue that *them* occurs as the counterpart of the Swahili emphatic pronoun *wao* 'they/them', not the clitic pronoun *-wa-*. A well-formed standard Swahili sentence would look like this: *a-na-wa-clear wao* (3s-Non-Present-them-clear + them). While *-wa-* is definitely a system morpheme, *wao* may be considered a content morpheme. Therefore, *wao* would be congruent with *them*, which is also a content morpheme. However, given the absence of *-wa-* (which is obligatory, at least in well-formed sentences in standard Swahili, while *wao* is optional), the second explanation seems just as plausible. (2) That is, the appearance of *them* may be a production error; as such, it stands as the sole counter-example in the Nairobi corpus to the System Morpheme Principle and the Blocking Hypothesis.

Other data sets need to be studied with the Blocking Hypothesis in mind. If pronouns are content morphemes in both the languages involved in CS, then EL pronouns should be possible in ML + EL constituents; but if they are not, EL pronouns should be prohibited. In [14], the English pronoun *somebody* appears in an ML + EL constituent, with Spanish as the apparent ML. The English pronoun is a content morpheme and functions as a subject here; it has a Spanish counterpart (*alguién*). Note that the morpheme encoding the object 'you' comes from the ML (*te* 'you'); it is best described as a clitic, which is a system morpheme and therefore is not congruent with the English content morpheme *you*. The Blocking Hypothesis would predict the non-occurrence of *you*, which is the case. Also note that the complementizer *que* comes from Spanish, the ML. This is predicted, because complementizers are system morphemes, as will be discussed below.

[14] *You didn't have to worry* que *somebody* te iba a tirar con cerveza o una botella *or something like that.*
'You didn't have to worry that somebody was going to throw beer or a bottle at you or something like that.'
(Spanish/English; Poplack, 1981: 170)

A cursory investigation turns up at least a handful of examples from language pairs meeting the test specifications (the pro-form is a content morpheme in both languages). Other examples (but only one each) of EL pronouns occurring as a single lexeme in ML + EL constituents are found in Moroccan Arabic/Dutch CS (Nortier, 1990: 135) and in English/Japanese (Nishimura, 1986: 136). In both cases, the EL pronoun functions as an emphatic. More study is needed, but preliminary investigations support the system content morpheme designations for pronouns and the predictions of the Blocking Hypothesis in this regard. Jake and Myers-Scotton (1992) includes an extended discussion of pronouns in CS data and the implications of these data as tests for syntactic theories.

Verbs and Congruence

In most language pairs, verbs from the EL appear in ML + EL constituents. These verbs are content morphemes, showing a plus setting for [Thematic Role-Assigner]. However, EL verb stems take ML inflections directly more readily in some language pairs than others (compare Swahili/English with Japanese/English). Also, as noted in Chapter 4, in a number of language pairs an ML *do* verb appears to take all relevant inflections, while the EL verb stem stands alone (e.g. from Shona/English CS with the Shona 'helping' verb -*ita*: *va-noka ku-ita catch up* (3PL-be late-INFIN-do-catch up) 'they are late to catch up'). In Shona/English CS, there are also many instances of EL (English) verb stems taking ML (Shona) inflections directly; however, not all languages with this *do* verb construction also inflect EL verb stems as well.

Note that neither *do* nor the copula qualifies as a content morpheme.

Both have a negative setting on the feature [Thematic Role-Assigner]. The prediction that the EL versions of these verbs will not appear in ML + EL constituents is supported in all data examined.

Modifiers: Adjectives and Adverbs

There are numerous examples in Chapter 4 showing that, while descriptive adjectives from the EL appear freely in ML + EL constituents, possessive adjectives and quantifiers do not. With the feature [+ Thematic Role-Receiver], descriptive adjectives are content morphemes, of course. In contrast, because they show the feature [+ Quantification], possessive adjectives and quantifiers are system morphemes.

Adverbs are also system morphemes, since they pick out individuals across variables. As would be predicted, there are no instances of EL adverbs (e.g. *very, too*) appearing as singly occurring lexemes in ML + EL constituents. In contrast, there are 20 EL islands which begin with an English adverb, notably *very* (e.g. *m-na-jua very well* 'you [PL] know very well'; *ni-ko very surprised* 'I am very surprised').

An Explanation for Two Sets of Agreement Prefixes

The following discussion applies only to Swahili, but it demonstrates that the system/content morpheme distinction has relevance beyond CS. Swahili has two different sets of agreement prefixes for most noun classes, one applying to descriptive adjectives and the second to other modifiers as well as the pronominal clitics in the verbal assembly. For example, in class 6, the agreement prefix on descriptive adjectives is *ma-*, but it is *y/ ya-* for other modifiers and on pronominal clitics. That is, all the forms which this analysis labels as system morphemes take the *y/ ya-* prefix, while the content morphemes take *ma-*. For example, compare *ma-embe ma-zuri* (CL 6-mango + CL 6-good) 'good mangoes' with *ma-embe y-angu y-ote ya-me-anguka* (CL 6-mango + CL 6-my + CL 6-all + they-PERF-fall down) 'all [of] my mangoes have fallen down'. Why these two systems exist has never been explained by grammarians; the content/system morpheme distinction points toward a solution.

The Case of Complementizers

Complementizers have been a subject for discussion in many studies of CS, as mentioned in Chapter 2. The constraints which were proposed earlier (e.g. Gumperz, 1982; Joshi, 1985) hold for many data sets; both say that complementizers cannot appear in the EL, but say little more.

Complementizers (COMP) are system morphemes because they are heads which fail to receive thematic roles and therefore have the feature [−Thematic Role-Receiver]. This leads to the prediction that the only way for EL complementizers to appear is in EL islands. What seems to distinguish complementizers from other system morphemes is that limited investigation has uncovered only one example of an EL COMP heading such an EL island, in Spanish/English CS from a Texas corpus (that in example (15)). It is likely there are more, but they seem to be unusual. Yet, also dealing with a Texas-based Spanish/English corpus, Pfaff (1979: 309) comments that full relative clause switching occurs very rarely in her data. (Still, recall that the prediction is only that, if EL complementizers occur at all, they will be in EL islands; it is not that they will occur frequently.)

[15] En hierbas, hay hierbas *that you can take for, you know, like for your nerves,* pa'los nervios.
'As for herbs, there are herbs that you can take for, you know, like for your nerves, for your nerves.'

(Spanish/English; Jacobson, 1990: 135)

A brief analysis across data set indicates that what is generally found can be summarized in this way: (1) either ML or EL complementizers (COMPs) are null (i.e. the sentential complement is headless); or (2) the only COMPs are ML ones, and in some language pairs, ML COMPs obligatorily head *even* EL sentential complements. For example, in the Nairobi corpus, there are both ML and EL sentential complements which appear as islands, but only null COMPs for all but one of both ML and EL islands. Islands involving sentential complements represent 8 per cent (10) of the EL islands (N = 121) in the Nairobi corpus. A relativizer occurs in one island (example [16]). Not surprisingly, it is from the ML. But all others have a null COMP (exemplified in [17a] and [17b]). In 5 of the cases, the EL island is the sentential complement (e.g. [17a]); for the other 5, the ML island is the sentential complement (e.g. [17b]).

[16] *It's only essential services* amba-zo   zi-na-   *-function right now.*
                                    COMP-CL 10 CL 10-PRES-
'It's only essential services which function right now.'

(Swahili/English No. 18)

[17a] Lakini unajua (ø) *it's very hard.*
'But you know [that] it's very hard.'

(Swahili/English No. 21)

[17*b*] *It doesn't mean* (ø) ukitembea utakuwa ukishikwa.
'It doesn't mean [that] if you stroll about you will be arrested.'

(Swahili/English No. 32)

In a limited Yoruba/English data set from conversations among two Yoruba university students in the United States, sentential complements are always introduced by the Yoruba COMP (*pe*) or (*ti*) and there are no English COMPs. Yoruba is the ML, and most of these Yoruba COMPs are part of ML + EL constituents. See [18].

[18] Awon nkan   ti   o *come naturally to me* ni mo *like.*
         those things that it   is I
   'I like those things that come naturally to me.'

(Yoruba/English; Oloruntoba, unpublished data)

As noted above, for some languages, available evidence indicates that *only* ML complementizers are possible. For example, Simango (1991) reports that only the Chewa COMP (kuti) may appear in Chewa/ English CS utterances (with Chewa as the ML). This is so whether COMP heads a Chewa or an English Complement (CP) (permissible patterns: E-C COMP-C or C-C COMP-E). Eid (1992) reports a similar finding for Egyptian Arabic/English CS. That is, the only possible CS configuration is an EL island in English followed by both the COMP and the sentential complement in Arabic (pattern: E-A COMP-A). Eid comments (p. 57) 'combination [AEE], which parallels combination [EAA] by reversing the roles of the two languages, does not occur. Nor do combinations [EEA] or [AEA] . . .'

The data for Lingala/French CS, however, is at variance with the above findings. Kamwangamalu (1989*b*) reports that the COMP may come either from Lingala (*'te*), or from French (*que*). (And Bokamba (1989: 282) seems to agree, pointing out that 'the Romance languages' complementizer *que* can occur in Kinshasa Lingala in structures where either the main or the subordinate clause is either in French or Lingala.') In addition, Kamwangamalu (1989*b*) states that *que* is preferred over *'te*, as does Nzwanga (1991).

Kamwangamalu cites an example in which the sentence is otherwise entirely in Lingala [19*a*], or in which a French matrix clause is followed by a CP in Lingala, but with *que* as its head [19*b*]. In all such cases, *que* appears to be optional (Nzwanga 1991), except in such configurations as that in [19*c*].

[19*a*] Oyebi *que* nazali na mionso mamu.
'You know that I have everything, Mamu.'

[19*b*] *Mais toi, on dirait que* ozokima te bajours oyo.
'But you, one would say that you do not job these days.'

(Lingala/French; Kamwangamalu, 1989*b*: 132)

[19*c*] Soki omoni   *que* okokoka   te, tika kaka.
    if   you-see-PRES that you-will-succeed not leave it

'If you see that you will not succeed, leave it.'

(Lingala/French; Nzwanga, 1991)

A possible explanation of this use of *que* may be that *que* has become an established borrowed form in Lingala and therefore is accessed as a Lingala system morpheme. This suggestion is raised again in Chapter 6.

In general, then, there is some evidence that EL complementizers are avoided. As indicated above, in the Nairobi corpus, there are only null COMPs in the 10 sentences with CPs as EL islands. Eid (1992) also noted the strategy of null complementizers for EL CPs in her corpus.

Obviously, complementizers warrant much more attention than I have given them here, but the direction of results seems likely: COMPs in ML + EL constituents come only from the ML (except in such cases as the troublesome Lingala one). Also, ML COMPs may head ML sentential complements; but EL sentential complements (as islands) are likely to have either ML or null COMPs. As maximal projections in Government and Binding theory, sentential complements are presumed to have unity with their heads (COMP). The presence of ML COMPs as heads of EL sentential complements calls into question this unity, and also raises questions about 'maximal projection' as a unit.

Double Morphology

The only exception to the Blocking Hypothesis is the presence of a singly occurring EL stem with affixes (system morphemes) from both the EL and the ML for the same function. That is, these forms show 'double morphology', such as plural affixes from both the ML and the EL, as already discussed in Chapters 2 and 4.

For example, some Bantu noun stems which are CS forms show the affixes of *both* the ML and the EL. See [20] from Shona/English CS, with the class 6 pluralizing prefix *ma-* from Shona as well as the English pluralizing suffix *-s*.

[20] . . . dzimwe dzenguva tinenge tichiita ma-*game-s* panze . . .
'. . . sometimes we will be doing games outside . . .'

(Shona/English No. 11)

Those writing on Lingala/French CS (e.g. Bokamba, 1988 and Kamwan-gamalu, 1989*b*) also report a number of examples, such as [21], in which *ba-*, the class *two* pluralizing prefix, precedes the French noun stem *parent* and the French pluralizing suffix *-s* follows.[2]

[21] Ba-*parent-s* na ye ba-zaka *riches*, yango ba-*promet*-t-aki ye te ba-ko-sombela ye *voiture* ya sika.
'His parents are rich, that's why they promised that they would buy him a new car.'

(Lingala/French; Kamwangamalu, 1989*b*: 160)

Eliasson (1989) and Backus (1990) discuss this phenomenon (with examples from their own data sets, Eliasson citing English forms in CS with Maori and Backus citing Dutch forms in CS with Turkish). They raise it as a possible challenge to the System Morpheme Principle. How can one tell which morpheme is 'relevant'? That is, which doublet is, indeed, dressed to go to the ball?

Yet, it seems that in most cases (all cases in the literature) there is evidence in the morphology of the rest of the sentence to indicate which language is supplying the system morphemes signalling relationships among the elements. By implication, it is this language whose doublet is the 'relevant' one in the double-morphology case as well, since the other affix must have, at best, only internal relationships with its head. And, of course, the evidence is unassailable in the case of the Bantu/English or Bantu/French plural nouns considered. This is because the noun-prefix itself is 'relevant' to signal noun class membership as well as plurality, and then also, typically, is copied onto all other elements in the sentence for which it governs agreements.

Stated more formally, the Double Morphology Principle is:

In cases where affixes from both the ML and EL appear with a noun or verb stem and therefore may be construed as competing, only one affix 'wins'. The doublet matching the language of other system morphemes controlling relationships in the constituent (e.g. affixes marking case, tense, etc.) will be the ML affix.

Chapters 2 and 3 include some preliminary remarks on how plural affixes arise in language production. Here, a scenario for how CS forms

[2] I thank Salikoko Mufwene for reminding me that it would be difficult to know, in spoken French, whether a plural marker is present or not, unless it is revealed through liaison with a vowel (when the following word begins with a vowel).

showing double-plural morphology come into existence is suggested. Five steps are hypothesized.

Step 1. One of three alternative processes results in an EL noun stem with its own EL affix undergoing the grammatical procedures specified by the ML.

(*a*) The noun stem is supplied to the formulator with the plural affix already attached. That is, the EL belongs to the class of languages in which the lemmas for noun stems provide a lexical item complete with a plural affix. As noted in Chapter 3, at least some psycholinguists argue that lemmas are structured so that certain ones contain frequently called inflectional affixes at the same address as a noun or verb stem. This argument is advanced especially for analytic languages such as English (Butterworth, 1989).

(*b*) Alternatively, there is a separate lemma address for the EL plural affix, and there is an EL procedure for calling it up which operates independently of ML affixing procedures.

(*c*) Or, an ML procedure provides the EL plural affix independently of the ML procedure which will supply the ML affix.

Under either (*b*) or (*c*), the one process is unaware that the other is taking place as well: (*b*) has the 'faulty' process resulting from EL procedures and (*c*) locates it with an ML procedure. In either case, the result is something of an 'access error'.

Step 2. The ML has its own procedures for assigning number with ML affixes. Recall that it is the ML which has been activated to supply system morphemes in the appropriate slots of the ML + EL constituent. That is, the ML formulator's procedures are blind to what has happened under step 1.

Step 3. The ML's formulator treats the EL lemma and its plural affix as a single unit. Its own pluralizing procedure (activated under step 2) is an 'if–then rule'. That is, if it finds an unfilled slot meeting its specifications, it fills it; if it does not, it passes by the lemma.

Step 4. Not finding a plural affix specification already in place *according to the exact specifications of its own roster*, the ML pluralizing procedure assigns a plural affix to the slot. (In the case of Shona/English CS, for example, it may help that Shona signals plurality with a prefix and English does it with a suffix. But linear differences in slot assignment definitely are not a necessary condition for double morphology to occur; recall double suffixes occur from Spanish and the indigenous language in the case of some Central and South American languages.)

Step 5. The result, a noun stem with two affixes having the same function (one from the EL and one from the ML), reaches the positional level (where surface features are assigned).

Levelt's (1989: 249) summary of the 'rationale' of the production model he presents is apt here:

The Kempen–Hoenkamp Incremental Procedure Grammar assumes the existence of 'syntactic specialists,' a collection of grammatical and functional procedures. These procedures . . . function in a highly modular fashion. They do their thing when called and provided with their characteristic input, and they deliver their own special kind of output to a particular address. They do their work automatically (i.e., without using the speaker's attentional resources) and in parallel fashion. And they are stupid. They blindly accept the wrong input if it is of the right kind. The speech errors discussed . . . testify to this witless automaticity of grammatical encoding.

Comparisons of established loan words with CS forms in the Shona corpus studied for this volume provides strong implicational evidence that double morphology may result from misfiring at some point in production. The evidence is that borrowed forms show fewer instances of double morphology than CS forms—just as one would expect under any of the proposed scenarios. The rationale is that, by the time a lexeme has become an established borrowing, the use of affixes would be more 'under control', with ML affixes winning out.

Along with Bernsten (1990), I studied English nouns placed in Bantu class 6 in Shona/English utterances. The analysis draws on a corpus of interviews offering about twenty hours of recorded speech. Interviewees were not aware that their language usage was of any interest. We classified any English-origin noun which appears in the standard Shona dictionary, or which appeared in three or more interviews, as a borrowed form; those English-origin nouns appearing in fewer than three interviews were considered CS forms.

Bernsten's interest was in the incidence of double-plural marking, i.e. forms showing both the *ma-* class 6 plural prefix from Shona and the English suffix *-s* (with the standard phonological realizations). She reports (1990: 82) that the double marking occurred on 17 per cent (136 out of 780) of the English borrowings into the Shona *ma-* class (e.g. *ma-part-s* [mapats] 'parts'). In dramatic contrast, double marking occurred with 69 per cent (86 out of 124) of those English nouns taking *ma-* which she identified as CS forms (e.g. *ma-hour-s* [maawaz] 'hours'). Note that all other (appropriate) slots for agreement with the class 6 noun class are filled with class 6 modifier prefixes.

The Blocking Hypothesis: Summary

The hypothesis has this first result: the syntactically relevant system morphemes in ML + EL constituents are only those which qualify as system morphemes in the ML. These include most prominently categories with the feature [+ Quantification], such as determiners and inflectional affixes. However, they also include categories with a minus reading for either [Thematic-Role Assigner] or [Thematic-Role Receiver]; therefore they include, for example, the copula.

Unless the frame is broken (by an EL island), the only other alternative is not to fill the system morpheme slot at all; that is, a bare form results (a noun or verb). The only way to realize the EL counterpart of the ML system morpheme is to do so in an EL island, as discussed later in this chapter.

An examination of data sets in the literature in regard to their ML + EL constituents and such categories as specifiers, quantifiers, relative pronouns, and clitics does support this analysis; that is, those categories which the analysis designates as system morphemes do not occur in the EL, with a few possible exceptions across a wide array of data sets.

A second result of the Blocking Hypothesis is that the appearance of EL content morphemes in these constituents is not totally free. EL members of the major categories designated as content morphemes (nouns, descriptive adjectives, and verbs) are found in many ML + EL constituents. These categories all have the feature [− Quantification] and a plus setting on the relevant feature of either [Thematic Role-Assigner] or [Thematic Role-Receiver]. However, lack of congruence concerning either their match with an ML morpheme or their thematic role structure (e.g. some pronouns) keeps some EL content morphemes from appearing at all in ML + EL constituents.

Matrix or Embedded Language Islands

Recall that part of setting the frame, according to the MLF model, is characterizing and constraining the occurrence of ML and EL islands. Only the constraints on ML + EL constituents have been discussed at length so far. But while these constituents are the ones for which the Matrix Language Hypothesis (and its accompanying Morpheme Order and System Morpheme Principles) and the Blocking Hypothesis are most relevant, these hypotheses are also applicable to EL islandhood.

ML and EL islands are entirely in one language, well-formed according to the grammar of their language. Example [22] illustrates all possible types of CS constituents, including islands.

[22] A Luo and a Luyia man are discussing their jobs. Both have secondary-school certificates.

LUO. Siku hizi watu wa-ta-ku-wa wa-ki-enjoy sana.
days these people they will be 3PL-CONT-enjoy very
'These days people will be enjoying very much.'
LUYIA. Kwa nini unasema hivyo?
'Why do you say that?'
LUO. hujasikia kutoka *next week* wafanya kazi wa serikali
you not yet hear from workers of government
hawatakuwa wakienda kazini on Saturdays.
they will not be they be going to work
'Haven't you heard that from next week government workers will not be going to work on Saturdays?'
(Swahili/English No. 27)

Wa-ta-ku-wa wa-ki-enjoy sana 'they will be enjoying a lot' is an ML + EL constituent and *next week* and *on Saturdays* are EL islands. The other constituents are all ML islands.

ML Islands

Explaining ML islands appears to be a very straightforward matter, requiring little discussion. After all, it is the ML's set of grammatical procedures which is continuously active during the production of ML + EL constituents. The only EL activity comes when content morphemes are inserted into sites prepared by ML lemmas. Therefore, producing ML islands is simply a matter of never allowing *any* activity from the EL.

While ML islands have hardly been studied, and certainly not systematically, it seems they can occur at any point in an utterance. If anything, it seems more appropriate to speculate about what factors promote rather than inhibit them. A very general, functionally based hypothesis seems reasonable at this stage: the main arguments of any utterance will be encoded most frequently either by ML islands or by ML + EL constituents. That is, EL islands are hypothesized to occur for more peripheral material, or when they are required.

EL Islands

EL islands are the potential Achilles' heel of the MLF model. To avoid this, EL islandhood must be constrained so that islands are not characterized just as those cases of two or more EL morphemes to which the ML and Blocking Hypotheses do not apply. Note, however, that EL islands are inherently constrained: because they must show internal structural-dependency relations, all islands must be composed of at least two lexemes/morphemes in a hierarchical relationship. (And, since no single EL forms may be islands, this criterion sets aside singly occurring forms as clear tests for the ML and Blocking Hypotheses.)

However, just because EL islands do occur, the nature of ML + EL constituents is restricted. The ML hypothesis characterizing such constituents applies categorically only if the constituents are defined as containing singly occurring EL forms. When CS forms of two or more lexemes appear, they may or may not follow the restrictions of the ML hypothesis; they generally do not in the Nairobi corpus, for example. Whether this is a general characteristic of ML + EL constituents requires further study. Obviously, if EL islands could be more specifically characterized than just as 'recognized' counter-examples to the ML hypothesis, the MLF model would be strengthened.

After a brief examination of earlier proposals relevant to EL islands, I advance two specific proposals designed to limit, and thus predict, the occurrence and distribution of EL islands.

Earlier Interest in Islands

Constraints on the actual composition of islands are the least studied part of CS—by any researchers. Recall that many earlier researchers have been concerned largely, in effect, with where islands may *begin*; this is a focus of Poplack's (e.g. 1980) Equivalence Constraint and Sridhar and Sridhar's (1980) Dual Principle Constraint, although they do not mention islands as such. These constraints argue that there must be surface syntactic congruence at the boundary in order for there to be an island. In fact, I shall be arguing just the opposite, but from the standpoint of looking at congruence. That is, when there is *not* equivalence (= congruence) of an abstract nature, this is when there is a change in the basic procedures, resulting in EL islands.

Islands Within the MLF Model

Even though they are an important element in CS data and in the MLF model, EL islands are less studied under the MLF model than ML + EL constituents. The analysis has dwelt at length on constraining EL morphemes in ML + EL constituents. In contrast, I can only make some preliminary suggestions about EL islands. The following hypotheses are encouraging however, because, their connections to the more studied ML Hypothesis provide them with motivation and they avoid an *ad hoc* quality. The analysis of EL islands is based on 121 islands occurring in the Nairobi corpus, with limited discussion of other data sets.

Two generalizations about EL islandhood are possible, one structurally based and one with a functional rationale. The structurally-based hypothesis is discussed first because it also logically precedes the functional limits.

Obligatory EL Islands

Based on the earlier discussion of the obligatory composition of ML + EL constituents, one can hypothesize when EL islands must occur. What will be called the EL Island Trigger Hypothesis is 'incrementally based': its sub-hypotheses are of the form 'if x is accessed, then y must be accessed'.

> The EL Island Trigger Hypothesis: Activating any EL lemma or accessing by error any EL morpheme not licensed under the ML or Blocking Hypotheses triggers the processor to inhibit all ML accessing procedures and complete the current constituent as an EL island.

Recall that activating an incongruent EL lemma results in directions to the formulator to follow only EL morphosyntactic procedures; these will produce a well-formed constituent, an EL island. Under this scenario, EL islands are initiated at an abstract level. In addition, at a level much closer to the surface of the sentence (i.e. when morphemes are selected to fill slots already prepared in the sentence frame by ML morphosyntactic procedures), misfirings can occur. EL islands may be produced at this stage in two ways:

1. If an EL morpheme implicating non-ML morpheme order in a constituent is accessed as the initial element in a constituent, this triggers processing of the entire constituent in the EL, thereby forming an EL island. This prediction is a corollary to the Morpheme-Order Principle applying to ML + EL constituents and permitting only ML morpheme order in these constituents. For example, this hypothesis predicts for Swahili/English CS that, if an English adjective is accessed before its head, then the adjective + head must form an EL island. (Recall that Swahili requires head-first order in NPs with adjectives; this holds in all instances except for a handful of Arabic-origin adjectives.) In [22] above, *next weekend* is an example of such an EL island. This hypothesis predicts that such examples as **next mwisho wa wiki* 'next end of week' will not occur; and the data support this prediction.

2. If any EL system morpheme, or an EL content morpheme not showing correspondences to an ML content morpheme, is accessed, ML procedures are inhibited, and the entire constituent of which the EL morpheme is a part must be produced as an EL island. This restriction complements the System Morpheme Principle and the Blocking Hypothesis. The System Morpheme Principle allows only ML system morphemes in ML + EL constituents, and the Blocking Hypothesis stops even EL content morphemes which correspond to an ML system morpheme or which, if they correspond to an ML content morpheme, do not show congruence with that morpheme.

In [23] below, the EL island *at the usual place* illustrates how this sub-hypothesis applies. Having accessed the preposition *at*, a content morpheme in English which assigns objective case to its head noun, the processor must go on and complete the PP as an EL island. In Swahili, it is the verb stem which assigns thematic role to the locative NP. The English preposition and the Swahili verb are not both content morphemes, and are not congruent at the level of abstraction involving subcategorization for thematic-role properties. Therefore, this sub-hypothesis predicts that examples such as *at mahali pa kawaida* 'at place of usual' will not occur. The data support this hypothesis. While English PPs occur as islands, English prepositions do not occur heading Swahili material in PPs (except as cited in [8] and [9], when the prepositions of the two languages show congruence).

Examples Supporting the EL Island Trigger Hypothesis
Examples [23]–[26] offer empirical support for the EL Trigger Hypothesis. In particular, [24]–[26] illustrate impossible ML + EL constituents, and show actually occurring ELs from the Nairobi corpus. In [23] the EL island *this evening* occurs. Because demonstratives have the feature [+ Quantification] and therefore are system morphemes, the only way for *this* to occur is if an EL island is being constructed. In addition, even if the accessing of *this* was an error, note that the Morpheme-Order Principle also predicts that, once *this* has been accessed, the constituent must be finished as an EL island, since it does not follow ML morpheme order, and therefore cannot be finished with an ML head for the NP.

[23] Wache mimi nielekeee tauni, tukutane   *this evening at the usual place.*
                                let us meet
'Let me go so that I may reach town, let's meet this evening at the usual place.'
(Swahili/English No. 34)

Thus the provisions of the MLF model allow only certain permutations in constituents in CS corpora. In the case of Swahili/English, two permutations are permitted, the one discussed as an EL island (*this evening*) and an ML + EL constituent, *evening hii*. This second possibility combines an EL content morpheme (*evening*) with a Swahili system morpheme, the demonstrative marked for class 9 (*hii*); also this shows Swahili morpheme order in accordance with the Morpheme-Order Principle. Three permutations are not predicted and do not occur in the Swahili/ English data studied: (1) *evening this* can not be a possible ML + EL constituent because it is entirely in the EL; however, it also is not a possible EL island because it is not well-formed according to the EL grammar. (2) *jioni this* 'evening this' is not a possible ML + EL constituent because *this* violates the System Morpheme Principle. (3) *this jioni* 'this evening' is not allowed because it violates both the System Morpheme Principle and the Morpheme-Order Principle. Specific predictions for other language pairs would differ, depending on the congruence of their grammars; the principles governing predictions would remain the same universally, however.

> [24a] *Sikuona *your* barua ambayo uliipoteza.
> 'I didn't see your letter which you lost.'

Because *your* is accessed, the EL Island Trigger Hypothesis predicts that it must be followed by an English head (e.g. *your letter*) as an EL island. The reason is that possessive adjectives are system morphemes (i.e. [+ Quantification]). Note that three EL islands with possessive adjectives, exemplified by [24b], actually occur in the Nairobi corpus:

> [24b] Tu-na-m-let-e-a   *our brother* wa Thika.
>   1PL-PROG-him-take-APPL-INDIC   of Thika.
> 'We are taking [it] to our brother of Thika.'
> (Swahili/English No. 6)

It seems that some islands are so unusual (even though required by the EL Island Trigger Hypothesis) that when they occur, they provoke comment. Example [24b] comes from a long conversation between two young people and police officers about a record-player which they are carrying. The sentence in [24b] elicits the response from the policeman, *unasema nini, sister, na hata Kiswahil chenyewe hujui?* 'What are you saying, sister, and you don't even know Swahili itself?'

Examples [25a] and [25b] are repeated from the discussion of system morphemes above.

[25a] *Nikamwambia anipe ruhusa niende ni-ka-*check*   *for* wewe.
                                      1S-CONSEC-check for you
'And I told him he should give me permission so that I go and check for you.'

Rather than this sentence, what actually occurs in the Nairobi corpus with *for you* is [25b]:

[25b] Nikamwambia anipe ruhusa niende ni-ka-*check for you.*

(Swahili/English No. 38)

[26a] *If* hainyeshi mvua . . .
'If it doesn't rain . . .

Note that English *if* in [26b] corresponds to a system morpheme in Swahili (*-sipo-* occurring as a prefix in the verbal assembly, or *kama* + a negative verb form). Therefore, the only way to produce a sentence beginning with *if* is to make its constituent an EL island. Such a sentence actually occurs in the Nairobi corpus as [26b]:

[26b] Hakuwa mpango maalum, lakini *if it doesn't rain*, nitakwenda huko Kangeni kuona ndugu yangu.
'There are not special plans, but if it doesn't rain, I will go to Kangeni to see my brother.'

(Swahili/English No. 32)

Obligatory EL Islands: Summary
The EL Island Trigger Hypothesis predicts exactly where EL islands must occur. Its predictions are supported by data on what types of island actually occur. For example, since quantifiers are system morphemes, it is expected that EL islands will often include them, since this is the only way in which EL quantifiers may appear at all in CS utterances. Also, PPs will be expected since, again, EL prepositions which do not correspond to ML prepositions can only occur in EL islands. And, indeed, a distinctive feature of EL islands in the Nairobi corpus is that many involve quantifiers or are temporal PPs (or both). Some examples initiated by quantifiers appear below as [27]–[29]. Some examples of EL islands initiated by prepositions include *ameshaweka msichana for six months* 'he already stayed with [a] girl for six months' and *nitatry kuwa nyumbani throughout the day* 'I will try to be at home throughout the day'.

In fact, it will turn out that, except for set phrases, few EL islands occur which are not *required* by the EL Island Trigger Hypothesis. The only two-lexeme CS forms in ML + EL constituents (i.e. not EL islands) include nouns and their descriptive adjectives. The EL Island Trigger

Hypothesis does not predict that these will be EL islands because they include morphemes which show class congruence and a match as content morphemes in both languages (e.g. *timing proper, table long*). More study is needed, but I would predict a statistically significant difference in the composition of EL islands between those containing quantifiers (i.e. system morphemes) and those with descriptive adjectives (i.e. content morphemes).

Even among 'required' EL islands (if the material contained therein contains an EL system morpheme), there are few examples of certain types. For example, *for you* cited in [25] is the only example of an EL island including a pronoun in the Nairobi corpus. There is also only one example of the copula (a system morpheme) heading an EL island (*hata kupalilia is impossible* 'even to weed is impossible', in a conversation about the rain). There are only two examples of NPs as EL islands in subject position (e.g. *Most people watakuwa wataelekea . . .* 'Most people will head towards . . .'). Note that *most people* begins with a quantifier.

A Functional Explanation of Island Occurrences

A functional analysis may explain which of the potential EL islands tend to occur. There are two distinct typologies characterizing EL islands which provide preferential hierarchies. The first is based on the grammatical function of the constituent, as core or peripheral. The second recognizes that idioms and set expressions from the EL are likely EL islands. These ideas are very briefly discussed in Myers-Scotton (1991*a*). Treffers-Daller (1991*a*; 1991*b*) works along similar lines, but goes further in developing the argument of a hierarchy. A major difference is that the hierarchy of Treffers-Daller applies to all constituents involving CS, whether islands or otherwise. Her data come from Flemish/French CS in Brussels.

Admittedly, *any* hierarchy must be less satisfying than the ML and Blocking Hypotheses and the EL Island Trigger Hypothesis, because these hypotheses make unconditional claims within their terms of reference. But I suggest it is 'in the nature of the beast' that when EL islands will be initiated cannot be predicted categorically, beyond stating the conditions under which they must occur. The same can be said of ML + EL constituents. While their structure can be predicted, when such a constituent will be produced cannot be predicted—except within the terms of the discussion of social motivations for CS raised in Chapter 8 and in Myers-Scotton (1993).

The EL Hierarchy Hypothesis

Thus, an implicational EL Hierarchy Hypothesis is proposed. It can be stated as two sub-hypotheses:

1. The more peripheral a constituent is to the theta-grid of the sentence (to its main arguments), the freer it is to appear as an EL island.

2. The more formulaic in structure a constituent is, the more likely it is to appear as an EL island. Stated more strongly, choice of (any) part of an idiomatic expression will result in an EL island.

The EL Hierarchy Hypothesis places the most accessible constituents for islandhood at the top of the hierarchy, and proposes that an implicational relationship from bottom to top is in force (i.e. if there are subject NPs as EL islands, there are also object NPs as islands, and so on).

Implicational Hierarchy of EL Islands

1. Formulaic expressions and idioms (especially as time and manner PPs but also as VP complements);
2. Other time and manner expressions (NP/PP adjuncts used adverbially);
3. Quantifier expressions (APs and NPs especially as VP complements);
4. Non-quantifier, non-time NPs as VP complements (NPs, APs, CPs);
5. Agent NPs;
6. Thematic role- and case-assigners, i.e. main finite verbs (with full inflections).

This hierarchy is suggested by data from the Nairobi corpus, and by theoretical claims in other areas of linguistics and data from other CS studies. For example, the idea that the most central constituents of a sentence are the least accessible to EL islandhood receives support from theories of functionalism in grammar (e.g. Hopper and Thompson, 1984; Givón, 1979; 1989), as well as from psycholinguistic experimentation (cf. Bock, 1987). These constituents would be the subject NP and the VP.

The argument is that the central constituents carry the main semantic weight of the sentence; it makes sense that they should be either in ML islands or possibly in ML + EL constituents. For the reasons outlined above (in Chapter 3) in defining the ML, the ML has more psycho-sociolinguistic dominance in the discourse under consideration. And to allow elements which are peripheral to the core of the communicative intention to appear in the EL (as islands) seems a likely corollary.

Table 5.1. *EL islands in the Nairobi corpus*

Type	No.	%
Copula VP complements	31	26
Prepositional phrases	24	20
Time adverbials	20	16.5
Non-copula VP COMPs	16	13
Set expressions	12	10
Main clause with CP	5	4
Complement clause	5	4
Miscellaneous[a]	8	6.5

[a] Possessive pronouns, 2; Subject NPs, 2; Conditional clauses, 2; Copula + COMP, 1; Interjection, 1.

Functionally Peripheral Islands

In the case of the Nairobi corpus, the evidence is overwhelming that functionally peripheral elements are most favoured for EL islandhood. Of all EL islands (N = 121), 29.5 per cent (36) are time adverbials, most as two-word expressions or as brief PPs (e.g. *next Saturday, every morning, after four months*). Many of these are almost formulaic (e.g. *next weekend, on Saturdays*); or one of a limited set of time-oriented modifiers appears (e.g. *first* in *first time, last* in *last month*). Almost 10 per cent (12) are set expressions (e.g. *old habits die hard, in fact, for personal purposes*). Most of the other islands are VP complements; many of them begin with quantifiers. In addition, many of them are complements of a copula consisting of an intensifier adverb + an adjective (*very fast, very late, very surprised*). In fact, 11 per cent (14) of EL islands involve *very* in a copula complement.

Table 5.1 classifies the EL islands in the Nairobi corpus from a more structural point of view. In assessing the functional role's weight in whether a constituent becomes an island, one must recognize that some constituents *must* become islands because of the EL Island Trigger Hypothesis, their functional status notwithstanding. That is, when an EL morpheme is accessed which is prohibited from ML + EL constituents by the Blocking Hypothesis, the only alternative is to complete the constituent as an EL Island. Thus, the presence of some categories (e.g. VP complements) among islands may have more to do with this hypothesis than their status as central or peripheral.

And, as already noted, quantifiers are predicted in EL islands in the Nairobi corpus, and there are a large number of them. Ten out of the

16 islands which are objective complements of finite verbs begin with quantifiers, exemplified below.

[27] Wana *some problems.*
'They have some problems.'
(Swahili/English No. 40)

[28] Ulikuwa ukiongea *a lot of nonsense.*
'You were talking a lot of nonsense.'
(Swahili/English No. 21)

[29] Ni-*check all that particular day's constructions.*
'I should check all that particular day's constructions.'
(Swahili/English No. 38)

Still, note how few EL islands are central in either a structural or a functional sense. First, there are very few finite verbs in EL islands and relatively few arguments of the verb in islands as well (i.e. agents, patients, beneficiaries, etc.), especially NPs which are agents in subject position.

Second, it is worth reiterating that the many (91) finite verbs in the Nairobi corpus with English verb stems and Swahili prefixes do not trigger English islands. Only 13 per cent of these verbs (12) are followed by one or more English lexemes, and of these, several are phrasal verbs (e.g. *a-na-make lunch yake* 'he makes his lunch').

Also, other evidence in the Nairobi corpus suggests that time expressions are not favoured as islands primarily because of their semantic content; I would argue they are accessed instead because they are very close to being set expressions. Note that this is a much more production-based argument; if they are set expressions, they should require less production effort. If their 'time' quality were most important, this would lead to the hypothesis that English numbers in general would be favoured, since numbers are the ultimate expression of time which can be adopted from the Western world. But this is not the case in the Nairobi corpus. It stands in sharp contrast to the Zimbabwe corpus in its non-borrowing of English numbers, as will be shown in Chapter 6.

Several additional examples of EL islands follow from the Nairobi corpus and other African data sets.

[30] Mimi ni-ta-*try* kuwa nyumbani *throughout the day. I'm sure* hi-zo
    EMPH 1S-FUT- to be home   these-CL 10
sherehe   zi-ta-onyeshwa kwa TV.
celebrations will be shown on TV
'As for me, I try to be at home throughout the day. I'm sure those celebrations will be shown on TV.'
(Swahili/English No. 32)

This example has an unusual amount of English in it, with *throughout the day* is counted as an adverbial PP and *I'm sure* introducing an S-bar complement.

[31] Hata siyo mwezi jana. Ilikuwa *early this month.*
'Not even last month. It was early this month.'
(Swahili/English No. 36)

[32] *Le matin de bonne heure* ngay joge Medina *pour* [pur] dem julli.
                                                    in order to
Suba tee   nga fa war a joge.
early in the morning
'Early in the morning you leave Medina to go to pray. Early in the morning you should leave then.'
(Wolof/French; Swigart, 1992: 27)

The French EL island 'early in the morning' is, of course, a time expression. Note that it is repeated in Wolof in the second sentence.

[33] ɔ- [sɪɪ t -í- -ì]   ne [é gzáɱs] nó *last year.*
     3s   V PART POSSES   DET
'He sat his exams last year.'
(Asante/English; Forson, 1979: 159)

Examples such as *nó last year* 'the last year' indicate that one can speak about EL islands within an ML + EL constituent. (Such 'internal islands' will be further discussed below.) This NP shows the Asante system morpheme *nó* for its determiner, but the order of the noun and its adjective do not conform to the Morpheme-Order Principle since Asante requires the head to precede the adjective. Again, since the Morpheme-Order Principle only applies categorically to single lexeme CS forms, such two-lexeme forms as *last year* are possible as islands. And the EL Trigger Hypothesis states that, because the constituent is initiated with *last* (a quantifier and therefore a system morpheme), EL procedures must complete the constituent as an island. Again, recall that set expressions which are also time expressions are frequent EL islands.

EL Islands: Summary

The EL Island Trigger Hypothesis is proposed, requiring that EL islands be formed under certain conditions. What makes it especially attractive is that it complements the ML and Blocking Hypotheses which apply in ML + EL constituents. It predicts that, whenever an EL morpheme is accessed which violates these hypotheses, the formulator will produce an

EL island. All evidence from the Nairobi corpus, as well as other data sets examined, support the EL Island Trigger Hypothesis; it successfully predicts when EL islands must appear.

The point of the discussion of system morphemes is to show that, when an EL morpheme is a system morpheme or when it is a content morpheme without a match in the ML (e.g. its counterpart is a system morpheme in the ML), the only way for it to occur is in an EL island. For example, it is suggested that the Blocking and EL Island Trigger Hypotheses explain some of the distribution of data which Eid (1992) finds in her Egyptian Arabic/English CS data. While relative pronouns from either Arabic or English may occur, they only occur introducing an entire relative clause which they must match in language. That is, for Eid's data, the Blocking Hypothesis explains why English (EL) relative pronouns must introduce English (EL) islands, if they are to occur.

In some ways, the EL Island Trigger Hypothesis makes opposite predictions from the equivalence constraint and similar constraints discussed in Chapter 2. Those constraints predict that there will be CS phrases (i.e. EL islands) only when there is surface syntactic congruence between the two languages at the point of the CS utterance. However, as has been argued, there is much evidence that such constraints do not hold. In contrast, the EL Island Trigger Hypothesis predicts that EL islands will appear precisely because there is *lack* of congruence. The difference in claims stems from the fact that more abstract types of congruence are at issue in the MLF model—one relating to whether ML or EL lemmas are directing morphosyntactic procedures for the constituent being constructed, and one involving the content/system morpheme distinction. And, as has been shown, the EL Island Trigger Hypothesis is supported by available data.

In addition, a functionally based hypothesis, the EL Hierarchy Hypothesis, is offered to predict when the speaker is likely to initiate a procedure resulting in an EL island. This hypothesis sets up an implicational hierarchy, suggesting that speakers are likely to encode core (versus peripheral) constituents in either ML islands or ML + EL constituents. Again, this hypothesis is supported by data on islands from the Nairobi corpus.

These hypotheses help to solve the biggest problem about EL islands: how to constrain them. The Trigger Hypothesis predicts which constructions *must* be islands and the Hierarchy Hypothesis predicts which are *likely* to be islands. Yet, since the class of EL islands is still open-ended, the problem of constraining them has only been reduced in size, not solved.

Remaining Problems Relating to EL Islands and System Morphemes

Although this chapter and Chapter 4 have presented strong empirical support for the MLF model, not all the data fit neatly under the various components of the model. In some ways, this is not surprising since, as I remarked in Chapter 3, CS itself can be thought of as extraordinary language production, if not even as akin to speech errors, especially in the case of EL islands. This does not mean that CS is therefore necessarily unorderly. In fact, as I have tried to demonstrate, CS largely follows the hypotheses of the MLF; but, as language produced under 'psycholinguistic stress', it is no wonder that it contains what might be some misfirings. Three problems are the most easily identified.

First is the omnipresent issue of bare forms, extensively discussed in Chapter 4. Bare forms are either nouns or verbs without either the specifiers or the inflectional morphemes required by the ML. Their production is one of the strategies which preserves the two parts of the ML Hypothesis, the Morpheme-Order and the System Morpheme Principles. Because they do not violate these principles, bare forms are not counterexamples to the MLF model.

However, bare forms pose a problem for several reasons:

(*a*) The MLF model cannot explain their occurrence other than by observing that accessing bare forms is a way to use certain EL content morphemes without violating the model. More study is needed to try to explain why morphological integration into the ML is avoided in these cases but not in most others. At the same time, the issue of congruency gives us a clue. That is, bare forms seem likely when there is a lack of congruence between the ML and the EL regarding the system morphemes which 'ought to' accompany an EL noun or verb stem. This idea was suggested when the accessing of English nouns in the locative case in Swahili/English CS was discussed earlier in this chapter.

(*b*) The occurrence of bare forms may be variable, even within a category. Far from all members of the same category occur as bare forms, and those which are bare forms are not necessarily in the same morphosyntactic contexts (Nortier, 1990 explores this matter very systematically). For example, why are some EL nouns bare and others not (from the same EL in the same language pair)? Or, why do some EL verb stems appear only with helping ML verbs (which carry the necessary system morphemes as affixes) while others appear inflected with the affixes themselves?

(*c*) In the Nairobi corpus there are three bare forms in EL islands. These bare forms violate the definition of EL islands, since the islands are no longer well-formed according to the EL grammar. Consider *such amount of cash* in [34] (target: *such an amount of cash*). Any assessment of the importance of these examples has to take into account the fact that they contrast with 118 EL islands in the Nairobi corpus which *are* well-formed according to the EL grammar. That is, they are probably best explained as simple production errors. Yet, these misfirings are an indication that there is some 'leakage' of the ML to EL islands.

[34] Several secondary school students (a Kikuyu, Kisii, and a Luyia) are talking about going to a football match at the city stadium.

LUYIA. Kuingia *centre stand* ni *one hundred*.
'To enter the centre stand is one hundred [shillings].'
KIKUYU. Sioni kama watu wataenda huko. Mtu hawezi kumaliza *such amount of cash* kuenda stadiumu.
'I don't think people will go there. A person can't spend such an amount of money to go to the stadium.'

(Swahili/English No. 35)

Second is the issue that ML conditions of well-formedness are sometimes modified in ML + EL constituents. Romaine (1989) certainly implies recognition of this phenomenon in her overall discussion. And some specific evidence comes from Ewe/English CS (Dzameshie, 1989; 1992). The Ewe copula *lē* is obligatory before English adjectival complements, but would not be present before Ewe adjectival counterparts (cf. [35*a*] and [35*b*], or the concept expressed by *lē* + English adjective would be expressed otherwise in Ewe (cf. [36*a*], [36*b*]; [37*a*], [37*b*]). The copula does occur in monolingual utterances before some other Ewe adjectives (e.g. *e-le yeye* 'it-is new').

[35*a*] e-lē *tall*
     he-COP

[35*b*] e-kɔkɔ
'He is tall.'

(Ewe/English; Dzameshie, 1992)

[36*a*] nye me-lē *sure* o
     1S NEG-COP   not

[36*b*] nye me ka   de   dzi o
     1S NEG swear PART on not
'I'm not sure.'

[37*a*] Wo nuto e-nya   be   nye me-lē   *very observant* o
      you self 2s-know that 1s NEG-COP   not

[37*b*] Wo nuto e-nya   be   nye me-lé-a   nkyu de nu nu tutu
      you self 2s-know that 1s NEG-fix-PART eye PART thing thing exactly

o
not

'You yourself know that I'm not very observant.'

Note: *-lé-* in [37*b*] is not the same morpheme as the copula *lē*; the two differ in tone.

(Ewe/English; Dzameshie, 1989: 3–4)

In some ways, this *be* + EL adjective construction resembles the *do* + EL verb stem constructions discussed earlier. It may be significant that neither *be* nor *do* verbs assign thematic roles; in this way, they differ from other verbs. Recall that the *do* construction also appears in monolingual utterances in some of the languages employing it in CS utterances. What is important here is that, in those cases where the pattern including either *be* + adjective (Ewe) or *do* + verb (many languages) is unique to CS utterances, then the pattern is outside the grammar of the ML. That is, it cannot be argued that ML morphosyntactic procedures are at work.

These cases are not enough to support any call for a 'third grammar' to describe CS utterances, of course. However, the empirical evidence obviously indicates that some alternations of ML conditions of well-formedness are being made. In a production model, at least the outlines of the adjustment are relatively easy to envision: they would involve adding special syntactic procedures which would be activated when certain EL lemmas are accessed to participate in ML + EL constituents. But why this happens in certain cases and not others awaits full explanation.

Third, there are a number of issues yet to be resolved concerning EL islands.

(*a*) There is the question of EL islands *within* ML + EL constituents, that is 'internal EL islands':

[38] dak *la chemise*
     that the shirt

(Moroccan Arabic/French; Bentahila and Davies, 1983: 317)

[39] FIRST SPEAKER. Hakanetse aka ka-*small thing* aka.
'It is not problematic, it is a small thing.'

SECOND SPEAKER. Vaienda kunoona imba, vanoda kutenga ma-*small house-s.*
'They were going to see houses, they want to buy small houses.'

(Shona/English; Crawhall, unpublished data)

At first blush, these seem quite confounding; but they can be handled as instances of a structurally assigned configuration under the Head Agreement Principle in X-bar theory (first discussed by Jakendoff, 1977; cf. Chomsky, 1986). Recall that, under X-bar theory, layered 'projections' have similar phrase structures and that in each projection in a phrase structure tree the top node is labelled X, plus a certain number of bars, with the topmost node having the most bars and forming the maximal projection. In cases such as [37] and [38], the maximal (i.e. phrasal or triple-bar) projection of the construction 'housing' the EL island is necessarily an ML constituent.

Fig. 5.1 gives structural trees representing relevant parts of [38] and [39]. In both trees, the top node is N′″ ('N triple bar'). It is projected as N″ ('N double bar') which determines two sister nodes (i.e. nodes on the same structural level in a binary branching configuration). One node is the noun complement (NC) or Specifier (SPEC); it is an ML system morpheme. The other node is N′ ('N bar'); this is the EL island. In turn, this N′ determines an NP (N + ADJ here).

For example, in [39] the N′ (*small thing* and *small house-s* in this case) is produced as is any EL island, by a switching from ML procedures to those of the EL. It is 'housed', however, by ML material (in this example the noun class prefix *ka-* for class 13 (a diminutive class) and the class 6 prefix *ma-*). These are projected directly from the head of the maximal projection, the N′″.[3] A similar solution could be used for [40a], an example from Cajun French/English CS in Brown (1986). The literal standard French version is given in [40b].[4]

[40a] Ça c'est le *highest class* français.

[40b] Ça c'est la classe française la plus haute.
'That's the French upper class.'

(Cajun French/English; Brown, 1986: 404)

---

[3] The analysis of Shona noun class prefixes in Myers (1990) seems compatible with these views about constituent structure.

[4] Cajun, of course, is a creole spoken in Louisiana, USA. Brown (1986) notes that this is the only instance in her CS data of English morpheme order; therefore, her data set would not support a claim that convergence with English explains this example.

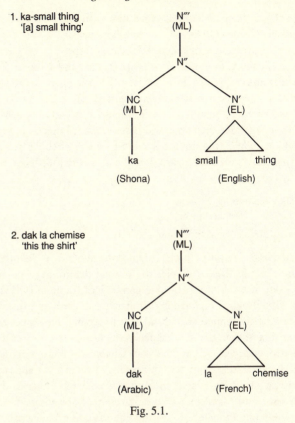

Fig. 5.1.

Brown herself suggests several alternative tree structures for [40*a*], including the structure consistent with the analysis suggested above for [38] and [39]. Under this analysis, *highest class* is an internal EL island of an ML + EL constituent. The overall constituent is projected from the ML under the topmost node, N‴. This projects N″, which goes to the sister nodes NC or SPEC and N′. SPEC is filled by *le* (from the ML). N′ projects two sister nodes, N and ADJ. The node N projects N + ADJ, which in this case is filled with (*highest class*), and the node ADJ is filled with (*français*). While the specifier node directly dominated by N‴ must be filled the ML, theoretically any of the other nodes could be filled with EL material; in this case only N under N′ is so filled. These solutions for internal EL islands is entirely consistent with other provisions of the MLF model. Nortier (1990) offers a similar analysis.[5]

(*b*) Another problem is that some EL islands, especially as 'internal EL islands', seem more favoured in some languages and in some language pairs than in others. A case in point is an EL island from French of an article + N. (Often the article is a definite article.)

This French constituent is a very frequent EL island in North African Arabic/French CS (cf. Bentahila and Davies, 1983; Poplack and Sankoff, 1988; Lahlou, 1989). It is also reported in French switching with various North American Indian languages. It is illustrated in [38] above and here in [41]:

> [41] rəbça dja:l *les appartements*
>   four of   the apartments
>
> (Moroccan Arabic/French; Lahlou, 1989: 3)

Note that Arabic requires both a demonstrative and a definite article in certain cases; in these examples the French determiner + noun fits in an island slot in the larger ML + EL constituent frame of [DEM ——].

Heath (1989) points out striking similarities in form and function between the French definite article and that in Arabic. He argues that this gives French a 'foot in the door' as far as the borrowing of French nouns is concerned; his ideas are discussed in Chapter 7. Here, one may note that this chance similarity in determiners may facilitate the appearance of such constituents as EL islands in Arabic/French CS. That is, the preference for such an island may be a language-pair-specific matter.

In a related, but ultimately quite different, case, Kamwangamalu (1989*b*) claims that constituents consisting of article + N from French may not occur as EL islands in Lingala/French CS.

> [42*a*] Ezali *probleme* monene te.
> 'It's not (a) big problem.'

---

[5] Nortier (1990: 27) produces a similar analysis, not in regard to 'internal' EL islands, but rather as part of her overall introduction to the (monolingual) grammars of Moroccan Arabic and Dutch. She analyses the Arabic definite NP with an N''' as head which is realized as a demonstrative (Determiner *a*). Under this head is an N'', with a second determiner (Determiner *b*) and an N' (realized as N + ADJ). Thus, *wahed l- bent sgira* (DEM + the + girl + little) illustrates this configuration. In my analysis, CS is possible within this configuration in one of two ways. (1) The N''' is an ML + EL constituent and the N'' is an EL island, i.e. the potential exists for the Arabic determiner (*wahed*) to 'frame' an EL island in Dutch in Nortier's data. (2) Alternatively, the N'' is an ML + EL constituent and the lower N' is an EL island, i.e. the N + ADJ would be realized in the EL.

[42*b*] *Ezali un probleme* monene te.
'It's not a big problem.'

(Lingala/French; Kamwangamalu, 1989*b*: 118–19)

Another example shows the 'missing' article in another context:

[43] Oleiki *direct* na (**la) chambre à coucher.*
'You go straight to the bedroom.'

(Lingala/French; Kamwangamalu, 1989*b*: 138)

The absence of the French article—indeed, the prohibition of this article, according to Kamwangamalu—may be caused by the fact there is no slot in the frame set by the ML for such a system morpheme, since Lingala has neither definite nor indefinite articles. It may also be because articles carry notions of gender and number in French and these are carried by nominal prefixes in Bantu languages, a point Kamwangamalu (1989*b*: 119) also makes. Yet an EL island consisting of an article + N is not prohibited by any of the constraints proposed. The EL Island Trigger Hypothesis refers only to obligatory islands, not prohibited ones.

However, the 'no (subcategorization) slot in the frame' suggestion may not be a very satisfactory explanation, because there are two parallel cases in the Nairobi corpus of an EL island consisting of either an English definite article + N or an indefinite article + N ([44] and [45]):

[44] . . . na alikuwa *the best.*
'. . . and he was "the best".'

(Swahili/English No. 19)

[45] . . . utaona *a change.*
'. . . you will see "a change".'

(Swahili/English No. 21)

Now, it is entirely possible that examples [44] and [45] are 'structurally marked choices' which take the form they do for socio-pragmatic purposes. The possibility of producing structurally marked constituents in CS utterances with such a motivation will be discussed further in Chapter 8. Certainly, the context of these examples makes it clear that *the best* and *a change* are meant to be marked with prominence.

That French EL islands of DET + N occur in some language pairs but not in others considerably weakens earlier suggestions that, for languages such as French, frequently used affixes/modifiers are stored in the same lemma as the head noun and therefore are accessed with them. If, in fact,

DET is stored with its head noun in French, why does it only appear in CS examples in some language pairs, not all?

(*c*) What can be considered a related problem is that sometimes a final ML particle seems to 'frame' an EL island. Some of these islands are very brief, such as *very observant* in [37*a*] above, which is so framed with a negative particle from Ewe (*very observant o*). But there are at least a few examples in the literature with what must be called very extensive EL islands; for example, an entire sentence except for a 'framing' particle or two may be an EL island. Forson (1979) gives several examples such as the following:

[46] *In fact, all along* nó, *I was under the impression* sɛ *things were not going well for her, the way she walked so mournfully* nó.

(Asante/English; Forson, 1979: 174–5)

Forson indicates that [nó] is a definite article, but also says it is the same morpheme as the obligatory second part of the distal demonstrative (*saa/ dɛm . . . nó*) 'that'.

Examples such as these seem to be similar to the *ka-small thing* cases. Again, these EL islands can be treated as structurally assigned configurations under the X''' convention.

(Note that the single ML morpheme which is sentence-internal is [sɛ], which, significantly, is a complementizer (and of course a system morpheme).)

Finally, there is the issue of CS in convergence situations. I will make only a few observations. First, even though *convergence* is routinely mentioned as a possible outcome in language contact situations, I suggest that syntactic convergence is actually quite an *exceptional* outcome in these situations. 'Syntactic convergence' is defined as syntactic compromise: the resulting variety shows exactly neither the phrase structure rules of one participating language nor those of the other(s). Such convergence occurs only when the varieties in question are typologically similar and perhaps also closely related genetically. For example, German/English convergence meets these criteria. More usual in language-contact situations is CS and lexical borrowing and then, given the requisite social conditions, language shift. Alternatively, but also in rare instances, the types of cases discussed in Chapter 7 may result—the maintenance of a language, but the substitution in that language of many of the morphosyntactic structures of the other.

When syntactic convergence does occur, will the MLF model correctly predict the distribution of ML and EL morphemes and their order? A very brief examination of some German/English convergence data indicates that the answer must be qualified. The prediction is that system morphemes in ML + EL constituents will come from the ML, as the System Morpheme Principle would require. However, morpheme order will be the area of true convergence between the ML and EL; that is, so-called ML morpheme order does not hold. Rather, order is that of a type of interlanguage which predominately reflects ML order, but with incursions from the EL. Further, it is entirely possible that this interlanguage will eventually establish its own set of system morphemes, although that is not yet the case in the limited data examined.

Consider the German/English convergence data cited below. Example [47] comes from a German-origin community in Australia, while [48] comes from a 'Pennsylvania German' community in Delaware, USA, and [49] is from a German-origin Amish community in Ohio, USA.

[47] Wir müssen sie *report*-en zur Polizei
                     report   to
'We must report her to the police.'

(Austrian German/English; Pütz, 1991)

German (*or* a German-based interlanguage) would appear to be the ML. Yet morpheme order in reference to the verb does not completely correspond with standard German, which would require the verb in final position. Rather, it corresponds to English order. An alternative explanation for the non-final position of the verb suggests itself. Since extraposition of sentential complements to the right of the verb is acceptable in standard German, it is possible that extraposition can be extended to non-sentential complements *as a marked order*. Thus, what occurs in [47] may be considered as a marked order for German and an unmarked order for English. The generalization which emerges from this argument is very compatible with the claim above, that syntactic convergence is very much a compromise. This argument is reminiscent of the claim in Chapter 4 for Swahili/English CS that the Morpheme-Order Principle is often preserved in the case of DEM + N by using an order which is marked for the ML (Swahili), but unmarked for the EL (English).[6]

[48] Die Kich   is voll ge-*peil-t*   mit Hundsfutter.
     the kitchen is full PPART-pile-PPART with dog food

---

[6] I thank Janice L. Jake for this observation about possible marked orders in German, as applied to this example.

'The kitchen is piled full with dog food.'

(Pennsylvania German/English; Enninger, 1980: 345)

In this example, *mit Hundsfutter* is not in the unmarked order for standard German. Although the morpheme *is* may be considered as the English morpheme, it is also a German dialectal variant of standard German *ist*, just as *Kich* is variant of standard German *Küche*. If it is the English-origin morpheme, then one would have to argue that Pennsylvania German is an interlanguage which has its own set of system morphemes, many—but not all—of which overlap with those of German.

[49] Er hat immer uns ge-*teach-ed*/ge-*teach*-t   mir sel   unser shtof
     he AUX always us PAST-   -PAST we should our   stuff
geschmiert habe
greased   AUX
'He always taught us [that] we should keep our stuff greased.'

(Amish German/English; Van Ness, 1992)

Note that Van Ness uses a partially phonetic rendition (cf. *shtof* 'stuff', which would be *stoff* in standard German).

In [49], *uns* 'us' would follow *hat* directly if the sentence were in standard German. Yet *uns* is not placed according to English morpheme order, either. This is an indication that an 'interlanguage' has developed (i.e. a variety clearly related to the original ML, but not identical to it). *Mir* is a dialectal variant of *wir*, and *sel* corresponds to standard German *sollen*.

Whether the verb *ge-teach-ed* or *ge-teach-t* shows a variation on double morphology is in question; that is, the suffix is definitely pronounced [t], and Van Ness herself indicates that it stands for the English past-tense suffix. Yet the form is ambiguous, since the German form and the English allomorph in this phonological context are pronounced the same. (Obviously, the use of [t] to represent the English past-tense morpheme would be non-standard, since *teach* takes the suppletive form *taught* in standard English.) Other data in Van Ness's corpus show that there is no consistent use of any past-tense suffix, either German or English. Elsewhere, she has an example, *aber er hat ge-farm* 'but he farmed' which shows no past-tense suffix at all, although it has the German prefix also marking a past participle. In Enninger (1980: 344), however, there are examples of suffixes which may represent the voiced allomorph of the English past-tense suffix (e.g. *g'happen-ed* 'happened'). A problem, however, is that the local scribe's transcription may reflect English orthography, not actual pronunciation, Enninger notes.

To return to the question posed above, does the MLF model correctly predict CS data in convergence cases? That is, are the designations of ML and EL still relevant? In order to answer this question, the morphosyntax of the interlanguage of the convergence situation first must be studied and compared with the morphosyntax of monolingual renditions of the dialects of the two languages involved. In the limited German/ English data examined, the active system morphemes are projected from a German variety close to standard German at least in its system morphemes; this is the likely ML in the CS conversations which presumably led to the development of the interlanguage. Thus, the System Morpheme Principle makes correct predictions for these convergence data: syntactically active system morphemes come from the ML. This indicates that the variety in place as the ML when the interlanguage begins developing remains relevant in the interlanguage in reference to system morphemes. The only possible exception results from the possible presence of the English past-tense suffix. What is its role? The assumption is that the German prefix *ge-*, which is categorically present, carries all the past-tense information, with the English suffix analysed by speakers as part of the verb stem. With respect to the Morpheme-Order Principle, while order in the interlanguage certainly reflects ML order more than EL order, correct predictions cannot be based entirely on ML morpheme order.

More study is needed, but except for all details of morpheme order, these data largely can be explained under the MLF model. The data also suggest the following hypotheses about language production and language change: (1) Different sets of production procedures project system morphemes versus morpheme order, and the system morpheme procedures are at a more abstract level. (2) Possibly because morpheme order is more of a surface procedure, it is more open to change.

CS and Modularity

There is an interesting error in the Nairobi corpus contained in [50] which illustrates how a blind syntactic procedure may read its input. A schoolboy is describing his awakening habits on non-school days.

[50] Mimi siku hizi   ni-ko *used* ku-amka   *very early.*
  I   days these I be   to-awaken
'These days I am used to awakening very early.'
(Swahili/English No. 24)

One can hypothesize this set of procedures. In the production process, there is a morphosyntactic 'specialist' whose job it is to insert the EL phrasal verb *used to* into the complement slot following the -*ko* construction. But when it performs its operations, it finds that there already is an ML morpheme in place in a contiguous slot signalling the infinitival concept of 'to' (the infinitival prefix *ku-*). Finding this ML system morpheme in place *and* operating under the overall specification that system morphemes are to come from the ML in any case, the 'specialist' reinterprets *used to*, not as a phrasal verb, but as including an unlicensed system morpheme (*to*) as an infinitive marker.

Note that the specialist does this on the basis of purely syntactic co-occurrence restrictions, since in its module, the specialist has no access to the semantic aspects of the lemma for *used to* at this point. It re-forms *used to* as *used*. This example shows that some of the modularity posited in current language-production models may result in errors in CS. When two systems are 'on' at the same time, the potential for 'mistakes' should be high. But the evidence for CS shows little high-level variability and many regularities instead, indicating a rather obliging relationship between modularity and CS.

That is, there is evidence that CS, at least, implicates different degrees of modularity at different stages in production. First, there is rather strict modularity for global procedures (preference for the ML in morpheme frequency, and in morpheme order and system morphemes in ML + EL constituents). But CS also suggests that there is interdependence and feedback for both some high-level and some low-level procedures. For example, there is independence shown by the possibility of selecting either an EL or an ML lemma to call a content morpheme in ML + EL constituents, as long as both satisfy the ML lemma's congruence specifications.

There is both evidence *and* lack of evidence of possible 'look-ahead' when a Bantu language is the ML: how EL nouns (as CS forms in ML + EL constituents) are treated in regard to their modifiers. The EL noun is assigned to a noun class. There is 'look-ahead' shown when its ML modifiers receive structurally assigned agreement prefixes of the same class. However, sometimes there is a mismatch in these structurally assigned prefixes, either with their head noun or between the modifiers. This indicates no 'look-ahead'. For example, recall that in example [8] in Chapter 4 the English lexeme *movements* takes two modifiers with structurally assigned agreement prefixes from two different noun classes (i.e. *movements yake zote* (movements-her-all) 'all her movements'). *Movements* may be considered morphosyntactically integrated into Swahili as a Bantu class 10 noun, since its modifier *z-ote* 'all' shows the class 10 modifier prefix (*z-*). A zero allomorph is a possible realization of class 10 nominal prefixes. But while *z-ote* is structurally assigned to class 10, the other modifier, the possessive adjective *y-ake*, is assigned to class 9 (a singular class) or class 6 (a plural class), both of which show *y-* as a modifier prefix. Example [29] in Chapter 4 shows a related problem. The English lexeme *time* is placed in Swahili class 6 (*ma-time*), while the structurally assigned prefixes on its modifiers come from class 10 (*z-*, *zi-*), as in *z-ile ma-time z-ote z-engine* (those-times-all-other) 'all those other times'.

Recall the metaphor of a cafeteria (introduced in Chapter 4). To make certain types of major selection, one must get in certain lines (i.e. the ML line or the EL line; the system morpheme line or the content morpheme line). But there is also flexibility at lower levels. This fact highlights an important feature of the MLF model. The provisions of the model do not so much require a specific structure as offer a limited set of alternative strategies. Recall that both the Morpheme-Order and System Morpheme Principles can be satisfied by three different strategies (e.g. fabricating *do* constructions to accommodate EL verb stems, allowing some nouns to appear as bare forms).

Just as diners can change their minds even about the more pre-packaged items, some variability in CS is permitted. First, there is high-order variability in allowing EL islands to be formed at all; after all, they entail inhibiting ML procedures under the conditions specified by the EL Island Trigger Hypothesis. Second, there is middle-level variability regarding which strategy to follow, while still supporting the ML Hypothesis in ML + EL constituents. Third, there is lower-order variability. For example, in CS involving Bantu languages, not all EL nouns in ML + EL constituents are assigned to the same Bantu class. Also, there is evidence that ML morphosyntactic procedures are not always applied uniformly to the same EL nouns at the content morpheme insertion stage. For example, there are often two realizations of the same English-origin CS form, *for the same speaker*, as well as across speakers, in the Shona corpus studied for this volume. Bernsten (1990), who studied the corpus from the point of view of integration of borrowed forms from English into Shona, remarks on this. For example, she points out that the same English noun stem may be variably placed into Bantu class 6 (e.g. *ma-* as the class nominal prefix + the noun stem, i.e. *ma-fact-(s)*), or in class 10 (e.g. the ø allomorph of the class nominal prefix + the noun stem, i.e. *fact-(s)*). In either case, the class membership is evident, based on the agreements which the noun governs. It is on the basis of such evidence that the MLF model envisions CS production as similar to the cafeteria line; it explains the regularities of CS by using such conceptions of modularity. This theoretical position explains such matters as how it happens that the participating languages play different roles, how their morphemes are differentially accessed based on their status as content/ system morphemes, and how the frame for ML + EL constituents is assembled separately from its content morphemes, as well as when EL islands must occur.

6
Relating Lexical Borrowing and Codeswitching

Preliminaries

This chapter deals with the relationship between lexical borrowing and codeswitching (CS), concentrating on the two as processes but also considering their outcomes. The general argument is that singly occurring forms originating with the EL, whether CS or borrowed forms (hereafter B forms), are part of the same developmental continuum, not unrelated phenomena, as some have argued. Evidence is that they undergo largely the same morphosyntactic procedures (of the Matrix Language, or ML) during language production. Therefore, it turns out, the motivation for distinguishing them in order to assess models of morphosyntactic constraints on CS seems to evaporate, at least for content morphemes.

However, even though they are subject to the *same production procedures*, the *lexical entries* of CS and B forms must be different, since B forms become part of the mental lexicon of the ML, while CS forms do not. I follow Levelt (1989: 6) in his definition of the mental lexicon as 'the store of information about the words in one's language'.

The reason to explore differences in this regard is that status as a CS or B form affects a morpheme's distributional possibilities in CS utterances, if it is a system morpheme. Also, a difference in status affects frequency, and an exploration of this nature leads to an explanation of why CS forms have little recurrence value, in contrast with B forms.

Possible criteria for distinguishing borrowing and CS are considered, but the conclusion is that traditionally recognized criteria (i.e. dealing with degree of integration of B forms) yield mixed results and are not useful metrics for this reason. Thus, absolute frequency and also relative frequency of occurrence of the test items present themselves as the most reliable criteria.

I will propose some generalizations about borrowing *as it relates to CS*; that is, I do not claim to offer a comprehensive view of borrowing *per se*. However, in dealing with contact-induced change, especially in regard to such an open system as the lexicon, one cannot expect that any statements will hold categorically. Thus, the same type of principles (embodied in the ML hypothesis) proposed about constraints on CS as a synchronic process are not possible in discussing the products of lexical borrowing. This is because the shape the structural frame of CS utterances takes is governed by cognitive procedures (and note that I say the frame, not the details of performance, such as preferred patterns or overall frequency). In contrast, the ultimate forms lexical borrowings take have the additional feature of being affected by many extra linguistic factors. (For example, I suggest the degree of contact or the psycho-sociolinguistic dynamics of a contact situation will not alter the principle that the ML sets the frame in ML + EL constituents; but these factors may effect a change as to which language is the 'designated' ML, or influence the types of lexical form borrowed or their degree of phonological integration into the ML, for instance.) This means that, with borrowing, there will be more counter-examples to the proposed claims, although they must be limited cases or the generalizations will be vacuous. Still, I proceed on the assumption that it is more useful to attempt predictive generalizations than to remain at the descriptive level. This, of course, does not mean abandoning facts; the proposed claims must be empirically based.

Further, some substantive generalizations regarding the nature of lexical B forms are possible. For example, it will turn out that the content/system morpheme distinction and the need for congruence between languages regarding this distinction applies to B forms as well as to CS forms. Specifically, I will use these ideas to account for the universally evident fact that nouns are the most borrowed category.

Why Study Borrowing in Relation to Codeswitching?

Much of the flurry of research on structural constraints on CS has been marred before it begins because it excludes single-lexeme forms from consideration as CS forms and does not consider how such forms compare with B forms[1] during language production. Thus, I suggest, the data base is skewed in many studies.

---

[1] I follow standard usage in linguistics so that 'borrowed' forms, of course, are the same as 'loans'. Romaine (1989: 54) writes: 'What happens to lexical stems has been central to discussions of interference, transfer, and borrowing. It is usually in this context that the term "borrowing" is used.' I note that some African-language specialists use the term 'adoptives'.

Here, I argue against the claim that phonological, morphological, and syntactic integration unequivocally distinguishes B forms from CS forms, citing evidence showing that, especially in cases of heavy cultural contact, the two types of form resemble each other more than has previously been recognized. I also argue against the notion that only utterances of EL material which are longer than one lexeme represent 'true' CS.

Why This Discussion Comes Here

In many ways, the arguments of this chapter are 'pre-theoretical' in the sense that they address issues which ought to be settled *before* the CS researcher attempts to account for the structures present in CS data. That is, before attempting to deal with CS, the researcher needs to have resolved the issue of whether and how to distinguish CS and B forms. The reason I have left this discussion until this late in the volume is that the argument relies on familiarity with the provisions of the MLF model, the express subject of the preceding two chapters.

The Database

The major data sets considered are primarily a Zimbabwe corpus, along with the Nairobi corpus used throughout the volume, but especially in Chapters 4 and 5. Data from 129 interviews, for a total of about 22 hours of speech, make up the Zimbabwe corpus. Half of the interviews come from Chitungwiza, a working-class suburb about 20 km. south of Harare, the capital of Zimbabwe. Most residents work in Harare as skilled and semi-skilled workers or in clerical positions. The other half of the interviews were conducted near Mutoko, a farming community 120 km. east of Harare. At both sites, the interviewers were local residents known in the communities. My collaborator in gathering the Zimbabwe data, Janice Bernsten, concentrated on studying the integration of English loans into Shona (cf. Bernsten, 1990).[2]

The interview process was designed to produce as near to naturally occurring conversations as possible. Most importantly, interviewees were not aware that the real purpose of their being interviewed was to study their use of English loan words. All interviewees and interviewers were native speakers of Shona; the interviews were conducted in the

---

[2] Bernsten's statistics are based on a slightly larger corpus than mine—132 interviews, as opposed to 129.

interviewee's home or nearby. The interviewer himself was instructed to speak Shona, but was given the latitude to engage in CS or use loan words himself, since he also was told to speak as naturally as possible. No instructions were given to the interviewees as to the necessary medium of the interview.

The Matrix Language as Recipient

In the presentation of the MLF model of CS, the ML is identified as the language governing the syntax of the sentence in utterances showing CS. In the case of borrowing, this same ML is also the recipient language. The EL is the source of CS forms and also B forms.

As has been repeatedly pointed out in the earlier chapters, the ML plays the dominant structural role in CS. But it is important not to assume that the ML is necessarily the language of higher socio-economic/political prestige in the bilingual community in question. In fact, it would seem that more often it is rather the language more asso-ciated with solidarity-building functions. As Thomason and Kaufman (1988) point out at many junctures, the language with high socio-economic/political prestige is typically the major donor language in any lexical borrowing which takes place in such a community. However, this donor language plays the minor structural role in CS as the EL.

Borrowing as a Research Topic

Virtually every language's lexicon includes some items borrowed from another language, and there have been many articles in the linguistic literature which describe the effects of borrowing in a specific language. Also, and in contrast to CS, borrowing enjoys a long record of receiving some attention in almost all general linguistic textbooks. In the numerous textbooks on bilingualism/language contact which have appeared in the last ten years, borrowing claims even more space (e.g. Baetens-Beardsmore, 1982; Grosjean, 1982; Lüdi and Py, 1986; Appel and Muysken, 1987; Hamers and Blanc, 1989; Romaine, 1989).

But received wisdom, both about the empirical facts of borrowing and about the matter of which aspects repay study, still relies almost exclus-ively for information and insight on the classics of this century: Haugen (1953) on English loans in the Norwegian of immigrants to the United

States, and Weinreich (1953) on language contact in Switzerland. The fact that the definitions and categories these scholars proposed are still used attests to their value; further, many of their insights still ring true, such as Haugen's comments about conditions promoting bilingualism. Haugen and Weinreich do detail how the shapes and meanings of borrowed lexical items are altered. But, as might be expected, they reflect the prevailing view at the time of their writing—that the systems of a language are so tightly organized that borrowing must be only a peripheral factor. Thus they concentrate on lexical borrowing, and are largely silent on subjects which become probable research questions only within a theory which sees languages as sets of modular subsystems (or sets of production directions), some more open to external influences than others. Examples of little-addressed questions in this era include: what specific factors (structural or sociolinguistic) demonstrably constrain or facilitate borrowing, or are there lexical categories which are more susceptible to borrowing than others, and why?

In addition, under the premiss that all linguistic systems are tightly organized, the prevailing view has been that the major function of B forms is to fill gaps in the lexicon, the one subsystem in a language welcoming change (and then only additions for new objects/concepts, for the most part).

Even in the major debate in creole studies (i.e. between universal grammar and substrate/superstrate languages as sources for creole grammar), those creolists arguing for substrate influences have concentrated all their efforts on finding substrate sources for specific forms. The result is that the more basic issues of how substrate effects come about in the first place, or how they are constrained, has not been a major research question. Still, the flurry of interest in pidgin and creole development may have helped spark new interest in structural borrowing, just because it could not help but call attention to the processes giving rise to structural evolution or expansion.

Current Interest in Borrowing

Whatever the motivation, in the last twenty years, and increasingly of late, researchers are studying data sets in terms of research questions which lead to the conclusion that the morphological and syntactic linguistic subsystems are much more open to borrowing than previously acknowledged, and that not all lexical B forms are equally integrated into the recipient language. These studies call for a reassessment of views on

borrowing. This scholarship includes attempts to explain the borrowing of basic vocabulary as a sociolinguistically motivated process (e.g. Scotton and Okeju, 1973; Heath, 1981; Lüdi, 1986; Mougeon and Beniak, 1987; 1991); or to discuss structural constraints on borrowing (Moravcsik, 1978; Mühlhäusler, 1985; Campbell, forthcoming) or to clarify and classify types of borrowing (Van Coetsem, 1988). Also, differentiating the effects of borrowing from those of language shift is a major topic in Thomason and Kaufman (1988).

The extent of lexical and structural borrowing is treated in several book-length treatments of bilingualism in a specific language community (e.g. Karttunen, 1985; Hill and Hill, 1986; Heath, 1989), as well as in articles on specific types of borrowing in a language (e.g. Campbell, 1987 on syntactic borrowing; Nurse, 1988 on morphological borrowing; Mougeon and Beniak, 1991 on differential borrowing patterns across bilinguals with different use patterns; and Bernsten and Myers-Scotton, forthcoming, on differential phonological integration across social groups and differential morphological integration across form classes). The data bases of these studies and the conclusions they engender inform the following argument, which compares borrowing with CS.

Borrowing: Two Different Types and Processes

As indicated in Chapter 2, few CS studies even consider comparing borrowing and CS as an issue.[3] Those that do acknowledge that there are two types of EL-origin form typically decide that separating out B forms is desirable, and tend to throw out the baby with the bath water, discarding *all* single-lexeme EL items as B forms—although there is also some hedging. When CS models exclude singly occurring EL lexemes, they do not account for what I have argued are bona fide CS forms. For example, the status of *innocent* in [1] is at issue, with this chapter making the argument that it is a CS form.

[1] Anaonekana kama ni mtu *innocent. I don't believe he has stolen that thing.*
'He appears to be an innocent person . . .'
(Swahili/English No. 11)

While earlier researchers on borrowing recognized that there are two types of B form, what I will call 'cultural' and 'core' B forms, few current

---

[3] Scotton (1988c) is an earlier attempt to differentiate CS and B. While it may make some useful points, I now think its overall objective (i.e. to distinguish CS and B) was ill-advised.

CS researchers do this (Scotton, 1988*b*). Even researchers dealing only with borrowing do not often explicitly mention the distinction. The division is important, however, because the two may be incorporated into an ML through different processes, one related to CS but the other not. (Both, however, undergo the same synchronic *production* processes.)

Cultural B Forms

Cultural B forms represent objects or concepts new to the ML culture (e.g. *baisikeli* 'bicycle' in Swahili or *bhajeti* 'budget' in Shona). When two (or more) languages share a long cultural tradition (e.g. in some places in Europe or Asia), most B forms between them may well be core B forms: that is, any cultural B forms either language takes in are more likely to come from more distinctly foreign cultures. And, of course, when the new objects or concepts which stimulate core B forms enter the ML culture, their encoding in the ML can be handled instead by other means, such as paraphrase or calquing.[4]

Core B Forms

In contrast, core B forms are items for which the ML always has viable equivalents.[5] Thus, core loans meet no real lexical needs and may be largely or entirely redundant (e.g. the case of the borrowing of English numbers by Shona discussed below). This means that, in the initial stages, they have a different status from cultural B forms with regard to competition with ML lexemes; it is a status identical to that of CS forms. At this stage, just as CS forms do, core B forms may appear only once or twice in a large data corpus, with no predictability as to their recurrence; they are used initially almost exclusively by speakers with fluency in both languages.

Since most CS researchers show little interest in differences between B forms, it is no surprise they are largely also silent on the issue of a connection between borrowing and CS. Until very recently, the following views were widely accepted (and certainly still have currency):

---

[4] Of course, some languages use their own resources to come up with lexemes for new objects/concepts and produce paraphrases or calques. e.g. when bicycles were introduced into Ghana, Ewe innovated the paraphrase *gaso* 'iron horse' for this new object. Other mechanized vehicles receive similar treatments (e.g. *yamevu* 'air vehicle' for 'aeroplane'). I thank Alex Dzameshie for these examples.

[5] There is always the issue of what, in fact, is a 'viable equivalent'.

Intrasentential code switching is sharply distinguished from other interferences, such as borrowing, learned use of foreign words, and filling lexical gaps, all of which can be exhibited by monolingual speakers. (Joshi 1985: 190).

The nonce loan hypothesis, which basically states no more than that borrowing, whether nonce or established, is a phenomenon of language mixture distinct from code-switching and is operationally distinguishable as such, at least at the aggregate level . . . (Sankoff, Poplack, and Vanniarajan, 1990: 97)

Of course those writers are correct who distinguish between CS as a bilingual's behaviour and B and other phenomena which are within a monolingual's ability (although even here the line may not be so distinct). But claiming a 'sharp distinction' between B and CS *as processes* and *how they undergo morphosyntactic procedures in language production* is poorly grounded, as I will claim below. Treffers-Daller (1991*a*) also argues against the CS/borrowing distinction at many points.

A Misguided Assumption

The problem with statements of a sharp line between borrowing and CS is that they seem to presuppose that all B forms are cultural B forms. Cultural loans, of course, are the usual textbook example of B forms.

Such loans undoubtedly *are* most common in most cases of borrowing. And, among all loans, nouns are typically most common, reflecting the high percentage of signifiers for new objects and concepts. The latter claim of the dominance of nouns is supported convincingly by Bernsten's analysis of the Zimbabwe corpus. She found (1990: 76) that, out of all B form types (N = 391), 78 per cent (306) were nouns. Verbs follow next, at 13 per cent (52), with numbers at 5 per cent (21) and function words at 3 per cent (12). Nouns also tower over other form classes in a count of tokens.[6] In their Canadian study, Poplack, Sankoff, and Miller (1988: 63) found that 64 per cent of what they identified as B forms from English into French were nouns, followed by verbs (14 per cent).

As a test of the claim that cultural B forms are much more common than core B forms, I compared the two types in Bernsten's (1990) listing of B forms in the Zimbabwe corpus. Out of 391 B forms 68 per cent (267) are clearly cultural B forms (e.g. [bohoro]/[boro] 'borehole'; [nes]/[nesi] 'nurse').[7] Some of the remainder (32 per cent, or 126) are borderline cases

---

[6] Bernsten's (1990: 76) token counts are the following: 6,294 total, with nouns at 73% (4,598); verbs at 5% (333); numbers at 20% (1,253); and function words at 2% (119).

[7] Material enclosed in square brackets represents a very broad phonetic transcription which may often be identical to a phonemic transcription.

(e.g. [beg]/[begi] 'bag'; [oda] 'to order'), while others are more definitely core B forms (e.g. [wan]/[wani] 'one'; [taim] 'time').

Still, common though cultural B forms are, there is no reason to take them as representing all B forms. Yet this has been the case, often in general and certainly in many of the earlier discussions of CS and structural constraints. A typical statement about loans is found in Sridhar and Sridhar (1980: 409) who state that one of the ways code-mixing (CM = CS) is different from B is that, in CM, 'the mixed elements do not necessarily "fill gaps" in the host language'. That B forms fill gaps is clearly a characterization fitting cultural B forms, but not core ones.

Of course, there are many examples of cultural B forms which 'fill gaps' in any current data corpus on CS. For example, in the Nairobi corpus the following examples are typical: *salvation* in [2] represents a new concept (i.e. related to Christianity), and *lunch* and *mapeni* in [3] and *school* in [4] encode new objects/concepts. Cultural B forms often occur in the same sentence with CS forms, as they do here.

[2] Kama mimi naweza kusema *salvation* kwangu ni ugumu—*hard* kabisa . . .
'As for me I can say that salvation for me is *hard*—very hard . . .'
[Note: *hard* is a CS form.]
(Swahili/English No. 1)

[3] Si ninyi mtaleta *mapeni* za *lunch*?
'Isn't it that you [PL] will bring money for lunch?'
(Swahili/English No. 8)

[4] . . . maanake alikaa huko *only four days* akarudi, akasema kuwa hati hiyo *school* ni mbaya . . .
'. . . because he stayed only four days and came back, saying that, oh, that school is bad . . .'
[Note: *only four days* is an EL island (CS).]
(Swahili/English No. 10)

The Near-Categorical Nature of Cultural B Forms

In terms of their relationship to the ML, cultural B forms are best characterized as at the categorical end of any continuum of B. That is, once the lexeme encoding a new object/concept is used in the ML, it is predicted that those speakers who first used it will use it again when the need to signify the same referent comes up. Therefore, the claim is that cultural B forms enter their ML lexicon *abruptly*. This does not mean that the new cultural B form will be used without exception by 100 per cent of the speech community. Certain groups of speakers may always resort to calquing or paraphrase. Thus, the term 'near-categorical' is only used in regard to the form's *relative* frequency, specifically for those social groups in the community initiating its use when the need to use its referent arises. Consider the recent case of *glasnost* entering English from Russian at the end of the 1980s, and standing for 'a change/warming of the political climate'. For those speakers who talk about such matters, nothing but *glasnost* is used for the concept/state of affairs in question. And in the Zimbabwe corpus, those respondents referring to *school fees* categorically use the English compound noun to do so; the only variation is in its degree of phonological integration (as [skurufiz] or [skulfiz]).

Why Borrow Core B Forms?

If cultural B forms have the instrumental role of filling lexical gaps in the ML, core B forms have a 'gratuitous' nature (Mougeon and Beniak, 1991: 199) since the ML always has close enough equivalents for them. Core B forms are borrowed because certain types of contact situation promote desires to identify with the EL culture, or at least with aspects of it. Making words used in that culture part of one's own repertoire is an obvious means of such identification.

A discussion of the psycho-sociolinguistic ingredients of those situations is beyond the scope of this study; but the existence of core B forms supports the insight of Haugen (1953: 373) that borrowing 'always goes beyond the actual "needs" of language'. Haugen (1992: i. 199) is more specific:

Words are often borrowed because they are felt to be prestigious or just novel. This is especially true if the speakers feel inferior to the speakers of the other language, as did the English when they were ruled by the Norman French. The loanword may cause native words to seem inadequate and gradually be disused. Hence the many loanwords from Anglo-Norman French in English and from Low German in Scandinavian.

While the tendency to overlook the frequency of core loans is motivated by the prevailing model of language as impervious to external influence except at the peripheries, such studies as Thomason and Kaufman (1988) now directly challenge these views. From impressively diverse sources, they amass empirical evidence of contact-induced change in all systems of a language. And such an eminent typologist as Comrie (1989: 91) now states flatly:

in principle anything can be borrowed. Although some phenomena are relatively unlikely to be borrowed, given sufficient time the probability of such phenomena being borrowed increases.

But while Thomason and Kaufman offer convincing evidence that borrowing can touch all parts of a language, both they and typologists are largely silent on the mechanisms of structural borrowing. This issue will be addressed in Chapter 7.

Core B Forms as a Link with Codeswitching

Because cultural loans do enter the ML abruptly, they are 'instant' B forms and unrelated to CS as a phenomenon, except that the same types of contact situation often promote B and CS simultaneously. The relation of core B forms to CS, however, is another story. Of course, some core B forms may enter the ML in the same way as some cultural B forms: a prestigious person uses them and others then slavishly follow suit.

However, I argue here that the unmarked mechanisms for introducing core B forms are the same production constraints as those on EL material when CS takes place. These constraints give primacy to the ML in CS, especially in ML + EL constituents, according to the MLF model. That is, the ML sets the frame for such constituents, supplying all active system morphemes and morpheme order. But—and here is the point relevant to this discussion—recall that, once the frame is set, content morphemes may be accessed from either the ML *or* the EL. That is, the lines are 'open' to both ML and EL morphemes at this stage. Thus, the fact that most B forms are content morphemes is entirely predictable within the MLF model, if they start out as CS forms in ML + EL constituents.[8]

Note, however, that the Blocking Hypothesis (discussed in Chapter 5) restricts the totally free entry of EL content morphemes. For this reason, there is a preference for ML morphemes, even at this step of content morpheme insertion. In fact, recall that I use the overall greater frequency of ML morphemes as a defining feature of the ML; I will return to this point later in the chapter when the frequency of B forms is raised.

---

[8] System morphemes, of course, in some instances are also borrowed. The MLF model certainly does not prohibit such possibilities. Conditions promoting such borrowing are not discussed here; however, even though EL system morphemes only appear in ML + EL constituents as instances of 'double morphology', they appear regularly in EL islands. Since this contiguity between ML and EL material exists, borrowing is possible.

One can refine predictions about lexical borrowing by offering a Content Morpheme-Borrowing Hypothesis along these lines. Content morphemes make up the bulk of borrowed words because they are generally more congruent with subcategorization specifications of slots in a recipient language (the ML) than system morphemes. Further, among content morphemes, more congruency (and therefore more ease of borrowing) is predicted for nouns and descriptive adjectives, since they receive, but do not assign, thematic roles. For such content morphemes as verbs and prepositions, which are potential thematic role-assigners, there is a greater chance that they will not match the recipient language in regard to subcategorization for these roles. Therefore, it will be more difficult to borrow them. Conversely, they may be borrowed if their category assignment in the borrowing process is changed to make them more congruent with the donor slots. This offers an explanation why, for example, borrowed verbs often become nouns.

CS as the Gate for Core Borrowing

The empirical evidence supports the scenario of CS as the gate by which content morphemes as core B forms enter the ML. In any situation of cultural contact between speakers of different languages where CS is a frequent mode, especially in those communities where CS itself is the unmarked choice for ingroup conversations, core B forms from the EL appear readily in conversations. These same conversations also include sentences showing CS. The hypothesis is that, before they were B forms, these core lexemes from the EL were CS forms. Consider these examples showing core B forms:

> [5] (female secretary from the Luo ethnic group, about 30 years old and with some secondary-school education):
>
> Nilikuwa na shughuli kidogo hapo *town*. Kwanza nilipeleka barua zangu kwa *posta*. Huko nikakutana na wasichana wengine wa kwetu.
> 'I had a little business here in town. First I took my letters to the post office. And there I met some other young women from our home place.'
> (Swahili/English No. 36)

The lexeme *town* [taun] appears in 12 out of the 40 conversations in the Nairobi corpus, clearly establishing it as a B form. (Note that it is not phonologically assimilated to Swahili phonotactics (requiring open syllables) in any of these occurrences.) Note also that *posta* 'post office' is a cultural B form.

[6] INTERVIEWER. Matambudziko api amunowana pakuenda kubasa?
'What kind of problems do you have getting to work?'
RESPONDENT [36-year-old male, who is a receptionist in an office and who has reached 'O' level in school, i.e. secondary school diploma]:
Ndee *transport*, *especially* kana wava kudzoka ndopanonyanya kunetsa zvikuru. Dzimwe nguva wasvika pa-*bhazi* na *half past four* unogona kuzowana *bhazi* ku-ma-*six*.
'It is of transport, especially when you are coming back, that's when we have too many problems. You can get to the bus stop at half past four, you are likely to get a bus at around six.'
(Shona/English No. 1)

In this conversation, *transport* and *bhazi* 'bus' may be considered cultural B forms. (The lexeme *transport* occurs in 72 interviews for 140 tokens, while *bhazi* appears in 89 interviews for 414 tokens.) The numbers are core B forms, with *six* occurring in 67 interviews for 116 tokens. These statistics are from Bernsten (1990: 111, 125, 123). (As will be discussed below, 86 per cent of the numerals in the Zimbabwe corpus were from English, including well over 90 per cent of those referring to time.) In addition, *especially* is also a core B form, occurring 10 times in 10 interviews (Bernsten, 1990: 114).

The argument that the initial admittance of (most) core B forms is as CS forms is the following. Since core B forms stand for meanings for which the ML has its own referents, there is no 'urgent consensus' mandating use of the new EL forms on the same scale as new cultural B forms would be used. Initially, therefore, the frequency of core EL forms is relatively low, satisfying only individual style. Those EL forms with low frequency and lacking predictability are CS forms, by definition. As a core form's frequency increases in relation to that of the ML form it duplicates, it is on its way to becoming a B form. (I will argue below, for example, that *because* and *but* show enough frequency relative to their Shona counterparts to be considered more than CS forms. What is 'enough', in labelling a form a B form? This will be discussed below; however, to an extent, it becomes a trivial and, at this point, only an arbitrarily determined issue.)

This argument leads to the following hypothesis: if entrance into the ML is the issue, a longitudinal study will show that most core B forms first appear with only one or two occurrences as CS forms, with their frequency building up gradually. This process contrasts with that of cultural B forms, which appear with a high relative frequency more suddenly.[9] (Of course, *some* cultural B forms may enter the ML first as CS forms, not as abrupt loans; and *some* core B forms may enter abruptly. But they are the exceptions.)

It is possible that many language-contact researchers simply have always assumed such a connection between B and CS forms, even if they did not differentiate cultural and core B forms. Researchers who speak explicitly of a dynamic continuum include Lüdi and Py (1984), Gardner-Chloros (1987), and Thomason (1988), with diachronic movement taking place so that CS forms become B forms. Gardner-Chloros (1987: 102) writes:

it would appear that the distinction between code-switching and loans is of a 'more or less' and not an absolute nature . . . If it is an innovation on the speaker's part, it is a code-switching. If it is frequently used in that community—whether or not in free variation with a native element—then it is at least on its way to becoming a loan. In short, a loan is a code-switch with a full-time job.

Differentiating Borrowing and Codeswitching

If CS and borrowing fall on a continuum, however, how is it possible to differentiate the two? Arguments typically suggested will be reviewed below. I will suggest that the criteria of absolute and relative frequency of occurrence are the only criteria which hold in all cases. But I will also conclude that there seems little reason to differentiate CS and B forms *as processes*; however, there may be a motivation to do so in regard to how the forms are entered in the mental lexicon.

A First Solution

Chapter 2 has already discussed some earlier views of CS. When Spanish/English CS researchers in the 1970s discussed CS, they generally dealt only with EL material comprising at least a phrase or preferably longer constituents. For example, Pfaff (1979: 296) notes that both Reyes (1974) and Gingras (1974), early researchers in Spanish/English CS, classified *all* instances of single words from the EL as B forms.

---

[9] The only way that one can produce a relative-frequency statistic for cultural B forms is to compare them to possible indigenous calques or paraphrases.

This view of CS (i.e. accepting as CS only extended stretches of EL material with its own internal consistency) still persists, helped along by folk views that, after all, CS in general can be explained as no more than 'searching for the right word' (the *mot juste*).

The position of Poplack and her associates has been very influential. While their views have shifted somewhat (understandably so with more study), in general their arguments include these five points: (1) CS and B are based on different mechanisms (Sankoff, Poplack, and Vanniarajan, 1990: 74): 'borrowing is a very different process from code-switching, subject to different constraints and conditions'. (2) The clearest cases of B forms are those forms showing phonological, morphological, and syntactic integration into the ML, but phonological integration may not always be complete (ibid. 73). (3) CS usually involves more than singly-occurring EL forms: 'When fragments from both codes alternate within a single sentence, this is often called intrasentential code-switching, especially if each fragment consists of more than a single noun or other content word' (ibid. 71). See Poplack (1988*b*: 97) for a similar statement. (4) 'Nonce borrowings' are exemplified by single-word forms showing morphological and syntactic integration (e.g. ML case marking and/or determiners) into the ML in Tamil/English and a Finnish/English corpora (Poplack and Sankoff, 1988: 1178): (5) But not all singly-occurring EL forms represent either established B forms or even nonce forms: 'Single-word code-switches are theoretically possible' (Poplack, Sankoff, and Miller, 1988: 53).

While I will argue against the views of Poplack and her associates, they deserve credit for seriously considering the issues from a number of perspectives.

Not All B Forms Are Phonologically Equal

While most established B forms may well be phonologically integrated into the ML, by no means all B forms show such integration. I suggest that the same psycho-sociolinguistic factors favouring the borrowing of core lexemes from an EL often also favour the non-integration of any type of B form from that language. That is, when the EL is the language of the group with more socio-economic prestige, such a situation seems to arise. One major mechanism promoting non-integration may be the 'flooding' of power-laden speech events by the EL, given its dominant position. Further, a related motivation not to integrate B forms results if the EL is also prominent in the educational system. I have argued elsewhere that educated bilinguals practise 'élite closure' (Myers-Scotton, 1990) by making their speech and use patterns different from that of the masses. Surely for bilingual élites to produce loans as close to the originals as possible is one form of élite closure.

Note that this prediction of (some) non-integration is *counter to* received wisdom on B forms. While phonological integration does mark most established loans, the assumption that phonological integration is a necessary conclusion, given time, is not always supported. Some earlier researchers certainly recognized the effect of other independent variables overriding longevity. For example, Haugen (1950) states that time-depth is not as important a factor in determining integration as the borrower's bilingual ability or the sociolinguistic situation. Ansre (1971) makes a similar argument in reference to the lack of phonological integration of some English loans into Ewe in Ghana.

Van Coetsem (1988) offers a lengthy essay on phonological integration and B forms, and there are numerous discussions in the borrowing literature on the specifics of phonological integration for a given language; but these observations seem largely based on individual examples. Further, *quantitative* support for arguments is missing in most of the literature on borrowing.[10] This makes Bernsten's recent study of the integration of English loans into Shona especially valuable. Bernsten works out an integration index for Shona, which takes account of two factors: (*a*) whether B forms observe the Shona open-syllable rule, inserting epenthetic vowels where necessary word-internally (in consonant clusters disallowed in Shona) and adding a word-final vowel where necessary (to preserve Shona's requirements for open syllables only) and (*b*) whether they include phonemes not attested in standard Shona. She arrives at an integration index of .37 for all speakers (N = 132) for all loan types (N = 391).

Just 35 per cent of the tokens of those B forms requiring phonological integration (N = 347) receive full integration for all speakers (Bernsten, 1990: 49); but 20 per cent (71) are not assimilated at all. Among her many findings is that more tokens appear *without* an added final vowel than *with* an added vowel (e.g. [yez] versus [yezi] 'years').[11]

[10] Poplack, Sankoff, and Miller (1988) do discuss at length a number of issues relevant to borrowing, including phonological integration. However, it is difficult to interpret their findings since they include under B what they call 'nonce borrowings'. These are, typically, singly occurring lexemes which are likely to be CS forms, I argue.

[11] Carter (1991) points out that discussion of the final vowel in Shona is complicated by the fact that the penultimate lengthening often leads to reduction or whispering of the final vowel, especially at the end of a sentence. Bernsten (pers. comm.) took this fact into account in assessing whether a final vowel was present at all, working with linguists at the University of Zimbabwe who are also first-language speakers of Shona.

One could argue that non-integration is due only to the time-depth of these English B forms in Shona, that these new loans will gradually become more integrated. And it is true, as Bernsten notes, that the more integrated forms are those which are attested in the dictionary of standard Shona (Hannan, 1974).[12] But there are many persuasive counter-examples to the 'just wait for integration' view. First, some long-established B forms in many languages show far from complete phonological integration. Consider *shlep* 'walk' from Yiddish, which is produced in English with the non-English consonant cluster /šl/. Also, some long-established Arabic B forms in Swahili violate Swahili syllable structure constraints; e.g. the consonant cluster /št/ in the Arabic-origin verb stem *-shtaki* 'accuse' is retained in Swahili where the only native CC cluster is NC.

Second, just as subjective reactions to linguistic varieties may change over time, attitudes toward the desirability of loan-word integration may change. For example, Bernsten (1990: 50) points out that some English lexemes receive quite different renditions in two different forms, presumably depending on attitudes/type of contact situation when they were borrowed. Cases in point are the Shona versions of English *school* and *school fees*, both of which have been in the language long enough to be attested in Hannan (1974). *School* is integrated as [čikoro] *chikoro*, but in [skulfiz] 'school fees' it takes quite a different form. The earlier B form (*chikoro*) is completely integrated, with a class 7 prefix (*chi-*), which introduces an epenthetic vowel to divide the initial consonant cluster. Further, English /l/ is assimilated to Shona /r/, and a final vowel is added. In the compound noun /skulfiz/, the /sk-/ cluster is not disturbed, the lateral /l/ does not assimilate, no vowel separates the /lf/ cluster, and there is no final vowel. Also, it shows no overt Shona noun-class prefix (it is presumably in Bantu class 9, for which the prefix has a zero allomorph). (The standard Shona orthography for this lexeme is *sikurufizi*; the lexeme occurs five times in the data set, three times as /skulfiz/ and twice as /skurufiz/. Note that it never occurs with a final vowel or with the /sk-/ cluster broken up.)

Other examples illustrating changing practices regarding integration come from Nahuatl in Mexico. Of the Third-World languages being inundated by a Western language, Nahuatl is one of the few for which written records extend back to the sixteenth century. Karttunen and Lockhart (1976) trace the incidence and form of Spanish loan words in these documents. Writing about contemporary Mexicano (Nahuatl), Hill

---

[12] When forms are attested in the dictionary, speakers' pronunciation of such forms may well be influenced by orthography.

and Hill (1986: 198) point out that loan words *today* show *less* phonological integration than did the same loan words 400 years ago, as attested by Karttunen and Lockhart: 'we can see a trend for nonnative forms to replace nativized ones and for speakers to pronounce new loan items exactly as in Spanish'. Mougeon and Beniak (1991) use the term 'disintegration' to describe the same phenomenon taking place in Canada in some areas regarding English loans into Canadian French.

Thus, the prediction is that far from *all* B forms can be distinguished from single-lexeme CS forms on the basis of their full phonological integration into the ML. Of course, it is true few single-lexeme CS forms show much phonological integration into the ML. And this is not to deny that *most* established B forms do show such integration. The point is simply that phonological integration cannot be used as a criterion to distinguish B from CS.[13]

Morphosyntactic Integration: A Feature of *Both* B and CS Single Lexemes

Those CS researchers who seem to recognize that phonological criteria will not definitively differentiate borrowing and CS turn to morphosyntactic integration to do the job. Such claims are based on the a priori assumption that 'true' CS will consist of phrases, clauses, or full sentences. I have no quarrel with the claim that CS of phrasal length or longer will regularly show only the morphosyntax of the EL (as EL islands) and therefore can easily be distinguished from ML material. But the problem is that *much* EL material in CS consists of singly occurring lexemes (in ML + EL constituents). This is the view followed in providing examples in Chapters 4 and 5. And many, even most, recent studies also are based on this premiss. For example, Park, Troike, and Mun (1989: 7) remark that 60 per cent of the entire set of 516 switches in their Korean/English CS data set consist of single nouns. Single nouns were also the most frequent CS unit in Berk-Seligson (1986) on Hebrew/Spanish CS. Also, regarding her corpus of Moroccan Arabic/Dutch CS, Nortier (1990: 140) comments, 'By far the largest group of switches concerns insertion of

---

[13] Bernsten (1990: 96) reports the following differences for the average integration index of high-frequency English-origin nouns and verbs (3 or more interviews) versus low-frequency ones (2 or fewer interviews). For types, high-frequency forms have an index of .41, but low-frequency ones have an index of .36. For tokens, the high-frequency form index is .49 while the low-frequency form index is .36. While these statistics clearly indicate differences in phonological integration, they are just as clearly not large.

single words in one language (usually Dutch) in sentences of the other language.'

Why do these single-lexeme/bound-stem EL forms differ from longer stretches of EL material (EL islands) in showing the morphosyntax of the ML? The commonsensical answer would be that they are vulnerable to the ML because they are stranded in a sea of ML morphemes. This is true, but it misses the underlying point: they behave differently from EL material in EL islands because they are parts of different types of CS constituent. And, in language-production terms, this means that the syntactic procedures which direct them are different.

Recall that the MLF model assigns different morphosyntactic require-ments to these different types of constituent (ML + EL constituents versus islands). The production frame procedures activated as a first step in ML + EL constituent construction impose ML morpheme order and ML system morphemes on all material in these constituents. This is why single lexemes/bound stems from the EL (including 'nonce borrowings') always show ML morphosyntax. In contrast, EL material in EL islands must conform to EL morphosyntax.

Nonce Borrowings

The category 'nonce borrowing' is identified with Poplack and her asso-ciates in the current CS debate. They recognize the resemblance between single-lexeme CS and B forms by assigning the name 'nonce borrowings' to forms whose occurrences have no predictability and which are part of the speech of bilingual speakers.

Poplack, Sankoff, and Miller (1988: 50) distinguish between forms 'that occur only once in our corpus ("nonce" borrowings) and those used by many speakers (widespread loans)'. A few pages later they elaborate (p. 52), to all appearances, on nonce borrowings:

Coexisting with words which presumably satisfy . . . criteria for loanword status . . . are others which are equally integrated from the linguistic point of view (such as *coper* [*see* [7] *below*]) . . . but for which the frequency and acceptability criteria are unclear or nonexistent.

[7] Je serais pas capable de *coper* [kəpe] avec [*sic*].
   'I couldn't cope with it.'

(French/English; Poplack, Sankoff, and Miller, 1988: 52)

The problem with creating such a category as nonce borrowings for such forms seems obvious: (1) No explanatory value is gained in exchange for adding another category of description. (2) Creating a category of quasi-borrowings masks similarities between ML content morphemes and 'nonce borrowings' in ML + EL constituents in reference to the production processes which they both undergo. (3) Introducing 'nonce borrowings' also blurs distinctions between B forms and CS forms *as end-products*, in reference both to their frequency and to their status in the language. EL-origin lexemes which are B forms have become part of the ML mental lexicon of those ML speakers who use them. As already noted, this fact will affect their frequency of appearance. (Scotton, 1988*b* makes a similar argument against nonce forms.)

But, also, their status in the ML mental lexicon means that B forms can be accessed as ML morphemes in CS; that is, EL-origin B forms are not governed by the restrictions which the MLF model imposes on EL-origin CS forms. For example, a number of Swahili nouns have been borrowed into East African English. As B forms in English, *not* Swahili forms (ML forms) in Swahili/English CS, they may occur with English system morphemes. Therefore, for example, such constituents with English system morphemes modifying Swahili-origin nouns (but now B forms in English) now occur (e.g. *her bwana* 'her boss/husband', *my shamba* 'my garden/farm', or *their safari* 'their journey').[14] The implications of this state of affairs will become clearer below when B forms which are system morphemes are discussed.

The only obvious motivation for taking 'nonce borrowings' out of the CS arena is that it permits Poplack and her associates to set aside the single lexeme items which figure prominently in counter-examples to the two constraints they have proposed, namely the equivalence constraint and the free-morpheme constraint discussed in Chapter 2. The cost of preserving these constraints is excessively high and not well-motivated.

A Fundamentally Different Approach

Note that recognizing a continuum between borrowing and CS reflects a model of language-contact phenomena quite different from one which separates CS and borrowing as processes, but still puts nonce borrowings in a way-station. Under the MLF model proposed here, CS forms may become B forms through an increase in their frequency and their adoption by monolinguals; nothing more is required. They already resemble each other in the morphosyntactic procedures they undergo during language production. This is not to argue that all CS forms become B forms; some may appear once in the speech of a single speaker and then never again.

---

[14] I thank Carol Eastman for this observation.

True, one type of B form (i.e. cultural forms) can be distinguished from CS forms in terms of how many of its members enter the ML, as I have indicated above. But all three types of contact phenomenon (cultural and core B forms and CS forms in ML + EL constituents) will be subject to the same morphosyntactic procedures—those of the ML—which they must not violate.

The Possibility of Incomplete Morphological Integration

A major reason to argue against morphological integration as the categorical criterion which will separate CS and B forms is that there are many cases of partial integration for B forms as well as for CS forms. (Note that 'partially integrated forms' and the 'bare forms' discussed in Chapters 4 and 5 are sometimes synonymous.)

Central versus Peripheral Morphological Marking

It is true that B forms typically seem to show *more* morphological integration than CS forms; but it seems to be a difference in degree, not in kind. Further, it seems that CS forms will be as integrated as B forms in regard to overtly signalling the more 'central' grammatical relations versus the more 'peripheral' ones; that is, if the ML has overt inflections for central relations, CS forms will also carry them, *or* a special strategy will be used, such as employing an ML 'helping verb' to carry inflections along with a bare EL verb stem. This claim is related to the argument and its supporting evidence in Hopper and Thompson (1984), who offer a functional explanation for the types of grammatical relation which are generally marked on nouns and verbs. They argue convincingly that nouns and verbs, which are central to the meaning of any sentence, typically carry the most inflections, to distinguish them one from another and to indicate their relationships to other items in the utterance. For example, in regard to verbal inflections, they claim that a representative study of the world's languages indicates that the more central or unmarked mood, indicative, is more likely to be accompanied by overt signals of tense differences and polarity than subjunctive, as a more peripheral or marked mood.

In an extension of their claims, I hypothesize that the more central ML inflections will appear with CS forms, while B forms may show relatively more peripheral ones as well. In Bantu languages, for example, verbs carry a number of affixes. The two most central affixes generally are the subject prefix, indicating agreement with the subject of the verb, and the tense/aspect prefix. These are categorically present in all CS forms (and

B forms) in data sets or in the literature which I have studied (or these affixes appear on the ML 'helping verb' accompanying the CS verb). However, the final vowel, an affix carrying little functional load in most cases, is often absent in CS forms, although it is present in B forms. Consider [8] from the Nairobi corpus and [9] from a conversation in Harare:

[8] Several women, who all have at least some secondary school education, are discussing an accident.

Wakati alifunga *brakes*, matatu i-   li-   *overturn* na kugonga basi.
when he applied brakes,   CL 9-3s-PAST-   and hit   bus
'when he applied [the] brakes, [the] matatu[15] overturned and hit [the] bus.'

(Swahili/English No. 40)

[9] Two Shona men, with secondary level education or more, are discussing why to get married.

SHONA 1. *It is another factor*, wa-ona. U-ka-ona a-chi-famba apa
                               you see if you see she-walking here
u-nga-guess   kuti mukadzi uyu anogona kubika here?
2S-able-guess that woman   this she can to cook INTEROG
Ti-no-da ku-taura   ma-*facts*.
we want to speak [about] CL 10-facts
'It is another factor, you see. If you see a woman walking can you guess whether she can prepare [good] food? We want to speak about facts.'
SHONA 2. Ndizvo zviri pauri izvozvo   futi mu- -no- *criticize because*
         it is   CONT on you those also very 2PL HABIT
majaira   kubika mega   siteriki *for a long time*.
you are used to cook you yourself really
'The same applies to you, you criticize because you are used to preparing your own food for a long time.'[16]

(Shona/English; Crawhall, 1990)

The English verb stems in these examples, Swahili/English CS (*-overturn*) and Shona/English CS (*-guess*, *-criticize*) are not inflected with final vowels. This leaves the verb stems unintegrated from a phonological point of view. Recall that Bantu languages have only open syllables, so that all indigenous verb stems end in a vowel.

More relevant to the discussion here, these verbs lack complete

---

[15] A *matatu* is a vehicle smaller than a bus and larger than a car, typically a pick-up truck with a cab on the back. Small businessmen own such vehicles, and drivers are notorious for over-packing them with passengers. According to my sources on popular lore, the name *matatu* comes from Kikuyu, meaning 'thirty cents', the amount charged for the ride in the early days; but others have heard different origins for the term.

[16] Carter (1991) points out that there are 2 words from Fanagalo in this extract: *futi* 'very' and *siteriki* 'really' (Afrikaans *sterk*). Thus, 3 languages are involved in CS here.

morphological integration, since the missing final vowel marks a grammatical relationship. But, in fact, the final vowel carries a minor morphological load. True, it often signals (positive) indicative (as it does in these examples), clearly a central concept; however, it does not do this on its own. The entire combination of affixes (as well as tone in many Bantu languages) is what signals the meaning of indicative. That is, particular configurations of prefixes (and at times tonal patterns) only occur with the indicative mood. Thus, the final vowel could be considered redundant.

There are many examples in Crawhall's data set from Harare of English verb stems without the final vowel; most seem to be CS forms. And none of the CS forms in the Nairobi data has final vowels except for three types which also have an 'extended' suffix.[17]

These data are at odds with data on B forms in both languages. For example, the verb -*check* is a B form in Swahili and always seems to take a final -*i*, as in *Ni-ta-i-cheki* literally 'I-FUT-it-check' or 'I will check it'. (Note that this final -*i* is not a regular option in Swahili morphology to encode positive indicative.) Arabic verbs borrowed into Swahili also satisfy Swahili phonotactics by showing final vowels, even though these vowels also are irregular, according to Swahili morphological patterns.[18]

And in the Zimbabwe corpus, English verb stems as B forms *always* receive a final vowel (e.g. for renditions of *inspect* (verb), [inspekta] occurs three times and [insipekita] occurs once). For the Zimbabwe corpus, Bernsten (1990: 54) found a distinction between verbs and other form classes in regard to the final vowel. It was added to 100 per cent (311 tokens) of the 48 verb types. This compares with only 35 per cent (1,297 tokens) of all other form classes (in which the final vowel serves no morphological function).

B Forms Falling Short of Complete Morphological Integration

An obvious topic for future comparative studies of CS versus B forms is a systematic study of the central and peripheral aspect of morphological integration. However, for the present argument it is valuable just to recognize that much evidence exists that all B forms are not completely morphologically integrated into the ML. And this is not a matter of a few

[17] Simango (1991) has noticed that whether an EL verb stem received the requisite Bantu final vowel in Chewa seems to depend on whether the verb is a bare form (with a *do* construction, as discussed in Ch. 4) or is inflected with Chewa system morphemes. Compare *Mwina ku-nyanja ti-ka-njoy-a* (1PL-FUT-enjoy-INDIC) *ti-ka-pit-a*, 'Perhaps we'll enjoy ourselves when we go to the lake', with *Mwina ku-nyanja ti-ka-chita* (1PL-FUT-do) *enjoy ti-ka-pit-a*, 'Perhaps we'll do-enjoy ourselves when we go to the lake'.

[18] It has been suggested that vowel harmony determines the shape of the final vowel on Arabic-origin verb stems. Such considerations are not part of this study.

exceptional examples, such as the fact that the semi-learned nouns borrowed into English from Latin and Greek may not take regular English
plurals (e.g. *syllabus/syllabi* or *datum or data/data*). For example, it is the
rule, not the exception, for B forms for persons in Swahili to lack entry
into the traditional Bantu 'people' classes (singular class 1 and plural class
2, marked by the prefixes *m-* and *wa-*). Rather, along with most other B
forms in Swahili, they are placed in classes 9 and 10, in regard to their
nominal prefixes. (Classes 9 and 10 have a zero allomorph for the prefixes.) Such B forms regularly take some agreements from classes 1 and
2, but others from classes 9 and 10.

For example, one must analyse the two occurrences of *chick* in the
following example as showing a zero prefix from class 9. The first instance governs the class 1 verbal prefixes (object prefix (*mw-*) and subject
prefix (*a-*)); also, its demonstratives (*yu-le*; *huyo*) are from class 1. But
its possessive adjective (*y-ako*) comes from class 9. Note that, in all
instances, ML morpheme order (Swahili) is followed.

[10] Several young men are conversing about a dance.

c. Ben, pia wewe u-mw-ambi-e yu-le   *chick* y-ako
       also you 2s-her-tell-SUBJ CL 1-that chick CL 9-your
   a-chungu-e   sana
   she-watch out-SUBJ very
   'Ben, you should tell that girlfriend of yours she should watch out carefully.'
A. *Chick* y-angu gani hu-yo?
   chick CL 9-my which CL 1-DEM
   'Which girlfriend of mine?'

(Swahili/English No. 16)

Long-established B forms for persons, such as *rafiki* 'friend' from Arabic,
show an identical lack of an overt prefix and take the same agreement
patterns. Many of these B forms are placed in class 6 for their plural form
(e.g. *ma-rafiki*, although *rafiki* as a plural is also heard), but then they
govern a mixed agreement pattern, involving prefixes from both classes
10 (the plural of 9) and 2 (the 'people class' plural). Consider:

[11] Ma-rafiki   z-angu   wa-li-   ondoka
     CL 6-friend CL 10-my CL 2 3PL PAST leave
   'My friends left.'

(Myers-Scotton, unpublished data)

Long-Standing Partial Integration in Swahili.
There are many other cases of entire classes of long-standing B
forms which show only partial morphological integration. Consider

both Arabic-origin nouns and adjectives in Swahili. In classes 9 and 10, Swahili allows the zero allomorph for noun stems beginning with the voiceless consonant; those beginning with voiced consonants take a homorganic nasal as their prefix. But consider the case of *bahari* 'sea' from Arabic. It does not receive the nasal prefix which indigenous Swahili class 9 nouns with a similar phonological shape take (cf. *m-bata* 'dry/ripe coconut'). Of higher frequency are a number of Arabic adjectives, fully established B forms in Swahili, which never have been fully integrated into the Swahili system of agreement: consider *hodari* 'clever'; compare *m-toto m-nene* 'child fat' with *m-toto hodari* 'child clever'. Other frequently occurring examples are the borrowed numbers, *sita* 'six', *saba* 'seven', *tisa* 'nine', and *kumi* 'ten'. While all the Bantu numbers below ten receive noun-class agreements, these do not (compare *wa-toto saba* 'children seven' with *wa-toto wa-nane* 'children eight').

Alternative Morphology for Zulu B Forms

Further evidence that B forms do not always totally conform with indigenous morphological patterns comes from Zulu. Consider B forms in class 9. In Zulu, this class is obligatorily marked by /i-/ plus a nasal homorganic with the stem-initial consonant. Canonici (1990: 57) notes that, while many foreign nouns have been incorporated into Zulu class 9 (e.g. *in-kampani* [iŋ] from *company*), there is 'a vast number of nouns which make use of the prefix /i-/ *without the homorganic nasal* . . . These are borrowed nouns, of which some are fully phoneticized while others are not' (my emphasis). He goes on to argue that, for other reasons regarding their morphosyntactic behaviour (the locative is inflected in a marked way and their plural formation is irregular, in that they form their plurals in class 6), 'We are clearly witnessing the surfacing of a new subclass in spoken Zulu, often reflected in written popular literature'. An example follows.

[12] I-*bharathoni* icula kahle kwi-*khwaya* yesonto lakithi.
'The baritone sings well in our church choir.'

Both *ibharathoni* and *ikhwaya* lack the homorganic nasal of class 9, but receive class 9 agreements. In addition, *ikhwaya* shows an unusual locative form.

B Forms Also May Be Bare Forms

The fact that some singly occurring EL lexemes as CS forms are bare forms was discussed in earlier chapters. Such forms show incomplete morphological integration, not by showing irregular/innovative allomorphs, but rather by showing no allomorphs *at all* in a given case; that is, the requisite ML system morpheme is not realized at all.

That numbers of apparent B forms *also* may be bare forms merits attention. For example, in writing about Spanish material in sixteenth-century Nahuatl and Mayan texts, Karttunen (1985: 64) notes that sometimes Spanish material in these meso-American languages appears with Spanish particles and sometimes not. After detailing some of the Spanish particles found in these texts, Karttunen writes (p. 65):

A curious fact about Spanish loan particles in both Nahuatl and Maya is that although they are most often seen, especially in the early contact period, in what appear to be unanalyzed Spanish phrases, they are even more notable for being omitted from such phrases. There are almost as many phrases in which all the words are Spanish but with particles missing as there are unremarkable Spanish phrases.

Karttunen goes on to point out that the most frequently omitted Spanish particle is *de* 'of'. She notes that from 1557 such forms as *oxppel aroba vino* 'three arrobas [of] wine' appear in Maya, and in Nahuatl *corte madrid* (1598) 'court [of] Madrid'. Karttunen is at pains to point out that lack of *de* cannot be attributed to ignorance of it, that *de* has been borrowed into Maya and Nahuatl, but may function differently. Sometimes the Spanish possessive phrase takes the Mayan or Nahuatl possessive inflection (a prefix), as in *i-armas ciudad*, literally 'its arms city' meaning 'arms of the city'. In these cases, of course, the Spanish B form is more fully integrated into the meso-American language, taking its system morpheme and dropping the Spanish (EL) one. But what is of interest here is the possibility of bare forms as well. Karttunen adds (p. 66): 'Attested from the earliest period of contact, Spanish phrases with missing particles are to be found in texts up until today and are rather characteristic of Nahuatl and Maya.'

Integration in Moroccan Arabic

Heath's (1989) study of CS and B in Moroccan Arabic also yields some interesting examples of adoption strategies, especially in cases where there are resemblances between the morphology of French and Arabic. The French definite articles offer one such instance, since (*le*, *la*, *les*, and contracted *l'*) are phonologically similar to their modern classical Arabic (MCA) counterpart, the definite prefix [l-]. Heath makes several observations about such resemblances. First, they offer French lexemes 'a foot in the door' (Heath's term), once a particular B form occurs in what looks like an MCA shape; that is, chance morphological resemblances promote borrowing, he argues. Second, he also views CS as the forerunner of B forms, in at least some cases;[19] and, when the 'foot in the door' phenomenon is present, he sees a quick transition between CS and B status. He comments (p. 35),

> Given that an initially code-switched form like *l'ananas* 'the pineapple' (Fr) looks exactly like an MCA word with no further adjustment, we can easily understand how such words may, if semantically appropriate, develop additional morphological forms (Pl, Diminutive) within MCA and thus come to be treated as relatively well-integrated borrowings.

Third, those nouns with allomorphs of the French article which do not fit the Arabic system (e.g. [la-], [le-], and [lez]) receive differential treatment; some are fully integrated, but apparently a sizeable number are not. Those which are integrated receive the usual Arabic definite prefix. But Heath notes (1989: 36),

> However, some Fr feminine nouns which appear to be in the process of stabilizing as loanwords show fluctuation between definite /l-/ and a syllabic form /la-/ or /la-/ based on the French definite form, and a few important and highly stabilized earlier borrowings show /la-/ or /la-/ as the normal definite prefix . . .'

He cites /la-gar/ 'the train station' and /la-pisin/ 'the swimming pool', noting that /la-/ is a definite allomorph only (it is bleached of its feminine gender) and concord, in fact, is masculine. Heath goes on to comment (while noting that his data are limited) that in Algeria, where there is more Arabic/French bilingualism, most recent French nouns are borrowed with their French definite forms intact. He points out (p. 36): 'Moreover, nouns with /la-/ or /la-/ definite prefix based on french *la* are treated as FSg [feminine singular] for concord purposes even though most lack the Arabic FSg suffix /-a/.' Clearly, then, there is some evidence in the Moroccan and Algerian cases that not all B forms are equally integrated into the morphology of Arabic.

Double-Plural Marking

Finally we shall consider another set of data which, while also showing less than complete morphological integration of B forms, serves another

---

[19] It is not clear how Heath views the difference (if any) between B and CS. He mentions (p. 23) pronunciation and frequency as distinguishing criteria, but then says they are problematic. The definition he offers at one point (p. 24) is rather vague, and not necessarily followed elsewhere: 'We will normally apply the term code-switching to Ly forms (at the word level or higher) used in otherwise Lx contexts when the forms show little or no formal adaptation to Lx.' However, he does make it clear that his main interest is not in CS: 'our main concern in the present volume is in code-switching as an avenue to borrowing' (p. 2).

purpose. It indicates that, no matter how much evidence there is that B forms are similar to CS forms in not always showing morphological patterning identical with that of indigenous stems, *still*, B forms may typically show *more morphological integration than CS forms do*. The case in point is that of EL-origin forms showing double morphology in Shona.

Instances of double morphology involving plural affixes from both the ML and EL have been discussed in earlier chapters. As already indicated when double-plural affixes were discussed, a favourite strategy for morphologically integrating foreign plural nouns into many Bantu languages is to place them in class 6, a plural class with the prefix *ma-*. This choice of class 6 seems more prevalent in the southern Bantu languages, such as Shona, than in north-eastern languages, such as Swahili.

Thus, the Zimbabwe corpus offers an excellent comparison between B and CS forms in regard to their overall realizations when they are prefixed with *ma-*. The question is, do B and CS forms show a similar incidence of double morphology?[20] Results show that there is a significant difference. I repeat the findings reported in Chapter 5: Bernsten's particular analysis (1990: 82) shows that, of the 136 tokens taking *ma-* which are B forms, only 17 per cent occur with English *-s* as well. But 69 per cent of the CS forms taking *ma-* also show English *-s* (86 out of 124).[21] Both CS and B forms undergo the same ML morphological process (and both equally govern agreements on other elements in the sentence). But one can say that the CS forms are less morphologically integrated because they are still open to EL morphological processes as well.

An obvious subject for future research is a systematic comparison of the types and degree of morphological integration which B forms undergo in comparison with CS forms.[22]

---

[20] Carter (1991) points out a back-formation in Shona: *bhinzi* 'bean' from [ma-biynz] (i.e. *ma + beans*). There are similar examples from other Bantu languages. They reinforce the idea that the speaker perceives the English noun + plural suffix as a single unit, and that it is accessed as such.

[21] Bernsten follows the '3-occurrence rule' which I suggest to distinguish B and CS forms. That is, if a type occurs in 3 or more interviews, she classifies it as a high-frequency form or a B form; if it occurs in 2 or fewer interviews, it is a low-frequency form or a CS form. A form which is attested in the standard Shona dictionary is also called a B form.

[22] Simango (1991) relates the following anecdotal evidence regarding perceptions of B and CS forms in Chewa In a conversation with other Chewa speakers in Malawi, he reports that he said: *Ku-Lilongwe, ndikakhala ma-week a-wiri.* (CL 6-week CL 6-two) 'At Lilongwe, I will stay two weeks'. But his companions said: *Ma-week a-wiri? Ah! ma-week-s a-wiri!*, 'Two week? No, two weeks!'

In effect, they were saying, 'You can't produce *week* without an English plural marker'. Simango perceives *week* as a CS form (the Chewa form for 'week/weeks', *sabata/ma-sabata*, is in regular use) and explains the reaction of his friends as a feeling that CS forms must show the English plural *as well as the Chewa plural*, presumably to indicate the origin.

Morphological Integration: Summary

The problem with morphological/syntactic integration as a criterion for B forms versus CS forms is that several different patterns of integration occur, not just one. This survey has pointed out four patterns: (*a*) not all B forms show complete morphological integration; (*b*) most CS forms in ML + EL constituents regularly show near-complete morphological integration; (*c*) when there is incomplete morphological integration, it may characterize both B and CS forms *in contrast to* indigenous forms; and (*d*) both forms show syntactic integration. However, recall the MLF model and the ML Hypothesis with its Morpheme-Order and System Morpheme Principles. The prediction that those principles are followed means it should come as no surprise that B and CS forms may pattern together in terms of morphosyntactic integration. Also, those troublesome forms which are not completely integrated into ML morphosyntax (e.g. bare forms) *still* do not violate the ML Hypothesis (i.e. they follow ML morpheme order, and if any syntactically relevant system morphemes are present, they are ML ones) and therefore are acceptable. The Spanish possessive phrases in Nahuatl and Maya mentioned above as bare forms and the English borrowings into Zulu class 9 exemplify such partially integrated borrowings. And the hypothesis that core B forms start out as CS forms is supported indirectly by the fact that both types of form show the same types of incomplete morphosyntactic integration into the ML.

Predictability/Frequency as the Criterion by Which to Distinguish B Forms and CS Forms

In the final analysis, all of the above criteria—phonological, morphological, and syntactic integration—fail to distinguish B forms from CS forms with sufficient precision to be used as metrics. While it may be true that many, or even most, B forms are indistinguishable from indigenous forms, especially in the phonological processes they undergo, the extent of this lack of distinction remains an empirical issue. As indicated above, most claims of phonological integration have yet to be put on anything but an anecdotal basis, and the quantitative study of Bernsten (1990) certainly does not support anything near total phonological integration for all, or even most, B forms.

Why Distinguish CS and B Forms?

This leaves us with what is an empirically demonstrable state of affairs: in many cases, B forms and CS forms resemble each other, especially in the extent of their morphological integration into the ML. How, then, to distinguish them?

One might ask first, *why* should they be distinguished in the first place if they so resemble each other? There are two considerations.

First, as I have indicated in the course of this chapter, there seems to be little motivation to distinguish sharply between single-lexeme CS and B forms in terms of the production processes they undergo. Preliminary analysis, at least, provides evidence for the hypothesis that there are only differences of degree in the extent to which both types undergo the same ML morphosyntactic processes. But more quantitative study is needed to support any such claims. For example, it may be that, while both B and CS forms may be bare forms, there are significantly more such forms under CS.

However, a second issue must be considered: the structural statement of the MLF model implies a difference between the relationships of the B forms and CS forms to the ML mental lexicon. While a B form is part of that lexicon, an EL morpheme realized as a singly occurring CS form is not. The difference is a matter of lemma entries. Recall that I am following Levelt (1989) in using the term *lemma* to refer to 'the nonphonological part of an item's lexical information'. This information is used to 'construct the "framework" of an utterance without much regard for the phonology of words' (Levelt, 1989: 6). He goes on to say:

when we say that a speaker has retrieved a lemma, we mean that the speaker has acquired access to those aspects of a word's stored information that are relevant for the construction of the word's syntactic environment.

There would seem to be two types of differences between CS and B forms regarding lemma entries. First, a B form probably has entries in the mental lexicon both of the ML and of its parent, the EL. The two entries need not be identical entries, of course. Second, an EL-origin word which is a CS form is accessed in ML + EL constituents through an EL lemma, true, but only if it is congruent with an ML counterpart, while a B form is accessed directly (through its own ML lemma). In EL islands, a lexeme is accessed directly through its own lemma (since such islands result from activating EL procedures).

I hypothesize that the important difference is this. While the CS form may undergo many or all of the same ML morphosyntactic processes as the B form (and indigenous ML forms), the CS form is not entered in the ML mental lexicon. What types of evidence support this claim, and what are the consequences? Above, I argued that the degree of any type of structural integration was not a sufficient criterion by which to differentiate the two types of form. Now I will consider two other possible types of evidence to support the hypothesis about differential membership in the ML mental lexicon: the bilingual versus monolingual status of the speaker and the predictability of the form in question.

Types of Evidence, I: Who Is a Bilingual?

The observation that monolinguals in the ML do use B forms, but not CS forms, offers indirect support, of course, for the hypothesis that B forms, but not CS forms, are part of their ML mental lexicon. This may only be trivial support, however, since it is not clear who is a monolingual and who is not. To illustrate the problem of deciding who is 'capable of CS' (and therefore the problem of deciding how to label the products), consider the following example, admittedly anecdotal, but still illuminating. Lupenga Mphande, a lecturer from the University of Malawi on leave in the United States, is the source of the example:

I remember visiting my mother's local village in northern Malawi and talking with the local villagers. From all appearances, I was just another person from the area: we spoke in the local dialect of [Chi]tumbuka which I had learned from my mother and I was dressed very casually. But then someone mentioned that I was a university lecturer. First, there was a pause. Then, someone who may have studied English in school—although today he knew and spoke little English, I am sure—said [in Tumbuka/English], *ukasekunguza which school?* 'You teach [at] which school?' It would have been simpler to convey the meaning entirely in Chitumbuka, *Ukasekunguza apa?* 'Where do you teach?' But he preferred to switch to English in order to show me he was not just another villager.

Clearly, this man has uttered a sentence containing CS (*which school* is an EL island), both from the standpoint of the language and from his own individual perspective. That is, *which school* is not a B form in Tumbuka and presumably not something this man says habitually, even when the concept arises. But is this man a bilingual? Or is there even an answer which is not trivial? The quandary which arises in defining the speaker as bilingual or monolingual suggests that one should discount the speaker's status as a way to label the forms he/she uses as either CS or B forms.

Types of Evidence, II: CS Forms and Predictability

More promising is the observation that CS forms differ from all B forms in their lack of predictability. I suggest that the two forms can be distinguished in an empirically demonstrable way by their relative frequency when the concept they encode comes up, or even by raw frequency. It has long been recognized that a distinguishing characteristic of CS forms is that they occur possibly only once, and certainly not frequently, meaning that they have no predictability. And, of course, if a B form has been integrated into the ML to encode a particular concept, its occurrence can be predicted, at least part of the time and for some groups, when that concept comes up.

I will demonstrate how using relative frequency as a criterion is entirely possible, though admittedly somewhat involved. And, because of this, I also will suggest a more viable, but more arbitrary, alternative as well.

The Motivation to Consider Frequency

But first I must argue that relative frequency has independent motivation as a criterion. The motivation has to do with relative activation of the two language systems. When the ML is most activated, those procedures inherent to the ML are preferred. (Recall psycholinguistic findings reported in Chapter 3 from Grosjean (1988) and Burki-Cohen, Grosjean, and Miller (1989) on base language effects.) A principle may be formulated to express this tendency:

> The Preferential Path Principle: In bilingual production, lexical items from the ML lexicon will be more frequently accessed since they are inherently on the preferential path. Lexical items from the EL may also be accessed in CS under the conditions specified by the MLF model, but they are less preferred and therefore less frequent.

This principle leads to the prediction that, when EL-origin material is at issue, B forms (as part of the ML) can be identified as occurring with more relative frequency than CS forms. As already noted, it is generally accepted that CS forms are ephemeral, or at the very least show minimal recurrence. If B forms contrast with CS forms in recurrence, the following definition should hold: B forms are EL-origin material which show a minimal recurrence value of 5 per cent *relative* to that of their indigenous counterparts when the concept they encode comes up in a text. Five per cent is an admittedly arbitrary lower limit. It is certainly open to revision when sufficient motivations to do so become clear.

Case Studies of Relative Frequency

To show how the relative frequency of presumed B forms can be demonstrated, two cases from Shona, with forms from English which theoretically could be either B or CS forms, will be discussed. The first deals with numbers and the second with the encoding of the concepts of 'because' and 'but'. In both cases, data come from the Zimbabwe corpus of 129 interviews discussed above.

Numbers in Shona

Listening to the interviews in the Zimbabwe corpus (or reading their transcripts), one is immediately struck by the many instances of numerical expressions encoded in English. Using English for numerals is not a new phenomenon in Shona; this has been the case for at least forty years (Carter, 1991). But, as will be shown below, a 1988 study showed that, when numbers were used, 86 per cent of the time the English lexeme was used. This use is entirely spontaneous.[23] All instances of the encoding of numbers in the entire corpus were counted and identified as either in Shona or in English.[24] The numbers were studied in relation to several independent variables, including their semantic function and types of morphological integration into Shona.

Altogether, 86 per cent (1,079) of all numerical expressions (N = 1,257) were in English, leaving only 14 per cent (178) in Shona. Faced with such statistics, the conclusion that English numbers are B forms in Shona seems incontrovertible.[25] Unless otherwise indicated, all findings reported below are significant, using a chi-square test.

Specific findings support the conclusion that English numbers are omnipresent rather than limited to special uses. True, it is the case that two-thirds of the numbers occurred in the urban interviews (67 per cent or 839), but this is a function of the lives the urban respondents lead, not of their differential borrowing patterns. Urban workers are very preoccupied with time because they have many problems finding transportation to get to work on time. Recall that Chitungwiza, the research site, is

---

[23] Interviewers did not elicit English numbers by their own example in the interviews. They spoke mainly Shona, except for some Shona/English CS, but never using numerals.

[24] The only numbers excluded from this analysis were those which occurred in addresses (e.g. *Chitungwiza two*) or in the names of hybrid maize seed (e.g. *two fifteen*).

[25] Of course, some of the instances of English numbers could represent CS forms for certain individual interviewees, not B forms. I thank Georges Lüdi for this observation.

Table 6.1. *Language used by location*[a]

Language	Location		
	Rural	Urban	Total
English	313[b]	766	1,079
	74.88[c]	91.30	85.84
	29.01[d]	70.99	
Shona	105	73	178
	25.12	8.70	14.16
	58.99	41.01	
TOTAL	418	839	
	33.25	66.75	

[a] χ^2 (df =1) = 61.88, p = <.000.   [b] Frequency.   [c] Column %.   [d] Row %.

20 km. outside Harare, where most of them work, and public transportation is limited and always crowded. Also, urban respondents tend to have jobs where the parts of their work-day can be marked by specific times, while the rural respondents were farmers without a schedule by the clock. Still, whatever the differences in their life-styles, both types of respondent use English much more than Shona to speak about those aspects of their lives requiring numerical expressions.

For the urban respondents, fully 91 per cent of their numbers (766) were expressed in English. But the rural respondents were not that far behind, with 75 per cent of their numbers (313) in English. Therefore, it is clear that the borrowing of English numbers is not limited to special groups only (see Table 6.1).

The English numbers were also heavily used in all the semantic categories, not clustered in one. True, 'time' was almost exclusively encoded in English, with 95 per cent of time expressions (476 out of 500) in English. But this category of English numerical expressions accounts for only 44 per cent of all English numbers and 40 per cent of all numbers (both English and Shona). And for all semantic categories except 'counting', English is used for a minimum of 70 per cent of the entries. This includes 'stating one's age', 'stating educational levels', 'money', 'duration of time', and 'stating a room number', in addition to 'point of time'. The category 'counting' received most of its entries from statements about the number of one's children (e.g. *ndine va-na va-tatu* 'I have three children' or *va-na two* 'children two'). Still, more than half of the numbers to encode even this intimate relationship were in English (55 per cent or 91 versus 45 per cent or 73 in Shona). See Table 6.2 for more details.

One of the most interesting statistics is that for morphological treatment of the English numbers. Fully 52 per cent (561 out of 1,079) occur as 'bare forms' with no Shona prefixation. I have mentioned elsewhere in this volume that Bantu languages have a very robust system of agreement, and Shona is certainly no exception; thus it is something of a surprise that so many English forms occur with no prefixes. Part of the explanation is that many of these occur in EL islands and therefore are not subject to Shona constraints (e.g. *ten o'clock to half past ten* in response to the question, 'When do you have tea-time?'). I have no separate statistic for English numbers in EL islands versus those in ML + EL constituents or in ML-only constituents. Some forms in these constituents may well be considered nouns in class 5 or class 9 with a zero allomorph of the class prefix.[26]

But there are many cases which cannot be interpreted in this way; these include most prominently adjectives which should agree with their head nouns (e.g. *ma-kore twenty-six* 'years twenty-six' given as an interviewee's age, instead of *ma-kore ma-twenty-six*; or *va-na six* 'children six' given as the number of children, instead of *va-na va-six*). In contrast, nouns typically take a noun-class prefix (e.g. *Kazhinji ndowanzosvika ku-ma-nine* 'Mostly I get home around nine', with *nine* taking both a locative prefix and the prefix of class 6). Further analysis of these data is warranted because preliminary study indicates that, while heads (i.e. nouns and verbs) are generally morphologically integrated into Shona, modifiers are not. If this finding holds up under further analysis, it would indicate that different ML morphological procedures may be accessed for different form classes. This finding also relates to the claim made above that central, as against peripheral, B forms will show more morphological marking, since nouns are more central than adjectives.

Almost no English numbers are preceded by an English preposition (as this type of EL island), which is no surprise; only 3 per cent (29 out of 1,079 English numbers) are so marked. However, many occur with Shona particles or prefixes which serve the purpose of heading PPs (e.g. *na-one o'clock* 'at one o'clock'); and others occur with one of the three locative noun-class markers (*ku-*, *pa-*, or *mu-*) which also serves to head a PP, plus

---

[26] The numbers used by interviewees are not cardinal numbers, as used in counting, which have no prefixes in Shona. Rather, they were more typically used adjectivally; adjectives show agreement with their heads via prefixes in Shona.

Table 6.2. *Language used, by function*[a]

Function	Language		
	English	Shona	Total
Age			
Frequency	154	25	179
Column %	14.27	14.04	
Row %	86.03	13.97	14.24
Educational level			
Frequency	186	1	187
Column %	17.24	0.56	
Row %	99.47	0.53	14.88
Duration of time			
Frequency	123	53	176
Column %	11.40	29.78	
Row %	69.89	30.11	14.00
Point of time			
Frequency	476	24	500
Column %	44.11	13.48	
Row %	95.20	4.80	39.78
Count			
Frequency	91	73	164
Column %	8.43	41.01	
Row %	55.49	44.51	13.05
Money			
Frequency	44	2	46
Column %	4.08	1.12	
Row %	95.65	4.35	3.66
Room no.			
Frequency	5	0	5
Column %	0.46	0.00	
Row %	100.00	0.00	0.40
Total			
Frequency	1,079	178	1,257
Column %	85.84	14.16	
Row %			100.00

[a] χ^2 (df = 6) = 230.218, p = < .000.

the noun class 6 prefix (*ma-*), effectively putting them in class 6 (e.g. *ndinomuka ku-ma-five* 'I get up about five'). Just over 17 per cent (187) of all the English numbers occur with both a locative prefix and *ma-*. These largely stand for specific points in time (N = 177) but represent only 35 per cent of that category (N = 500).

If one looks at the degree of morphological integration according to semantic function, no categories stand out. For example, one might have expected more integration with numbers serving as quantifiers in an NP. But about as many quantifiers occur with no Shona morphological integration at all as occur with 'proper' Shona agreement (e.g. a noun class prefix on the number as an adjective, as in *va-na va-viri* 'children two'). Those with no agreement constitute 48 per cent of the semantic category (78 out of 164), while those with prefixation denoting noun-class agreement represent 49 per cent (81). The semantic class with the most bare forms is that referring to educational level (86 per cent, or 160 out of 187). Many references to educational level might be considered EL islands (e.g. *form two* in *ku-svika form two* 'to arrive [at] form two'); but islandhood is often a moot point, since the English phrase often does not violate ML morpheme order, and no system morphemes are involved. For expressions of duration, almost the same percentages show the number as a bare form (35 per cent, or 62 out of 176) as show the number with a class 6 (*ma-*) prefix (36 per cent, or 63).

Renditions of Numbers for Age

Bernsten (1990: 71), who also studied English numerical loans, looked specifically at the interviewees' rendition of the request for an age (either their own or that of their children). She found there were exactly 70 such renditions for the urban sample and 70 for the rural as well. Five different possible representations occurred: (1) the Shona word for the number, e.g. [ma-sanu] 'five'; (2) the Shona word for 'years' [ma-kore] plus the Shona number, e.g. [ma-kore ma-sanu] 'years five'; (3) [ma-kore] plus the English number, e.g. [ma-kore fayv] 'years five'; (4) the English number plus the English word *years* [yez], e.g. [fayv yez]; and (5) simply the English number on its own, e.g. [fayv]. The results appear in Table 6.3. The English number on its own had the most tokens (53 per cent of the rural and 40 per cent of the urban sample). Both groups also showed many tokens in category 4, which is an EL island composed of the English number + *years*. For the rural group, 21 per cent of its tokens fell in this group and 24 per cent of the urban tokens did. But 26 per cent of the urban tokens also occurred in ML + EL constituents (i.e. *ma-kore* plus the English number).

Table 6.3. *Shona/English variations*[a] *in age expressions, by location (%)*

Expression	Location	
	Rural (N = 70 tokens)	Urban (N = 70 tokens)
Shona no. alone	3	0
[makore] + Shona no.	16	10
[makore] + English no.	7	26
English no. + [yez]	21	24
English no. alone	53	40

[a] Statistics refer to % of tokens.
Examples of categories:

Shona no. alone:	[makumi] 'twenty'
[makore] + Shona no.:	[makore makumi] 'years twenty'
[makore] + English no.	[makore twendi] 'years twenty'
English no. + [yez]:	[twendi yez] 'twenty years'
English no. alone:	[twendi] 'twenty'

Source: Bernsten (1990: 71).

Non-Integration with Numbers

Bernsten (1990: 75) reports another important finding: the phonological integration of the English numbers is relatively low. For types, it is only .06 and for tokens it is .08. This compares to an overall integration metric of .37 and .41 respectively for all English B forms in the Zimbabwe corpus.[27] (Recall that Bernsten's integration metric gives a form a score of 1.0 if the B form is totally integrated; that is, its consonants must be part of the Shona indigenous inventory and it must show the indigenous phonotactics of open syllables, meaning that epenthetic vowels and word-final vowels are added.)

Shona Numbers: Summary

English numbers are firmly entrenched in Shona as B forms. This is attested by their very high relative frequency for the concepts they encode, but also by the lack of distinctive patterns in their distribution. Yet even though they clearly must be considered B forms, they are not 'classic' B

---

[27] Bernsten (p. 75) notes that both English-origin function words and numbers have an extremely low phonological-integration index. She speculates that, because such words are not attested in the standard Shona dictionary, speakers have no written model to guide them.

forms: they show relatively little phonological integration, and only show morphological integration just under half the time. Note that they do show syntactic integration when they occur in ML + EL constituents, as the MLF model would predict (e.g. *ma-kore five* 'years five').

Numbers in Swahili Compared

Why so many English numbers in Shona? The same situation holds in many other southern Bantu languages; many speakers do not even know the numbers in their own languages, in some cases above 'three' and in others above 'five'.[28] But this is not what is found in Swahili. For comparative purposes, numbers were counted in the Nairobi corpus. There are 126 tokens of numbers, but only 4 per cent (5) are in English. Why the difference? Part of the explanation lies in the fact that Swahili has borrowed from Arabic not only three of the numbers from one to ten, but all of the decimal numbers including twenty and above (*ishirini* 'twenty', *thelathini* 'thirty', etc.). The southern Bantu languages retain rather involved ways of encoding the higher numbers; thus, borrowing the English numbers makes the system more streamlined. But why they are giving up the numbers below ten is only open to speculation (since they are very similar to the Swahili numbers, which remain robust).

English *Because* and *But* as B Forms in Shona

Relative frequency also indicates that Shona is in the process of borrowing several discourse-markers from English, notably *because* and *but*. A study of the relative frequency of English and Shona morphemes for the relevant concepts shows that 7 per cent (24 out of 367) of the encodings of 'because' are with the English morpheme *because*. Also, 8 per cent (25 out of 315) of the encodings of 'but' are with the English morpheme *but*.[29]

While languages often borrow discourse particles, the case of *because* and *but* seems remarkable because they seem to offer no 'structural

---

[28] Ngara (1982: 78) comments: 'it is doubtful whether the generality of Shona children can count properly in Shona'.

[29] Of course, there are other ways in Shona apart from *nokuti* to express the concept 'because'. Those which were morphologically very close to *nokuti* were also counted (e.g. *pamusana pokuti* 'on account of the fact that'); dialectal variants were also counted (e.g. *nekuti*). In the case of 'but', other morphemes (in addition to *asi*) which expressed related concepts were not counted. For example, the verbal prefix *-to-* can mean, among other things, 'on the contrary'. However, such morphemes were not included in the count, partly because their meaning was not exactly the same as 'but', but also because they do not stand as *discourse-markers* in the same sense as *asi* is able to function.

advantage' over the indigenous Shona morphemes which seem to encode the same concepts. Shona has two free forms for these concepts, *nokuti* 'because' and *asi* 'but'. One may well attempt to make a psycho-sociolinguistic argument that the English morphemes have a certain cachet which the indigenous morphemes lack. But then one would also expect that Swahili might also be infected with the same lust for English flavour and would also borrow these morphemes. Such is not the case. The Nairobi corpus was studied in order to make a comparison with the Shona data. The analysis turned up only 7 tokens of the Swahili *kwa sababu* 'because' but no tokens at all of English *because*. And there are 41 tokens of Swahili *lakini* 'but' versus one token of English *but*. It is true that Swahili has already done its borrowing here, since both *kwa sababu* and *lakini* come from Arabic. But the fact that the present morphemes are already borrowed is no reason for English not to exert its pressure today.

A Structurally Based Explanation

Within at least some syntactic theories, *because* and *but* are considered logical operators. Logical operators are of two types. (1) Some are functions, such as quantifiers and *wh*-forms. These pick out individuals across variables. Thus, they have the feature [+ Quantification] and therefore are system morphemes. (2) The others do not involve binding a variable (i.e. they are not linked to some other variable, such as a noun). Rather, they are functions linking two propositions; they are, therefore, freer to stand on their own. Such English morphemes as *but, because, and,* and *or* fall into this second category. (They may be considered as content, not system, morphemes. Some, such as *because* in *because of the rain* clearly assign thematic role; the argument for some others is harder to make.)

While this approach to *because* and *but* is necessarily only tentative, it is attractive—largely because there are many known cases of the borrowing of discourse particles across languages. Certainly, this approach suggests the direction for further research.

In addition, the fact that these markers also are free forms possibly facilitates their borrowing. (Scotton and Okeju (1973) make this argument about the discourse markers from Swahili and Luganda which have been borrowed into Ateso.)

English words also occurred for a number of other discourse particles in the Zimbabwe corpus, but no relative-frequency study was done for them. All of these would also fall in the same class of logical operators as *but* and *because*. Those with the most tokens include *and* [ende/end] (10), *especially* [espesali] (11), *plus* [plas] (14), and *so* [so] (12). Bernsten (1990: 74) lists others.

No Triggers in the Environment

The environments of occurrences of *because* and *but* were studied via statistical tests. These tests support the general conclusion that it is not immediate prior use of English which triggers the use of *because* or *but*. That is, these forms occur without English primes. Furthermore, *because* and *but* are not primes which trigger English following them.

For example, in an utterance-internal position, *because* occurred 16 times both preceded and followed by Shona material. Only 4 instances of utterance-internal *because* were preceded by English and followed by Shona; in one case, *because* was followed by English and preceded by Shona. As an utterance-initial form, *because* occurred 3 times followed by Shona material. The distribution of *but* is similar.

Another indication that *because* and *but* are B forms, not CS forms, is the fact that their distribution across social groupings was general. That is, it was hardly associated with the social-group memberships of their users. True, for *because*, the classification of its users as urban or rural was significant (chi-square df = 1, value = 4.022, P > .045). This simply means that, while the prediction generated by the statistics program was that 6 urban residents would have used 6 instances of *because*, instead they used 9. And for *but*, the variable 'sex' was significant (chi-quare df = 1, value = 7.071, P > .008). What this means is that, whereas the prediction would have been that 9 males would have used *but* instead of *asi*, 14 males used it. But other factors studied (self-reported English proficiency, age, education) were not significantly associated with either lexeme's occurrence.

In summary, the occurrence of *because* and *but* is generally independent of the use of English as any type of CS; it is more likely that these lexemes will occur surrounded by Shona. Further, their use is not tied strongly to any social group. These findings support the relative-frequency argument that *because* and *but* are at least well along their way to becoming established B forms in Shona.

Frequency and Methodological Considerations

What are the problems with using relative frequency to distinguish B forms? Methodological issues come to mind. One may argue that it is all well and good to demonstrate that numbers and discourse-markers, as potential B forms, can be studied via the methodology of relative frequency, but what about lexemes standing for *much less* commonly expressed concepts or objects? That is, even if the suspected B form occurs even as much as 50 per cent of the time (versus the indigenous encoding for the same concept) when a specific concept/object is expressed, 50 per cent may only represent one or two tokens. After all, even in a very large corpus the encoding of a particular concept may only come up once or twice, so that even an attested B form may only occur once or twice. How can one distinguish a B form from the CS form, if *both* occur only once or twice?

It seems clear that relative frequency will not always prove a workable criterion. Further, deciding 'how much' relative frequency is 'enough' is, as I admit, an arbitrary decision. Still, this statistic is a useful diagnostic in many cases, such as those illustrated here. Further, taking into account the absolute number of tokens (e.g. 24 and 25 in the cases of *because* and *but*) strengthens the argument.

Changing the Focus to CS Forms

Another way to deal with the problem is this: many thorny issues disappear if one focuses on distinguishing B and CS forms and *not* on identifying B forms. That is, the problem is to be approached from the point of view of the CS form, not the B form. It is not that a B form *must* recur to be a B form; it is that a CS form must *not* recur in order to be a CS form. I suggest the following procedure, which was employed in detailing the Nairobi corpus.

1. In order to consider suspect lexemes for the CS pool, the first step is to remove B forms from consideration. I use three or more occurrences in different conversations in a corpus of a minimum of twenty hours of conversation as the mark of a B form. Admittedly, three is an arbitrary number. (Of course the relative frequency criterion would also remove from the potential CS pool the same lexemes which are eliminated by the three-occurrence rule.)

2. This leaves all forms which occur two or fewer times as either CS or B forms. This residue can be reduced by factoring out all lexemes standing for new objects or concepts as B forms; recall that I argued above that these B forms generally do not enter the ML through CS, but rather are typically abrupt loans, receiving instant membership in the ML lexicon.[30]

---

[30] The methodology of using independent coders to judge whether a form is a cultural B form may be employed. This was the method used in analysing the Nairobi corpus.

3. What remain now are the critical cases: lexemes encoding core concepts and occurring no more than twice in a relatively large corpus. These are called CS forms.

Importance to the MLF Model of Distinguishing CS and B Forms

The relevant claim of the MLF model here is that the two or more languages active in CS are not equally accessed. That is, there is a 'preferential path'. ML morphemes, not EL morphemes as CS forms, are on this path, as intrinsically part of the ML mental lexicon. While both B forms and CS forms may undergo the same ML morphosyntactic procedures, B forms are accessed more readily in constructions for which the ML is the frame. This is because B forms are accessed via their own lemma entries in the ML. In contrast, CS forms are accessed with more production effort: either via EL lemmas congruent with ML lemmas for ML + EL constituents, or when all ML grammatical procedures are inhibited and EL ones activated in order to produce EL islands.

If it can be argued (on the basis of a frequency study) that a specific EL-origin morpheme is a B form rather than a CS form, how does it matter? As I have indicated above, this is not an important theoretical issue if content morphemes are being compared. That is, either CS forms or ML forms (including B forms) undergo similar morphosyntactic procedures in ML + EL constituents. The difference in morphosyntactic behaviour between CS and B forms seems to be a matter of degree, but not of kind.

An ancillary claim of the MLF model, however, is that the difference in status (CS form or B form) will affect a system morpheme's distributional profile in CS utterances.

Recall the case of the French complementizer (*que*) discussed in Chapter 5 in regard to Lingala/French CS for which Lingala is the ML. The MLF model predicts that only ML complementizers can be heads of ML complements; evidence indicates that they also head EL complements in some data sets. In contrast, the model predicts that the only way for an EL complementizer to appear at all is as the head of an EL island. In Lingala/French CS utterances, however, both the Lingala complementizer and French *que* appear as heads of these constructions. As matters now stand, this is a counter-example to the model.

However, if a frequency study of a corpus of Lingala/French utterances demonstrates that *que* is not a CS form, but rather a B form, then the distributional predictions for *que* change: as a B form and therefore an ML form, *que* could occur as the complementizer heading an ML complement or even an EL complement. Such a study has not been done to date. However, researchers working on Lingala predict that *que* is the more likely choice when a complementizer appears than the Lingala-origin counterpart (Kamwangamalu, 1989*a*; Nzwanga, 1991). It should now be clear how demonstrating that *que* is a B form would eliminate the Lingala/ French complementizer case as a counter-example to the System Morpheme principle. This example shows the theoretical utility of establishing an EL-origin morpheme's status if it is a system morpheme.

CS versus B Forms: Summary

I have argued that there are both similarities and distinctions between lexemes as CS and B forms. One cannot speak in categorical terms about any area; but I suggest the following statements as hypotheses.

1. B forms and singly occurring CS forms undergo ML morphosyntactic procedures in the same way. B forms observe ML morpheme-order constraints, just as do CS forms in ML + EL constituents. Further, singly occurring B and CS forms are both apparently subject to the same morphosyntactic procedures in these constituents. Yet caution is necessary in drawing definite conclusions here. The two types of form fall along a continuum, with B forms apparently more under the direction of ML procedures than CS forms. While a systematic study of morphological differences between the two types of form is beyond the scope of this study, at least this discussion identifies an important area for further research.

2. B forms themselves divide into two groups, cultural forms and core forms. Core B forms are more closely associated with CS forms, with most core B forms entering the ML first as CS forms.

Thus, core B forms are dynamically related to CS forms in two ways. These B forms enter the ML through the process of CS; also, both types of form lie along a frequency continuum, with CS forms showing minimal recurrence values.

Cultural B forms, which stand for new objects or concepts, often do 'fill gaps', as is generally held to be true of B forms in general. The process by which such forms enter the ML has little relation to the process of CS; these forms often come into the ML abruptly, for the obvious reason that they are needed to fill gaps.

3. The separating of B forms from CS forms in order to assess morphosyntactic constraints on CS remains an issue only in the case of B forms which are system morphemes.

4. B forms and CS forms differ in their status in relation to the ML mental lexicon. B forms are entered in this lexicon, but CS forms are not. Support for this hypothesis comes from the empirical evidence that there is a difference in the frequency of EL-origin material in CS utterances. In effect, this hypothesis is another way of stating that B forms have a new status as ML forms.

5. The status of an EL-origin form as a B form or a CS form can be established by measuring the frequency with which it occurs representing the concept or object it encodes in relation to the frequency of the indigenous form for the same concept or object. Cultural B forms are predicted to show high (if not categorical) relative frequency, since there is no indigenous form in competition with them. Core B forms will show high frequency in relation to those EL forms which are CS forms.

While I have used a three-occurrence rule (any form occurring at least three times in a relatively large corpus is a B form), the cut-off point itself has little meaning. What is important is the relative lack of predictability of CS forms in comparison with B forms. This lack of predictability is a natural function of the fact that CS forms are EL morphemes appearing in ML frames.

7
Codeswitching and Deep Grammatical Borrowing

Introduction

This chapter deals especially with borrowing which goes beyond lexical items. I will suggest that CS is an important mechanism in at least some cases of structural borrowing, as well as in some cases of language shift and related contact phenomena. First, I will discuss in some detail one such case: spoken in East Africa, Cushitic-origin Ma'a is sometimes called a 'mixed language' because it shows deep Bantu incursions. Next, I will present a set of seven scenarios showing the possible role of CS in such cases, including that of Ma'a. It is *not* my claim that, if CS is present, any of these scenarios *necessarily* will unfold. My major hypothesis, however, is that a 'turnover' of the ML in CS can set into motion processes leading to one language's borrowing of structural features from another. In a 'turnover' of the ML, the former EL becomes the ML, and the former ML becomes the EL.

Much of this chapter is speculative; it largely presents hypotheses for further testing. However, speculative though they are, the arguments in this chapter are important because they show the implications of a synchronic model (the MLF model) for solving some diachronic mysteries.

Preliminaries and the Problem

In some situations of heavy contact between two languages, one language takes on not only cultural and even core lexical B forms from the other language, but also the syntactic patterns and/or inflectional affixes and function words of the second language. Or, heavy contact, in the right sociolinguistic climate, may lead speakers to shift from their first language (their L1) to a second language (an L2) as their main means of communication. When language shift occurs, a possible outcome for the L1 is language death.[1]

[1] This chapter is an extended version of the argument in Myers-Scotton (1992*c*). I would like to thank Janice L. Jake, Trevor James, Michael Montgomery, S. M. Simango, and John Singler for discussion of this version.

There is in East Africa an excellent example of the radical result of heavy cultural contact: Ma'a (Mbugu), spoken in north-eastern Tanzania. Those who have studied Ma'a agree that when its early speakers entered Tanzania, the language they were speaking was Cushitic. What makes Ma'a so unusual is that its system morphemes can largely be related to those in Bantu languages (including the noun-class system of prefixes). True, Ma'a also has many Cushitic elements, but it is notable that these are mainly lexical items only.

Cushitic, of course, is one of the five branches of the Afro-Asiatic family of languages. Most Cushitic languages are concentrated further to the North: Somali in Somalia and Oromo in Ethiopia, for example, are major Cushitic languages. Iraqw, also classified as a southern Cushitic language along with Ma'a by most researchers, is spoken in northern Tanzania as well. But its speakers do not live in a contiguous area to Ma'a. Further, there are no other Cushitic languages in the intervening area between northern Tanzania and the northern Kenya coast. Thus, Ma'a speakers today are surrounded by speakers of Bantu languages on all sides.

There are three major views in recent scholarship about Ma'a. The first is that the language defies genetic assignment, with Whiteley (1960) calling Ma'a a 'linguistic hybrid' and Goodman (1971) seeing it as outside the usual classification systems. However, Thomason (1983) and Thomason and Kaufman (1988) view contemporary Ma'a as a Cushitic language which has maintained itself while borrowing from a neighbouring Bantu language or languages numerous features of its morphosyntax. Brenzinger (1987) views Ma'a differently. He argues that contemporary Ma'a is the result of a language shift; that is, he claims Ma'a is now a Bantu language with a substrate of some Cushitic features, especially in its lexicon.

Less dramatic examples exist elsewhere in the world, languages with extensive morphosyntactic material from a language which is not the primary source of its lexicon. Some receive extensive discussion in Thomason and Kaufman (1988). These include the Greek variety spoken in scattered communities in Asia Minor (Dawkins, 1916), although the extent of Turkish grammatical material is less extensive than that of the Bantu input in Ma'a; Romani spoken by English Gypsies, consisting of a Romani lexicon with English grammar (Hancock, 1980); and Aleut as spoken on Mednyj in the Aleutian Islands, which has had its finite-verb morphology replaced by that of Russian (Menovščikov, 1969).

Less discussed cases are Media Lingua, an Amerindian contact language spoken in Ecuador, consisting largely of a Quechua morphosyntactic base and a Spanish lexicon (Muysken, 1981); the Javanese spoken by the

Peranakan Chinese of East Java, showing many Indonesian lexemes (Wolff, 1983); Maltese, an Arabic variety spoken on Malta with incursions from Italian (Tosco, 1990); and Dahalo, a Cushitic language spoken along the northern Kenya coast, showing serious encroachments from Swahili (Tosco, 1992). Similar situations can be found elsewhere in the world, e.g. for some of the languages in Arnhem Land in Australia discussed by Heath (1981), and for some Amerindian languages, such as those in northern Alberta discussed in Scollon and Scollon (1979).

CS: A Possible Mechanism?

Many researchers, of course, offer 'heavy cultural contact' as the reason for what I will call 'deep borrowing' (i.e. incursions into the morphosyntax). But a moment's reflection indicates that, while contact may stimulate such changes, it is not the mechanism or the means. A consideration of contact communities showing such changes suggests that, in some cases at least, CS may be the mechanism behind extensive restructuring, as well as language shift and language death. However, this is not to suggest that *all* cases of language shift and language death depend on CS, nor that CS *always* stimulates the outcomes to be discussed. I am only suggesting a plausible mechanism to explain how certain outcomes have arisen.

Behind this argument is the premiss, raised earlier in this volume, that there is at least some modularity in the subsystems of language. This possibility, as well as differences in language-use patterns and—crucially perhaps—language attitudes in different groups in a community, may result in discontinuities in the application of the morphosyntactic proced- ures of a language, or lack of uniformity of procedures across different speakers.[2]

Of course, the best example of modularity in grammars is the claim, embodied in the MLF model discussed in Chapters 4 and 5, that system morphemes are accessed separately from content morphemes; extensive empirical evidence from an array of language pairs makes it clear that ML + EL constituents in CS do contain system morphemes from the ML but content morphemes from both languages. Thus, CS is a clear mechanism of placing in contact content morphemes from one language (the EL) with morphosyntactic patterns defined by the system morph- emes of another language (the ML).

---

[2] Both Mühlhäusler (1985: 255–8) and Mohan and Zador (1986: 313) also refer to discontinuities between grammars when languages are in contact. Their references are to communities where pidgins and creoles have developed.

A less dramatic example of how CS can affect structures is the potential effect on nominal and verbal systems of the *do*-verb construction found in ML + EL constituents in CS in many language pairs. (Recall that these consist of the ML verb for *do* as a type of auxiliary, carrying all inflections and followed by a bare EL verb stem or nominalized verb.) In some cases, there is evidence that a category change takes place, with the EL 'former' verb stem behaving syntactically as a noun. Over time, the EL form may be borrowed into the ML.

The Possibility of Modularity and Substitution

Especially in the case of language shift and language death, the possibility of modularity in morphosyntactic procedures may prove crucial in cases of maintenance with deep borrowing. The general assumption in the literature regarding language shift and language death is that change in such cases is gradual, and that it results in *loss* of various types for the sociolinguistically minor language. I will suggest that a better way of looking at the processes involved is to highlight *substitution*. Also, I will argue that the way that language production is organized in CS, along with extensive CS existing in a community, motivate substitution. I concur with Denison (1977: 21), who raises the issue of whether rule substitution can, 'if it goes far enough, ultimately amount to "language death" '. As the MLF model views such phenomena, they are a matter not so much of rule substitution at the surface level, but rather of the projection of different frames at the lemma level.

Types of Contact-Induced Change

One of the major arguments in the Thomason and Kaufman (1988) model for contact-induced effects on a linguistic system is that different results come from a borrowing versus a shift situation. Under borrowing, the first language (L1) is maintained, but it receives B forms from another language, an L2. In most such cases, one can consider the L1 as the ML in CS and the L2 as the EL (to use my terminology). Under language shift, the ML is dropped and its speakers shift to the EL (their new ML). Basically, Thomason and Kaufman claim that, under the 'maintenance condition' (my term), contact phenomena first (and predominately?) consist of lexical loans; under the 'shift condition', however, ML speakers shift to the lexicon of the EL (an L2 becoming an L1), but may bring with them elements from the ML phonology and morphosyntax (i.e.

substrate elements). Thomason and Kaufman do allow, however, that, given much cultural pressure, even under the maintenance condition, an ML may borrow from the phonology and morphosyntax of the EL. This is the reason that they argue that Ma'a, with its Bantu morphosyntax, still can be considered the result of the maintenance condition. In effect, however, their claim about Ma'a weakens their own distinction between the maintenance and the shift condition, since this claim about Ma'a indicates that morphosyntactic material can be borrowed under maintenance as well as under shift.

I will suggest that a key to when morphosyntactic material is passed between languages and in which direction it goes—to the maintaining language or to the shifting language—depends on which language is the ML during CS.

Structural Borrowing

Thomason and Kaufman are most convincing when they illustrate with many examples their overall claim that incursions into all systems of a language are possible, given the 'right' socio-psychological condition. And, of course, many other researchers on borrowing (e.g. those mentioned at the outset of Chapter 6) also have made it clear that deep borrowing is not such an unusual phenomenon as some textbooks in historical linguistics make it out to be. But what has not been well discussed is *how* these contact-induced changes are accomplished, from the structural point of view. Of course, it is at least implicit in almost all studies that bilingualism and even perhaps CS are involved. But in what ways?

CS Playing a Major Role in Structural Borrowing

The purpose of this chapter is to show how the specific structural configurations of ML + EL constituents in CS utterances and the possibility to 'turn over' the ML suggest an explicit role for CS in borrowing and language shift (including language death). Further, its role can be extended to pidgin/creole formation.

At the same time, I stress that no data have been gathered with the hypotheses to be suggested in mind; therefore, the only support now available consists of data from communities where no information was gathered at the time on the presence or structure of CS in naturally occurring conversations. Therefore, this chapter can only suggest questions for future research. Still, some convincing empirical evidence is available to motivate the scenarios suggested. And further, the claims made are testable, requiring only the requisite field studies.

A Prime Ingredient: CS Itself as the Unmarked Choice

Since the proposed scenarios require CS to occur, a partial exposition of the social motivations for CS offers a necessary background to discussion of the following language-contact scenarios. Four explanations for CS are presented under the markedness model already discussed earlier in this volume (cf. Scotton, 1988*a*; Myers-Scotton, 1993). The most clearly relevant explanation here is CS itself as the unmarked choice (unmarked CS).

This type of CS does not occur in all situations or all communities. Largely, it takes place in casual, ingroup interactions between peers who positively evaluate for their own identification *both* the identities indexed by the two (or more) codes involved in CS. This is the case in many communities in bi/multilingual societies, but by no means in all. In those communities where the languages of CS may point to values (ethnic, socio-economic, or otherwise) which are seen as conflicting, speakers may wish to associate themselves with only their 'own' group's set of values. In their ingroup conversations, therefore, they will not engage in the type of CS displaying both languages, since it indexes both sets of values. This does not mean that these same speakers do not engage in CS *at all*; they may still show other types of CS for other motivations (e.g. CS as a marked choice to negotiate a change in the social distance).

It is unmarked CS which is of interest here because of its 'to-and-fro action', since it is the use of an overall pattern of CS which carries the social significance, not a specific switch point. That this overall pattern exists means that CS 'displays' both languages in the same utterance. Further, in those communities where it occurs, such CS is likely to be very frequent, since it is occasioned by a 'state of mind' (a perception of oneself and one's fellows as having dual identities). In contrast, other types of CS generally occur only at one point in a conversation to index a more specific interpersonal objective.

The Possibility that the Designation of the ML May Change

A crucial point in the MLF model is that one language (the ML) plays a much more important role in structuring CS constructions than the other(s) (the EL): the ML sets the frame of ML + EL constituents by governing the morpheme order, and also by supplying all system morphemes active in signalling relationships.

The psycho-sociolinguistic basis for setting the ML is discussed in Chapter 3. Recall that, although the ML can be identified using relative frequency of morphemes for the discourse type in question, the setting of the ML is socially motivated. These social conditions and psychological attitudes which set the ML can change over time, of course. And a crucial point for this argument is that, when this happens, the designation for a community of the ML for CS interactions also may *change over time*. Presumably, this will result from a change in the relative psycho-sociological unmarkedness of the varieties involved for such interactions, and possibly from a change in relative speaker proficiency. In order for the ML to turn over for the entire community, such a change almost necessarily is preceded by changes for specific interaction types only. For example, perhaps language X would replace language Y first as the ML for CS conversations at places of work, then in informal public interactions, and finally in the home.

For evidence that such changes do occur, one can look at variability in ML assignment in some communities today. This variability was discussed in Chapter 3. Recall, for example, that among some Spanish/English speakers in the American south-west in conversation with peers with similar backgrounds, bilingual speakers with an awareness of CS report that the ML changes for them from interaction to interaction, depending on the situational features of the interaction. If a complete turnover of the ML happens anywhere, one would expect to find it most frequently in an immigrant community. As the community becomes more assimilated into the L2 culture, the prediction would be that the L2 becomes the community's ML. Such a state of affairs seems to exist among at least certain Japanese-American immigrants to North America, for example (cf. Nishimura, 1986). That is, Japanese seems to be the ML for some interactions, but English is the ML for other interactions. The next step for these communities would be for a shift to English as the only ML, although variable ML assignment may also be maintained.

CS-Based Scenarios

Seven scenarios are presented, all involving CS. Whether they involve a maintenance or a shift condition is not so important as which language is the ML during CS.

Scenario I: Content Morphemes as Core Lexical B Forms

The L1 maintains itself and is the ML during CS with an EL. Core content morphemes enter the ML from the EL, but the borrowing of system morphemes is negligible.

Note that, although wide-scale bilingualism and regular use of both languages encourages such borrowing, they are not sufficient conditions to predict this outcome. If these were the only triggering factors, there would be no reason why numerous system morphemes would not be borrowed as well. This is not the case. (There is always the possibility of the occasional borrowing of system morphemes, of course.)

The reason that core content morphemes are borrowed, but not many system morphemes, is that only EL content morphemes occur productively in ML + EL constituents in CS, making them highly salient in an ML context, since they occur in CS in an ML frame. In contrast, syntactically relevant EL system morphemes occur only in CS when they are in EL islands, where they are immersed in EL material, lacking individual salience.

Unfortunately, data have not been collected in such a way as to test the hypothesis that there is a connection between the presence of many core B forms and much CS, especially CS itself as the unmarked choice. True, the massive study comparing French Canadian communities in Quebec and Ontario by Poplack, Sankoff, and Miller (1988) did find more borrowing in the Ontario communities, where there was also more CS. In this study, however, core B forms are not differentiated from cultural B forms, nor do the authors look at types of CS according to social motivations.

Another study of French Canadian speakers (Mougeon and Beniak, 1991) does offer evidence of an association between the use of a specific core B form and a pattern of alternating between French and English use. But they do not specifically study CS. They consider the English lexeme *so*, used either as a discourse-marker or as a consecutive conjunction. Considering the association between *so* incidence and a number of independent variables (including sex, socio-economic status, locality of residence, and an index of French maintenance), Mougeon and Beniak conclude that French maintenance is the best predictor. But the point relevant to the current discussion is that the association between use of *so* and speaking French is not a linear one. That is, the finding is not 'the more English spoken, the more *so* is used'. Rather, it is the *mid-level* French users, those who show roughly balanced alternation between French and English, who are the greatest users of *so*. Mougeon and Beniak suggest that *so* is found here because the linguistic behaviour of other speakers (i.e. high French or English maintainers) is more compartmentalized. They write (1987: 40):

> the low maintainers by definition speak little French in the private domain while the high maintainers speak mostly or only French in the said domain. In other words, it would appear that bilingualism has to be of the 'unpatterned' type . . . in order for [this] core borrowing to become prevalent.

Even though their methodology did not provide for investigating the amount or type of CS shown by these 'unpatterned' bilinguals, Mougeon and Beniak do conclude that CS is in general related to core lexical borrowing:

> that sentence connectors and other kinds of discourse organizers are often reported in lists of core lexical borrowings may not be a coincidence since these items all occur at prime switching points. If this view of things is correct, then core lexical borrowing (or at least some of its manifestations) would simply be a by-product of code-switching.   (1987: 43)

My own earlier research in Africa reinforces these findings and interpretations (e.g. Scotton and Okeju, 1973 on Swahili and Luganda B forms in Ateso, an eastern Nilotic language spoken in Uganda and western Kenya). And, of course, the study in Zimbabwe of the English lexemes *because* and *but* in Shona, which is discussed in Chapter 6 and in Bernsten and Myers-Scotton (1993), also finds discourse-markers being borrowed in conversations including CS.

Scenario II: Relexification with EL Content Morphemes

If Scenario I is taken a little further, one arrives at relexification. That is, the L1 still maintains itself as both the main language of the speakers and the ML of CS utterances, but the higher prestige L2 (the EL) begins making serious inroads into the content morpheme lexicon of the L1. Such extensive relexification seems to be a rarer outcome than Scenario I, but still is attested. For example, this scenario holds for Media Lingua, a contact language spoken in several communities in the Ecuadorian Highlands. According to Muysken (1981: 52), the language is Quechua in its grammatical structure and almost 90 per cent Spanish in its lexicon. He compares the renditions in Quechua, Spanish, and Media Lingua of the same sentence (p. 54),

[1] Quechua   yalli-da tamia-pi-ga,   mana ri-sha-chu
    Med. L.   dimas-ta llubi-pi-ga,   no-i-sha-chu
    Sp.   si lleuve demas,   no voy a ir
    'If it rains too much, I won't go.'

Other discussions of similar relexifications can be found here and there in the literature. Their presence promises that explicit searches for relexification might show this to be a regular pattern in certain types of contact situation. Further, relexification may be a regular stage at certain points in time for those cases resulting in eventual language shift. While not all instances of relexification need necessarily result in language shift, the typical immigrant scenario may be one of content morpheme relexification followed by shift. At least, in discussing the shift from Norwegian to English in America, Haugen describes the state of affairs in the very terms which this model would predict. Presumably Norwegian is still the ML at the stage Haugen describes. He writes (1969: 71, quoted in Romaine, 1989: 250):

> In becoming bilingual within the American cultural environment they [speakers of Norwegian] were forced to modify their Norwegian if they wished to continue using it. At practically every point they maintained the basic phonetic and grammatical structures of their native dialects, but they filled in the lexical content of these structures from the vocabulary of English.

Also, Tosco (1992) sums up his discussion of Dahalo as an endangered, but maintained, language in some of the exact words which the MLF model of CS would use. (Dahalo is a Cushitic language spoken on the northern Kenya coast, where Swahili is indigenous and also a dominant lingua franca.) Tosco writes, 'Taking into consideration both assimilated and unassimilated material, the net result is often some kind of Mischsprache [mixed language], in which Swahili is framed into Dahalo.' (My only quarrel would be with the use of *Mischsprache*, depending on its intended meaning; certainly, there is no non-systematic mixing under the MLF model's conception of CS.)

I would suggest that 'relexification' may not be the best term for the contact phenomenon taking place in these cases. Rather, I would hypothesize that a second look at these cases would show that, in fact, what is happening is that these speakers are simply engaging in frequent CS. That is, I hypothesize that what is called 'relexification' is really just *the extensive presence of EL content morphemes* in ML + EL constituents. I suggest that a study of such cases will show that CS (rather than either the ML or the EL) has become the unmarked medium of everyday, ingroup conversation for these speakers.

Scenario III: Initial ML Role in CS for an L2 in Intergroup Communication

The scenario to be suggested here is especially speculative. Still, it offers a plausible mechanism to explain a state of affairs otherwise not clearly explained.

In many of the cases of CS discussed in the literature, the ML is the first language of the speakers engaged in CS, and much of their CS is intragroup in nature. For example, in Nortier's (1990) study of CS by Moroccan Arabic recent immigrants in the Netherlands, these speakers engage in CS with each other, using Arabic, not Dutch, as the ML. And in CS among francophones in Canada, French is the ML. The first language is also the ML for Shona speakers in Zimbabwe engaged in Shona/English CS.

But in a case of multiple groups (with different first languages) engaging in CS, not everyone's first language can be the ML; only one language must surface as the ML. In Nairobi, a neutral solution is achieved, with Swahili as the ML in multi-ethnic conversations. A possible result of such a state of affairs would be the incorporation of system morphemes from the ML into the EL, just because in ML + EL constituents in CS there is a juxtaposition of EL content morphemes with ML system morphemes. But in the case of the Nairobi corpus, the EL also is a lingua franca and, furthermore, one of much higher socio-economic prestige than Swahili, at least at present. There is a good deal of evidence that the donor language in borrowing usually has higher socio-political prestige than the recipient language. Therefore, it is unlikely that English as the EL will be a major recipient of Swahili borrowings into its morphosyntax.

However, this scenario for intergroup communication might explain other cases where the borrowing of system morphemes has been attested but never satisfactorily explained. A celebrated case is reported in Gumperz and Wilson (1974) for Kupwar in India. They indicate that the local varieties of Urdu, Telegu, Kannada, and Marathi have very similar morphologies in terms of inflection and derivation, as well as similar phonetics, but different lexicons. Marathi seems to be the source, especially regarding morphology. A possible explanation for this state of affairs is that there is a good deal of CS in the community, with Marathi as the ML.

Another famous *Sprachebunde* mystery, the disappearance of the infinitive in largely unrelated Balkan languages, might be solved with a similar explanation. Seuren (1991) suggests that CS, as envisioned in the

MLF model, might offer an explanation. The usual story is that the infinitive was lost under the influence of Greek, which lost its infinitives in the first centuries AD. From there the loss spread over the Balkan area, affecting Macedonian, Bulgarian, Romanian, and Serbian in differing degrees. But the issue is: what is the mechanism by which Greek could exert such an influence? Seuren suggests one explanation. (1) Greek had high status in the Middle Ages because of the events of ancient history and the accumulated glory. (2) Suppose that there was a good deal of CS going on with neighbouring languages, with Greek as the EL. (3) ML infinitive positions would be likely sites for CS, but Greek could not oblige with an infinitive, not even with a stem form. It could only supply a subordinate clause with a finite verb and its subject ('He wants that he gets rich'). (4) The ML could accommodate the Greek subordinate clause as an EL island, headed with an ML complementizer. (5) If such CS became both frequent and prestigious, it could lead to the gradual disappearance of infinitives in the various MLs, in favour of finite subordinate clauses.

Another variation of this scenario is that, if Greek were the major lingua franca for intergroup conversations, then Greek may have been the ML in any CS in such conversations. In this case, its morphosyntax would have prevailed in ML + EL constituents from the outset of intergroup conversations. Gradually, the Greek pattern would have been copied into the other languages.

Identifying the ML in a case of structural borrowing between a set of Swahili dialects might also explain the resulting pattern of borrowing. Nurse (1988) reports on the borrowing of inflectional morphology from northern Swahili dialects into the Zanzibar dialect. Geographically and linguistically, the Zanzibar dialect (Ki-Unguja) is a southern dialect. While there are many resemblances between Ki-Unguja and the dialects of the northern Kenya coast and offshore islands (e.g. Ki-amu), their tense/aspect systems show considerable differences. Still, Ki-Unguja 'most frequently has the Northern variant' (Nurse, 1988: 110).

Nurse asks (p. 111), 'Why should the T/A systems of Unguja and the Northern dialects be so similar, when the communities using them are separated by some 500 kms of ocean, equivalent to several days of traveling by the traditional methods that obtained for centuries?' While Nurse suggests several possible explanations, he finds none of them entirely satisfactory.

The MLF model would suggest that the answer lies in considering which dialect was the ML during intergroup contacts. If the northern dialects were the ML, then northern tense/aspect morphemes would have appeared (as system morphemes) in ML + EL constituents. Nurse states that the northern dialects had more socio-political prestige up to the end of the eighteenth century (when these developments presumably took place). If this were the case, it is likely that the northern dialects would have been the ML in encounters between Zanzibaris and north-coast Kenyans.

Scenario IV: The Turnover of the ML in CS

While there is no empirical evidence that turnovers of the ML occur in CS for an entire community, recall that synchronic change in the ML is definitely attested as a feature of the CS of individuals. The reason there is no evidence of community-wide change may be (*a*) that few communities have been studied over time and (*b*) that, even where longitudinal studies have been conducted, no researchers have ever considered looking for a turnover.

The motivation for a hypothesis of the turnover is that it accounts in a principled way for the *mélange* of languages found in Ma'a, as well as for other dramatic cases of pervasive incursions of an L2 into the morphology or syntax of a maintained L1, as well as for many cases of less extensive incursions.

Under this scenario, speakers of an Ll take a step just short of shifting completely to an L2 which has become sociolinguistically dominant. Instead, they acknowledge the L2's dominance (in their own repertoires) by shifting to the L2 as the ML when they are engaged in CS.

Recall the role of the ML in ML + EL constituents, and it is obvious why this turnover of the ML is so important. Both morpheme order and active system morphemes in these constituents come from the ML. If the L1 loses its primacy as the ML in CS, with the L2 taking its place, the result is an 'outside goes inside' change. Denison (1977: 21) offers a vivid metaphor for such a replacement, recalling 'the Russian fable of the wolf which ate the sleigh-horse and thereupon found itself in harness as a horse-substitute'.

I now speculate on the steps leading up to (and beyond) such replacement of the Cushitic antecedent of Ma'a with a Bantu language in CS.

1. The first step would be for the Cushitic speakers to become bilingual in one or more of the Bantu languages in the area surrounding the Cushitic settlement. It is known that some Cushitic speakers assimilated to neighbouring Bantu groups, especially the Pare, shifting to the Pare

language as their own. An obvious motivation for the remaining Ma'a speakers to become bilingual would be their desire to speak to these ethnic brethren, as well as to Bantu-origin neighbours. Further, the sheer pressure of Bantu numbers would promote bilingualism. According to Nurse (1988: 108), all Ma'a are bilingual in one of these Bantu languages, Shambala.

2. The next step is some CS. Possibly the Ma'a engaged in Cushitic/Bantu CS with their Cushitic-origin neighbours; possibly they only used CS among themselves. The speculation is that Cushitic/Bantu CS replaced monolingual Ma'a as what must be called their L1.

3. But the crucial step would be to respond to environmental pressures by a turnover in CS to a Bantu language as the ML in ML + EL constituents. This would mean that the active system morphemes as well as morpheme order would come from the Bantu language.

4. Once this replacement is made, it is easy to see how the forerunners of today's Ma'a speakers could carry over the practice of using non-Cushitic system morphemes and syntax to non-CS renditions of proto-Ma'a.

This scenario fits present-day results, since in Ma'a almost all the system morphemes and morpheme order show every indication of coming from a Bantu source. As Thomason and Kaufman (1988: 224) remark,

In morphology, Ma'a retains only one systematic inflectional feature of Cushitic origin, namely, suffixed pronominal possessors . . . Otherwise, Ma'a preserves just a few fossilized Cushitic inflectional features, while the entire productive inflectional apparatus is borrowed from Bantu—the functional categories, their ordering, and the affixes themselves.

Ethnographic reports indicate that the Ma'a form a group wishing to distinguish itself from its neighbours in order to follow its own traditions. They live in a relatively remote area in the Usambara mountains. However, it is known that the Ma'a used to have regular interactions, including ethnic ceremonies, with their Cushitic-origin neighbours who live in the South Pare mountains further north. In order to make themselves understood, surely they must speak a Bantu variety part of the time, not Ma'a. (Pare and Shambala are Bantu languages spoken in the area, and morphological features in contemporary Ma'a most resemble Pare and Shambala features.) One way in which they could symbolize their ethnic distinctiveness would have been by *not* using a Bantu variety exclusively, insisting instead on a CS pattern. Still, the Bantu variety would have had to be the ML if this CS were to be intelligible to the others. That is, the frame of CS utterances would have had to be Bantu. From here it is an easy step to see how Bantu morphosyntax could enter their ingroup renditions of their own variety.

It does seem that the social situation has to be unusual to result in a language such as Ma'a. I am not, however, saying that the situation has to be unusual for there to be a turnover of the ML in CS. I suggest that this happens regularly in immigrant situations, as a step in the language-shift process, and there is every reason to hypothesize that it also happens wherever a minority language is overwhelmed by a neighbour with more sociolinguistic vitality. In fact, one may even say what makes the Ma'a case unusual is that the Cushitic element persists, *not* that the Bantu element is present. Note that this 'turnover' scenario (and therefore language shift) can be predicted *without* a content-morpheme relexification stage.

What is the final step in the scenario, maintenance or shift? So far, this scenario leaves a Cushitic language in place as the L1 of Ma'a speakers today, as Thomason and Kaufman argue, even though they offer no mechanism for the Bantu incursions. Their final statement on the subject (1988: 228)[3] is this: 'The only remaining line of development is massive borrowing from a Bantu language B into a (minimally) maintained Cushitic language A.'

But another ending to the scenario may be just as possible, related to that advocated by Brenzinger (1987). He sees present-day Ma'a as the result of a shift to a Bantu language, followed by some relexification with Cushitic elements.

I suggest a resolution between the two claims: present-day Ma'a is a Bantu language which retains Cushitic features (mainly in the lexicon) as part of its substrate. Even if they 'thought' they were speaking a Cushitic-origin variety, in fact the Ma'a had tipped the scales toward a Bantu variety.[4] The replacement is especially clear in the inflectional system, just where it would be most predicted. Over time, more replacement with Bantu features followed. The result is a language which was substantially replaced from the inside out, a result which must be called language shift to a Bantu variety.

The major rationale for this solution is that it brings the Ma'a case into

---

[3] Thomason has several earlier papers on Ma'a; Thomason (1983) is reported to be an elaboration of a case study written for Thomason and Kaufman (1975).

[4] Anecdotal evidence gathered among Africans who regularly engage in CS (involving their own language) may be representative of speaker perceptions of CS. Malawians who switch between Cheŵa (or another indigenous language) and English think of themselves as speaking a dialect of the African language, *not* as speaking English at all (Simango, 1991).

line with other language-shift situations; the Ma'a case only differs in the extent of the substrate features.[5] Both the Thomason and Kaufman claim of 'massive' borrowing and the Brenzinger claim of 'reborrowing' create an exception out of Ma'a.

Scenario V: Language Shift

Of course, language shift may occur without intermediate CS or, even if there is CS, without a turnover of the ML. Yet, CS, with the turnover, is an obvious mechanism which not only promotes language shift but also explains the process involved.

I do not pretend to detail language shift facilitated by CS; my only purpose here is to suggest that the mechanism exists. The details of shift, even facilitated by CS, must be varied. Even the turnover of the ML in CS, preceding actual language shift, need not be either categorical or abrupt. For example, it is possible that in CS the 'old' ML first gives way just to the morpheme order of the 'new' ML. Or only the system morphemes for one subsystem (e.g. the nominal system) may be given over to the 'new' ML.

These suggestions tie in with hypotheses about modularity in grammatical systems. They are supported by such empirical evidence as that reported in Hill and Hill (1986) in an extensive study of borrowing and CS in Malinche Mexicano (Nahuatl) in Central Mexico. Hill and Hill state flatly that Mexicano syntax has converged with that of local Spanish, and that system morphemes which are function words also come from Spanish. This finding implies that the Morpheme-Order Principle is lost first in language shift. Recall that the limited data on covergence discussed in Chapter 5 also suggests this order.

It is possible to speak an intelligible (although not an elegant) Mexicano by simply inserting items of either Spanish or Mexicano etymology, appropriately inflected in Mexicano, into Spanish sentence frames held together by Spanish function words.   (Hill and Hill, 1986: 233)

In regard to system morphemes, Hill and Hill report other findings which suggest that shift shows itself first among those system morphemes from Spanish (the EL) which are congruent with Mexicano counterparts.

Modularity is also suggested in another study of borrowing and

---

[5] The implication in the review of Ma'a grammar by Thomason and Kaufman is that, even with derivational morphology (which I do not discuss at all in reference to CS because it is not under the sway of the ML in CS), the productive derivational patterns are from Bantu.

codeswitching, this time in Morocco. Heath (1989: 197) offers these concluding remarks:

we must recognize very different adaption strategies for borrowings depending on their word-class affiliations . . . even a full structural analysis of L1 and L2 does not permit us to predict the detailed treatment of borrowings, since there may be several distinct but interacting levels of structure, each pointing toward a different type of adaption strategy.

Scenario VI: Language Death

When a language reaches any (or all) of the previous scenarios, a further possible scenario is for all of its speakers to shift their language, or for remaining speakers to die themselves: either way, death overtakes the 'old' L1.

Let us compare the turnover case with language shift and language death. When speakers abandon a language for an L2, this is a case of language shift. Language shift also involves language death when *all* speakers of language X abandon that language. The Ma'a turnover case can be thought of as a variation of language shift and language death. As such, it shows 'arrested language shift', a true shift to a Bantu language in the morphosyntactic system, but not in the lexical system. (It also represents arrested language death, since there are no other speakers of Ma'a.)

Many speak of language death as if it results from morphosyntactic loss. According to the line I have taken here, the dying language need not so much *lose* features as it may *substitute* features (i.e. from the invading language). What the investigator 'finds' may be a product of the methodology of studying language death. The issue is whether the true focus is on the data source or on the data-collector. If it is known that the investigator is interested in having informants speak the dying language, those informants who no longer speak that language fluently may respond by producing little data. The investigator may equate little production with 'loss'. Such speakers may simply be avoiding producing the substitutions they have incorporated from the invading language. Again, as with the other hypotheses of this chapter, testing is only possible with naturally occurring conversations, not with elicitations.

A scenario for language death, with CS in the community, would include the following parts. First, those fluent speakers, who produce the dying language in its near-full form, would be found not to engage extensively in CS as an unmarked choice. Their fluent production of the dying language implies special loyalty to the identity associated with that language. Recall that speakers must identify positively with the attributes of both languages in order to engage in CS as an unmarked choice. (This does not mean that fluent speakers are not able to speak the invading language, or even use it in CS patterns. For example, Dorian (1990) reported that fluent speakers of Scottish Gaelic engaged in what I call CS as a sequence of unmarked choices, i.e. CS according to situation.)

The argument made here predicts that, for fluent speakers, the dying language must remain their ML in all CS utterances. Thus, the mechanism for extensive incursions into the morphosyntax from the invading language is not even available to fluent speakers.

Second, other speakers in the community, however, have quite different speech patterns (it is hypothesized). Again, this claim is based on the premiss raised earlier that discontinuities exist in any speech community between special groups or individuals.

These speakers use the dying language very little *except in a CS pattern*. And when they engage in CS, it is the invading language which is the ML for ML + EL constituents. That is, they certainly do not see their identities as tied to the dying language in any important sense. Dorian (1977: 24) does report that those individuals whom she calls 'semi-speakers' were 'very much more at home in English' than in Gaelic. This scenario is reminiscent of that reported for many American Indian languages, although, unfortunately, few researchers cite much linguistic data. For example, Miller (1971) reports that the Shoshoni show very little language loyalty. He states that some Shoshoni do state that they wish they or their children had control of the language. But he goes on to say (p. 119):

But very few do anything about it. Some parents purposely use Shoshoni so that their children will learn the language, but this is not a common practice. Quite a number of families are proud of being Indians (not necessarily of being Shoshonis), but more often than not these are the families that use the most English.

Significantly, Miller also reports a good deal of CS (which he refers to as 'interlarding' Shoshoni with English words and phrases). Unfortunately, no details are given of the data.

In some communities there are no fluent speakers. In extreme cases, the only use of the dying language may be in formulaic EL islands when semi-speakers engage in CS.

Thus, the hypothesis is that language death comes about in two different ways, sometimes in the same community: (*a*) among the fluent speakers, their own deaths spells demise for the language; (*b*) among the semi-speakers, CS is prevalent, with eventual loss of the L1 as the ML. That is, CS takes over monolingual speech, just as it did in the Ma'a case. The difference is that in language death there is linguistic replacement of the dying language at all levels.

Scenario VII: The Development of Pidgins and Creoles

Consistent with the hypotheses already set down is a tentative one about the role of CS in pidgin and creole development. First, consider a hypothesis about pidgin development: if the L1 of speakers participating in pidgin genesis is also the ML when they engage in CS, then their L1 will set the frame for their ML + EL constituents when they try to speak to others (to whom the L1 is not known). That is, L1 morpheme order and system morphemes will be prominent (or those of whichever language is the ML; it may be a second language serving as a lingua franca).

This scenario leads to the hypothesis that L1 or the lingua franca's morphosyntactic features (or perhaps features from several different L1s) will compete to set the frame in pidgin formation. These speakers may try to plug in content morphemes from a 'target' language (the one of greatest socio-economic prestige in the community); but the frame will be a substrate creation. Which substrate features win out depends on the interaction of a number of factors, some sociological (e.g. numbers of speakers), some purely linguistic (e.g. the relative markedness/status in universal grammar of competing features).

Of course, there is an extensive literature on the substrate hypothesis versus other contenders, and I do not pretend to compete with it here. My purpose simply is to suggest that the role of the ML in CS also offers a mechanism for the resulting outcomes in pidgin and creole development.

Also, because the ML can turn over, CS may offer support in different quarters at different stages in development. In the initial stages of development, CS almost certainly takes place and the ML is most likely the speakers' own language(s); this scenario is strong support at this point in development for a substrate-based grammatical frame. Later, the original superstrate language or some other contender may become the ML. Turnover of the ML to a superstrate language will result in decreolization, with the superstrate now not simply a contributor of lexical items but the language providing the morphosyntactic frame.

One final suggestion: As is well known, a developing pidgin/creole receives much of its lexicon from the superstrate language. Since, in the early stages of development, the superstrate will be the EL, not the ML, it is predicted that most of these lexemes will be content morphemes. However, superstrate morphemes may turn up as system morphemes in the following way: content morphemes may be borrowed and then used with new meanings, as system morphemes.

Further discussion of pidgin and creole development is beyond the scope of this study; but these possibilities suggest that researchers should consider the role of CS.

Conclusion

When there is extensive borrowing (beyond the incorporation of cultural B forms into a language), some explanation beyond citing 'bilingualism' or 'contact' is needed. In communities exhibiting CS, specifically where there is a motivation for CS as the unmarked choice, an explanation suggests itself. Such switching includes ML + EL constituents in most cases, and these constituents consist of morphosyntactic frames from the ML, filled with content morphemes from either the ML or the EL.

Scenario I. Content morphemes are borrowed into the L1, which is maintained as the main language of the community. As long as the maintained language is the ML during CS, CS offers no easy means for EL morphosyntax to affect the ML, but it does provide a mechanism for EL content morphemes to enter the ML.

Scenario II. This outcome takes incorporation of EL content morphemes into the ML a step further. If many EL content morphemes are used in CS over a period of time, relexification from the EL occurs. Again, largely content morphemes are involved.

Scenario III. This outcome may arise through CS in a community with a good deal of intergroup communication. CS may become a type of lingua franca in such communities, with the ML for this CS as the first language of the most socio-politically dominant of the groups (in terms either of numbers or of socio-political prestige). System morphemes and phrase-structure rules from the ML may be gradually borrowed into the speakers' L1s (the ELs).

Scenario IV. This outcome rests on a more radical CS mechanism. Socio-political conditions are such that speakers 'turn over' the ML in their CS patterns: what was the EL becomes the ML. The result is that they will now use the morphosyntax from the 'new' ML in their ML + EL constituents in CS. This 'turnover' sets the stage for borrowing the new

ML's morphosyntax into the original ML (which is likely to be the speakers' L1). The case of Ma'a is placed here.

Scenario V. This scenario represents the next step. Under the influence of morphosyntax from the new ML in their CS utterances, speakers shift their main language to a second language, the new ML of CS.

Scenario VI. This is language death. The old ML is no longer used on its own by larger and larger numbers of speakers in the community. When it is used by most speakers, it occurs in CS utterances; but there has been a turnover of the ML, and the morphosyntax of the new ML influences the dying language. Substitutions are made from the new ML. Eventually, fluent speakers of the dying language die themselves, and semi-speakers use the dying language only in CS patterns and finally only in formulaic expressions.

Scenario VII. CS may also be a mechanism in the development of pidgins and creoles. The hypothesis is that speakers approach pidgin formation as an instance of CS production.

The hypotheses in this chapter are speculative. Further, there is no suggestion that they apply in *every* case of CS. Their potential value is that they do explain deep structural borrowing, when it does occur. Field testing, using naturally occurring data, is necessary. Certainly, the hypothesis that CS itself as an unmarked choice promotes extensive core lexical borrowing from the EL is open to testing in many communities in the world. Also, hypotheses about the effects of having a non-L1 as the ML in intergroup CS also can be tested, although there may be fewer communities showing this feature. In addition, the claim that a turnover of the ML in CS interactions triggers substitution borrowing in the morphosyntax of the old ML can be tested with longitudinal data, or even with generationally based differences in different situations.

8

Conclusions

The goal of this volume has been to offer an account of how knowledge of multiple languages is represented and accessed during intrasentential CS, the use of two or more languages in the same sentence. In what may be considered a companion volume (Myers-Scotton, 1993), I discuss how the knowledge of multiple languages is exploited for socio-pragmatic purposes; that is, I consider the socio-psychological motivations for CS.

Here I summarize the structural-constraints model, the MLF model, the main subject of this volume. I go on to suggest some ways in which the socio-psychological motivations and community norms for CS intersect with structural constraints.

Premises and Provisions of the MLF Model.

Crucial generalizations about structural constraints on CS can be captured by recognizing the interplay of two hierarchies.

1. One of the languages involved in CS plays a dominant role. This language is labelled the Matrix Language (ML), and its grammar sets the morphosyntactic frame for two of the three types of constituent contained in sentences showing intrasentential CS, ML + EL constituents (those showing morphemes from the two or more participating languages), and ML islands (constituents composed entirely of ML morphemes). The third type of constituent, the EL island, is produced when ML morphosyntactic procedures are inhibited and EL procedures are activated.

2. The major organizing device which the ML uses in setting the frame is the division between system and content morphemes. The way in which content and system morphemes are differentiated in the MLF model becomes a theoretical claim about some of the crucial distinguishing features of lexical categories in all natural languages. Recall that properties regarding quantification and thematic-role status are used to make this distinction. The model claims that the feature [Quantification], viewed from the perspective of a system of logic, is a property of all system morphemes, since they pick out individuals across variables.

Content morphemes are identified by their plus setting for the feature either [Thematic Role-Assigner] or [Thematic Role-Receiver]. Whether a morpheme from the other language(s) involved in CS may appear in an ML + EL constituent depends on its status as a system or content morpheme; whether it must appear in an EL island (that is, if it is to appear at all) also depends on this status. The congruence of an EL content morpheme with ML morphemes in various ways also determines whether that EL morpheme may be accessed in an ML + EL constituent.

The provisions of the MLF model are contained in a set of interrelated hypotheses. Each hypothesis, however, also stands on its own in that it makes specific predictions. These predictions make clear the type of evidence which would falsify the hypothesis; data regarding what would constitute counter-examples are discussed at relevant junctures in Chapters 4 and 5.

> The Matrix Language Hypothesis: The ML sets the morphosyntactic frame for ML + EL constituents.

This hypothesis is realized as two testable principles: the Morpheme Order Principle ('Morpheme order must not violate ML morpheme order') and the System Morpheme Principle ('All syntactically relevant system morphemes must come from the ML').

> The Blocking Hypothesis: The ML blocks the appearance of any EL content morphemes which do not meet certain congruency conditions with the ML lemma which directs frame-building in the constituent. (These conditions are spelled out in Chapter 5.)

> The EL Island Trigger Hypothesis: Obligatory EL islands result whenever an EL morpheme not permitted under either the ML Hypothesis or the Blocking Hypothesis is to appear in the sentence. There are two ways in which these islands which are entirely in the EL result: (1) The speaker's intentions lead to the selection of EL lemmas from the mental lexicon and to the direction to activate only EL morphosyntactic patterns and lexemes. (2) A 'misfiring' occurs, resulting in a syntactically active EL system morpheme; the constituent it initiates must be completed as an EL island.

In addition, an EL Implicational Hierarchy Hypothesis refers to optional EL islands. It states that generally only those constituents which are either formulaic or idiomatic or peripheral to the main grammatical arguments of the sentence will occur as optional EL islands. (EL islands are discussed in Chapter 5.)

The motivating principle behind the MLF model is that, from a production point of view, CS can be thought of as similar to monolingual speech production. The grammars of both the languages involved in CS are 'turned on'; the difference is that the ML grammar is designated as more active, and is therefore responsible for directing most CS structuring. This means that a hypothesis underlying the model is that only ML lemmas are accessed for much of the production of a sentence containing CS. Recall that lemmas (cf. Levelt, 1989) contain all the non-phonological information for entries in the mental lexicon of a language. I will return to the composition of lemmas later in the chapter, when I will speculate that socio-pragmatic information is also contained in lemmas and is highly relevant to the production process.

It is the ML grammar which directs the framing of ML + EL constituents, meaning that only ML lemmas are activated to produce these constituents. EL lemmas are only involved in supplying lexemes which are content morphemes at the content insertion stage. These lexemes must match the specifications set by the ML lemmas. And, of course, the ML mental lexicon (with the grammatical procedures it directs) is the solitary lexicon involved during the building of ML islands, which are constituents entirely in the ML. The only time EL grammatical procedures are activated is when the ML grammar is inhibited so that EL islands may be formed. Now EL lemmas are in control. This is the only 'switching' in the MLF model; but it is a switching of abstract procedures, not of linguistic material.

The MLF model of how CS is produced and structured helps explain other language contact phenomena, as discussed in Chapters 6 and 7. The differences in the roles played by the ML and the EL and the differences in how system versus content morphemes are accessed are also important in accounting for the morphological treatment of established borrowings, as well as for the structural steps leading to language shift and language death. For example, while there may be differences in degree, only ML morphosyntactic procedures apply to all singly occurring content morphemes from the EL, whether they are established borrowings (B forms) or singly occurring CS forms (also necessarily content morphemes). That is, ML system morphemes (inflections and function words) prepare the slots in the ML frame for both B forms and CS forms, and they follow ML morpheme order. Yet there are differences between the two forms in their degree of morphological integration, and especially in their frequencies of occurrence; these differences reflect their different statuses in the ML mental lexicon. Also, the strength of the ML in framing constituents in CS at any point in time suggests that the structural-dominance configuration of languages in CS over time (which one is the ML) may be a mechanism in language shift, or even in pidgin and creole development.

Intersections Between Structural Organization and the Social Motivations and Socio-Pragmatic Roles of CS

The premiss underlying the markedness model of the socio-psychological motivations for CS (cf. Myers-Scotton, 1993) is that speakers use code choices for socio-pragmatic effects; further, they use them largely to negotiate interpersonal relationships. True, sometimes speakers switch because of performance problems—they cannot think of the right word. But a good deal of evidence across many cultures indicates that speakers *choose* to use more than one language, even though it is more often an unconscious than a conscious choice. The markedness model offers motivations for the typical distribution of code choices for a given interaction type in any bilingual community.

Questions relevant to the current volume are: (1) Do the social functions of CS control in any way the types of structures which the MLF model claims to account for? (2) And, on the other side of the coin, do the constraints set up by the MLF model permit speakers to use CS, *according to the markedness model*, to negotiate their own identities and mutual rights and obligations sets with other participants in an interaction?

Identifying the Matrix Language

The MLF model depends on the specification of one language as the ML, since certain key structural patterns come from the ML. Designating the ML is largely a socially motivated decision, I argue. (The identification of the ML is discussed in Chapter 3.) It is true that the operational definition of the ML is a structurally motivated statement: the ML is the language with the higher frequency of morphemes in a discourse sample in which CS occurs. But this definition only defines the ML; it does not explain the choice.

Investigation of the socio-political factors in the community where CS is a pattern shows that the ML is preferred for social reasons in the interaction type where it is the ML. I have indicated above, in Chapters 3 and 6, that the ML need not be the language with official status or the highest socio-economic prestige in the community as a whole. For example, in the case of the Nairobi corpus, English has more associations with higher socio-economic status than Swahili. Yet Swahili is the ML for CS between members of different ethnic groups in casual, ingroup conversations. Both English and Swahili are second languages for the speakers involved; many—even most—of them are proficient in English. But it is the association of Swahili with a 'solidarity syndrome', including the view of Swahili as an 'African town language', which determines its use as the ML in CS, it seems. Consider also the case of Strasburg, in the Alsace–Lorraine region of France (Gardner-Chloros, 1991). While French is the official language and enjoys an image as the language of socio-economic mobility, Alsatian is the ML of at least many informal, ingroup conversations involving Alsatian/French CS.

Therefore, it is the particular domain or interaction type *and* its specific associations which are salient in determining the ML. In this way, social factors precede the provisions of the MLF model in accounting for CS patterns.

The Prevalence of ML + EL Constituents

Next consider the main preoccupation of the MLF model—constituents consisting of morphemes from both languages, ML + EL constituents. Their very existence can be attributed to large-scale socio-political factors. Recall that these constituents, showing alternation of morphemes from language to language within a single constituent, are distinguished from CS as alternation across constituents or even across sentences. Such switching seems to occur largely under the social type of CS which I have labelled 'unmarked CS' in my discussion of the markedness model (cf. Myers-Scotton, 1993). I argue that such switching occurs when speakers wish to index the social identities associated with *both* the linguistic varieties shown in the constituent. This desire to index two identities at once is why there is so much to-and-fro switching between the two varieties, rather than an alternation of full constituents or sentences.

Certain sociological conditions must be met for unmarked CS to be a frequent type of CS in a community, and therefore for a large number of ML + EL constituents to occur. First, the speakers must be bilingual peers; such switching typically does not happen where there are various socially based differentials between speakers. Generally, speakers share the same social-identity factors regarding age, education, and occupation, although not necessarily the same ethnic group, at least in the multiethnic communities in Africa which I have studied.

In addition, certain criteria regarding speaker attitudes must be met. The interaction has to be of the type in which speakers wish to symbolize the dual memberships which such unmarked CS calls up. Also, proficiency in the languages used in CS is not a sufficient condition. Speakers must *positively evaluate* for their own identities the indexical values of the varieties used in switching. Therefore, unmarked CS typically occurs when the interactions are private, informal, and involve only ingroup members. These are just the types of conversation which have produced the ML + EL constituents from Nairobi and Harare cited in this volume.

The hypothesis about unmarked CS predicts that such switching is at best infrequent in communities where ethnic rivalry along language lines is strong. This subject is discussed at length elsewhere (cf. Scotton, 1988*b*; Myers-Scotton, 1993). But it seems clear that the MLF model would have little grist for its mill were it not for the existence of communities where dual identities are positively evaluated and the unmarked CS which symbolizes such a state of affairs is prevalent.

The Usefulness of CS as a Social Index

One can also argue that the macro-role of CS as a social indexing device contributes both to the incidence of singly occurring EL morphemes in ML + EL constituents and to the incidence of certain types of EL island, as socio-pragmatically motivated discourse devices. That is, speakers use these structural types as 'reminders'; they remind the addressee of another identity apart from the dominant one being conveyed by the language which is the choice for the rest of the interaction.

For example, Southworth, who writes about switching between English and Malayalam between highly educated Indians (who are native speakers of Malayalam), comments (1980: 139):

We might ask . . . why people who are fluent in English bother to use Malayalam at all. The answer seems to be that to carry on a conversation entirely in English would create an extremely formal atmosphere. Making excessive use of English is, in fact, a way of keeping a person at a distance.

There are many examples in many data sets of ML or optional EL islands as parenthetical expressions. Their function is to 'remind' the addressee of the 'other' identity, I would argue. Bentahila and Davies (1983: 310; 1992) cite a number of examples of such islands from their Moroccan Arabic/French data set.

Certain types of discourse-markers also often occur in the EL for a similar function. The Spanish/English CS data in Jacobson (1990: 134, 137) yields examples of both English discourse-markers and parenthetical expressions:

[1] Y, *of course*, tambien yo no se hacerlo bien bien.
'And, of course, I do not know how to do it well either.'

[2] *Sometimes*, 'tamos comiendo y los sentamos y vienen los demàs y we start speaking English.
'Sometimes we are eating and we ask them to sit down and the others come and *we start speaking English.*'

Pandharipande (1990: 22, 28) goes so far as to make an argument for the dominance of social factors in determining structure in CS. In regard to her data on Marathi/English CS, she argues that there is a 'modernity continuum' in Marathi society and 'a correlation between the form and its sociolinguistic function . . . Marathi and English are the two opposite ends of the continuum'. Her examples along the continuum are given in [3]:

[3*a*] mi tyala sangitle vikayayla
    I him told   sell

[3*b*] mi tyala sangitle *sell it* karayala
    I him told   to do

[3*c*] mi tyala sangitle *sell it*
    I him told

'I told him sell it!'

Pandharipande's position that 'the functional constraint overrides the structural constraint' (p. 28) is too extreme, I argue. Social factors do affect choices in CS, but they do so within a structurally-determined framework. None of the variants in [3] violates the constraints of the MLF model. I would argue that it is within this frame that speakers are free to choose options to negotiate the subtle socio-psychological differences in their communicative intentions which Pandharipande has in mind.

The Possibility of Structurally Marked Choices

Yet the spirit of Pandharipande's claim is not without value. There are cases in which socio-pragmatic effect exploits structural constraints. Elsewhere I argue that speakers make socially marked choices for socio-pragmatic effect (cf. Scotton, 1983; Myers-Scotton, 1993). That is, they choose a linguistic variety which is marked, given the norms of the community for the interaction type in question. They do this to negotiate an 'other-than-expected' effect.

Just as marked choices in code *selection* are possible, so are marked choices in *structure* in CS. That is, to negotiate certain socio-pragmatic effects, speakers may violate the principles of the MLF model. Yet, in order for a marked choice to be noticed and even possibly effective, there has to be an unmarked choice as a reference point.

For example, the Nairobi corpus shows only one instance in 40 conversations in which the Morpheme-Order Principle of the MLF model is violated. Recall that this principle requires morpheme order in ML + EL constituents to come from the ML. Yet in [4] the order of N + modifiers comes from the EL (English), not the ML (Swahili), which requires head-first N + ADJ constituents.

> [4] A Kamba house servant is conversing about agriculture with the Luyia son in the home where he is employed.
>
> LUYIA. Sisi kwetu iko ng'ombe, kondoo, kuku, na wanyama wengine.
> 'At our place, we have cattle, sheep, chickens, and other animals.'
> KAMBA. Na hizi mbuzi, ni zile ambayo ziko kubwa, zile ambayo zina nyolewa manyoya, au ni hizi nyingine ambazo *no ordinary* mbuzi?
> 'Are the goats [sheep] big? The ones that people get wool from, or are they the ones which [are] no ordinary goats?'
>
> (Swahili/English No. 25)

From the surrounding discourse, it seems clear the speaker is making a structurally marked choice to draw attention to the details of his question. Marked word order does what marked code choices do; they draw attention to the content, or the speaker's attitude toward the content as 'something different'.

Thus, the hypothesis about structurally-marked choices is that further study will turn up other such examples in other data sets. If there were numerous violations of the Morpheme-Order Principle, of course, [4] would no longer represent simply a marked choice but would threaten the Morpheme-Order Principle. Note, however, that example [4] relies for its emphatic effect on the fact that there is an unmarked structure.

CS and New versus Given Information

Finally, another possible pragmatic function of CS has to do with the encoding of new and given information. Preliminary analysis indicates that many of the constituents containing CS occur in sentence-final position; certainly, many of the EL islands are complements or adjuncts of the VP. Normally, sentence-final is the place where new information is positioned in monolingual discourse; sometimes this is referred to as 'the principle of end focus'. For example, Leech and Short (1981: 212) observe:

In the tone unit, there is a general tendency for given information to precede new information; that is, for the speaker to proceed from a starting point of information which is assumed to be shared by the hearer, to information which is assumed to be 'news' to the hearer, and therefore communicatively more salient.

An obvious way to make new information even more salient is to switch codes to encode it. This observation is intended as only suggestive here; but it might stimulate systematic study of the new given information distinction and the specifically pragmatic functions of CS.

The MLF Model as a Set of Options

Let me conclude this section by extending an argument which I introduced in Chapter 1. I have argued in this section that socio-pragmatic forces at all social levels *do* have an effect on *performance*, i.e. on what is present as CS data. Everything from what is the characteristic pattern of CS found in a given community (e.g. are there many ML + EL constituents?) to how an individual uses a CS utterance to convey a certain socio-pragmatic effect in a specific interaction (e.g. is there a structurally marked choice in the CS utterance?) shows the effects of socially motivated factors.

But this does not mean that there are no generalizations to be made about the structural outlines of CS. Socially motivated variation does not obviate the fact that there are apparently cognitively based constraints which set the parameters for CS. Further, that these limits are universal is empirically supported by all CS data in the literature. These data support the argument of this volume: there are specific limits on which structural strategies are possible, no matter which of an unlimited number of social scenarios prevails. What the MLF model does is offer a set of claims about what the possibilities and limits are. In short, the model claims that '*not* anything goes'.

Implications of the MLF Model for Grammatical Theory

If one assumes that the distribution of ML and EL forms in CS utterances (notably ML + EL constituents) is based on grammatical distinctions, are these distinctions also recognized within current grammatical theory? That is, how well do competing current theories accommodate the empirical facts of grammatical organization in CS? The most central distinction to consider is that between content and system morphemes, of course. How well can current syntactic theories capture this generalization? Also, some of the CS data considered here suggest certain problems for some syntactic theories. These include the usefulness of the category 'maximal projection' regarding the status of the tie between complementizers and their complements.

It is beyond the scope of this volume to do more than raise such issues. Jake and Myers-Scotton (1992) discuss at some length the extent to which several current syntactic theories fit the CS data by accommodating claims which the MLF model makes about constraints on accessing. In general, the data and the MLF model support theoretical approaches giving prominence to the lexicon.

Organization in CS

The overall scenario for the organization of CS, taking account of data and claims which have been presented throughout this volume, also has implications for psycholinguistic theories of language production. The data present in CS seem to support an incremental and modular view of language production. For example, the building of ML + EL constituents certainly seems to proceed by increments; also, the presence of double morphology suggests misfirings because some morphosyntactic procedures are contained in modules blind to each other. More important, CS data seem to support a 'top–down' model of language production. The hypothesis which seems best to account for surface CS structures is that an initial choice of abstract lemmas, entries in some (as yet) ill-defined mental lexicon, directs all morphosyntactic and lexical insertion procedures (this is basically Levelt's approach (1989)).

I suggest, however, that this 'top–down' model includes socio-pragmatic intentions which affect the choice of lemmas. This information is either included in the lemmas themselves or present in the mental lexicon in some other form. Part of the lemma's entry, then, might be information about the socio-pragmatic values indexed by the choice in a given situation of the linguistic variety for which that lemma is 'tagged'.

As I indicated in Chapter 1, using the lemma and the procedures it directs as a major unit obviates the problem of whether one must conceive of languages as discrete systems. Language-contact phenomena such as CS seem best accommodated if one thinks of the grammar of a linguistic variety as a set of lemmas, with the conditions on accessing or modifying members of some subsets more limited than that for others.

'Trouble in the Works'

Continuing with the production question, one can think of CS as a type of 'trouble in the works' for the language-production system. Because the grammars of two (or more) languages are involved, the operation of CS puts special stress on the system. What makes CS so remarkable is that this 'trouble' results in extremely little disorder in the product. That is, one can account for the structure of almost all CS utterances rather parsimoniously, as I have tried to do with the MLF model.

Finally, the CS data suggest that CS as a structural phenomenon can be accounted for by constructing models employing the same categories as those currently used in psycholinguistic and syntactic studies to account for other forms of naturally occurring linguistic data. With the addition of the provisions of the MLF model, the alternative strategies resulting in CS data can be described and explained within the terms of the grammars of the participating languages.

Afterword

While most codeswitching research supports the predictions of the Matrix Language Frame model (hereafter MLF model) as it appeared in *Duelling Languages* (hereafter *DL*), the *DL* manuscript was written in 1991–92; thus, some comments on new developments in the model and on some intervening codeswitching research seem in order in 1997. Happily, the model's discussion in *DL* often even presages new developments; still, some statements do not match current thinking. In addition, parts of the model have been misinterpreted. The goal of this 'Afterword' is to bring the model up to date, to correct misstatements, and to clear up misunderstandings.[1]

The Competence versus Production Issue

Some researchers who would distinguish the MLF model from competing models to characterize constraints on codeswitching (hereafter CS) refer to the MLF model as a production-based model, while labelling a model which they prefer (often their own model) as competence-based. The curious result is that they thereby imply that language production is unrelated to linguistic competence. Surely any trained linguist cannot mean this. Certainly, to categorize the MLF model *only* as a production model is a red herring drawn across its profile. True, the model is introduced in *DL* as 'a production-based model' (p. 6). This early characterization was intended to show links between and evidence for underlying structure from psycholinguistic research on language production and what linguists were beginning to observe in large corpora of naturally-occurring CS data. Yet, the complete sentence which 'production-based model' comes from has been largely ignored. In full, the sentence characterizing the MLF model reads: 'It is a production-based model which sees CS constraints as

[1] I gratefully acknowledge NSF grant SBR 9319780 (Carol Myers-Scotton and Janice L. Jake principal investigators) which has enabled us to conduct extensive field work on CS in a number of language pairs. I thank Janice Jake for her helpful comments on this Afterword.

set by processes which operate *well before the positional level at which surface orders and structures are realized*' (italics added).

Clearly, those descriptions of the MLF model as production-based are at best incomplete and have distracted attention from the fact that the heart of the model explains CS data by referring to the abstract level of linguistic competence. The MLF model views CS, like monolingual speech, as a natural outcome of linguistic competence. The role of linguistic competence in the model should have been clear because the two abstract theoretical constructs structuring the model, the Matrix Language (ML) versus Embedded Language (EL) distinction and the system morpheme vs. content morpheme distinction, can only derive from underlying linguistic competence. Diverse evidence (e.g. speech error data, aphasic data, child language acquisition, second language acquisition, lexical borrowing) shows that the system vs. content morpheme distinction structures language universally. The ML versus EL distinction requires two codes in order to operate. When data from such bilingual language is examined (e.g. from interlanguage in second language acquisition to language attrition, as well as CS), the concept of an ML as structuring the morphosyntactic frame is a reasonable inference. Its effects are obvious implicational evidence that the concept of an ML is part of the linguistic competence of speakers who produce utterances involving more than one linguistic code.[2] If these constructs are universally robust in explaining configurations in CS production as well as in these other forms of language production, surely the basis of such production must be a universally-present competence.

Another aspect of the MLF model which relates competence to production is the assumption that speaker intentions support projections of lexical structure. The concept of congruence (i.e. a matching of lexical structure between the abstract lexical elements of the ML and EL) is introduced at many junctures in the 1993 model in *DL* and further explicated in Myers-Scotton and Jake (1995) (hereafter *Matching*). *Matching* argues that how EL linguistic material is inserted into a frame prepared by the ML depends on congruence between the ML and EL in the mental lexicon (i.e. congruence between information encoded in counterpart ML and EL lemmas, entries in the mental lexicon). Under this view, performance is not removed from competence.

In summary, a main goal of the MLF model is to explain how EL

---

[2] Although *DL* does not explore bilingual speech at the dialectal or stylistic level, the ML construct should be salient there as well as at the level of switching between languages.

linguistic material may appear in a CP framed by an ML *in the perform-ance of CS*. That is, does a given EL content morpheme appear as a singly-occurring content lexeme (either as morphologically integrated into the ML frame or as a 'bare form'), or does it appear in an EL island (a constituent morphosyntactically well-formed in the EL), if it appears at all? The model argues that the grammatical information at the abstract level of linguistic competence determines the answer to this question, *not the external conditions of the performance/production itself.* How similar grammatical information (e.g. features of tense/aspect) is 'bundled' in the lemmas along with the other features of lexical-conceptual structure and the 'match' of this bundling between the ML and the EL decides how EL material is realized in performance. This is a general claim of *Matching* and it is made more specific in Jake and Myers-Scotton (1996) (in refer-ence to a mismatch between English and Arabic verbs affecting the production of English verbs in CS when Arabic is the ML; see example [7] below). That such claims constitute hypotheses about how bilingual language production operates should not obscure the fact that it is linguistic competence which must underlie such processes.

The fact is that, at this time, all hypotheses about Language (of any type, in any context) regarding competence are supported by performance data. The question is whether the 'performance' is derived from exten-sive corpora of naturally-occurring data or, at the other extreme, gram-maticality judgements/native speaker intuitions by linguists with vested interests in a particular model.[3]

To return to CS, I see the MLF model best characterized in this way: because CS is part of the competence of the bilingual speaker, looking at how syntactic structures are projected from abstract lexical entries will provide explanations for the structure of CS. This view contrasts with predictions that language equivalences of certain lexical categories in syntactic projections at the surface level determine what constitute 'grammatical' CS utterances. Such predictions are at best motivated solely by the theoretical framework in which they are formulated. This is so whether such efforts rely on surface linear order (Poplack and associates, e.g. Meecham and Poplack, 1995) or more abstract phrase structure configurations (e.g. Belazi *et al.*, 1994; Mahootian and Santorini, 1996; Bhatia and Ritchie, 1996). Further, to date, such efforts have not succeeded descriptively either (i.e. there are many counter-examples).

---

[3] In general, Linguistics differs from most other social sciences in that developing a standard methodology for data collection has not been a priority. See Schütze (1996) for an interesting discussion.

In order to explain CS configurations, a model must 'begin' where bilingual utterances begin, with abstract lexical structure and its projections. Thus, a bilingual competence model which includes the notion that participating languages are matched for congruence, with implications for production, is required. The MLF model is such a model. Its goal is to provide an account for what must be part of the bilingual speaker's *universally-present competence* (innate component) which is necessary in order to engage in CS as it is *empirically-evident* (i.e. as it actually occurs).

The Proper Unit of Analysis for CS Constraints on Mixed Constituents

An important change in the MLF model since *DL* first appeared is that the unit of analysis now is the CP (X^{Max} of COMP). The CP has been used in extended versions of the MLF model (e.g. *Matching*, 1995; Jake and Myers-Scotton, 1996; Finlayson *et al.*, 1996). In *DL*, the implied unit of analysis is the sentence, since *DL* clearly states that intrasentential CS is the subject of study. However, in fact, the constraints presented as the MLF model do not refer to the full sentence, but rather to 'constituents'. These constituents are always maximal projections within a CP, although, of course, they are also within a sentence. Therefore, the constraints presented (e.g. the Morpheme Order Principle, the System Morpheme Principle, the Blocking Hypothesis, and the EL island hypotheses) are not invalidated at all by my stating that the proper unit of analysis is the CP. That is, the theoretical discussion in *DL* of these constraints needs no modification; explicitly stating that CP, as opposed to Sentence, should be the domain of analysis simply allows for more precision in testing the constraints since what counts as switching within a CP is clearer than what would be 'intrasentential' switching.

Why use the CP as the unit of analysis? First, as a recognizable unit in syntactic theory, the CP is less ambiguous than either 'sentence' or 'clause'. Second, CP is the syntactic unit at which parameter settings and universal principles are realized (e.g. conditions on binding). Note that since many sentences involving CS contain more than one CP, these may be a mixed CP and a monolingual CP.

I will still speak of 'constituents', with the understanding that a constituent may be part of a larger constituent, i.e. an NP may be a constituent of a VP which is a constituent of an IP which is a constituent of a CP. In [1], *team* occurs in the mixed NP *ein team* 'a team' in a larger mixed constituent, a VP composed of the mixed NP and the ML separable prefix verb *an-ge-fangen* 'begin (past participle)'.[4]

[1] [$_{CP}$dann hab-en [$_{IP}$sie [$_{VP}$ [$_{NP}$ein   *team*] an-ge-fang-en],
     then have-3P   they   a/N/ACC team (to)-PP-begin-PP,
[$_{NP}$ein   *AIDS care team*]]; [$_{CP}$dann hab-en sie   mir
     a/N/ACC AIDS care team,   then have-3P they 1S/DAT
ge-sag-t, . . .
PP-say-PP, . . .
'Then they started a team, an AIDS care team; then they told me, . . .'

(German/English; Fuller, 1995 C2: [52])

How is a CP containing CS identified? As *DL* makes clear, the MLF model provides for three types of CS constituents: (1) ML + EL constituents consist of morphemes from both the ML and EL (typically including only singly-occurring content morphemes from the EL) in a grammatical frame set by the ML; (2) ML islands are constituents which consist only of ML morphemes and which follow ML constraints on well-formedness; and (3) EL islands are constituents which consist only of EL morphemes and which follow EL constraints on well-formedness. Since EL islands occur *within* a CP, EL islands cannot be CPs themselves.[5]

In order for a CP to qualify as a mixed CP, it must contain minimally either an ML + EL constituent or an EL island; the remainder may be in the ML. Example [8], discussed below, illustrates how superficially complex CS data involving Zulu/English CS receive an explanation when analysed in terms of the CP as the unit of analysis; its 'complex' structure conforms to the predictions of MLF model.

The 'centrepiece' of a CP containing CS (a mixed CP) is generally an ML + EL constituent, and a larger ML + EL constituent may well contain either ML or EL islands. In particular, the idea that such a larger mixed constituent may contain an EL island, in addition to the singly-occurring EL lexemes which qualify it as an ML + EL constituent, has not been well understood by some commentators on the model. Example [2] illustrates such configurations, with Arabic as the ML. In the first CP in [2], *including labor* is an English EL island in a larger mixed constituent. A singly-occurring lexeme *dollar* also occurs in a mixed NP constituent in the CP. The remainder of the CP is from Arabic. Arabic also frames the

---

[4] This VP occurs in an IP, out of which AUX (*haben* 'have-3P') has raised into COMP. An adverb *dann* 'then' is in SPEC of CP.

[5] In a few cases of identifying EL islands, I do refer to a full CP as an EL island. Under my current thinking, of course, full CPs cannot be EL islands since islands occur *within* a CP. Fortunately, the examples incorrectly labelled as islands are few.

second CP. An EL island predicate adjective phrase *too much* occurs in an otherwise null IP; Arabic requires neither a copula nor a subject. The demonstrative *hada* is in a discourse emphatic position preceding IP.

[2] $[_{CP}[_{IP}$dafaʔ $[_{VP}[_{NP}$alf *dollar*] $[_{AP}$*including labor*]]]];
  PERF/3M/pay thousand dollar including labor
$[_{CP}$hada $[_{IP}$*too much*]]
  this   too much
'[He] paid [a] thousand dollars including labor; this [is] too much'

(Palestinian Arabic/English; Okasha, 1995, 5:3)

The ML controls grammatical configurations within all constituents of a mixed CP. Note that this is a more general claim than the one made in *DL* about the role of the ML. In ML + EL constituents (mixed constituents), this control is formalized in the Morpheme Order and the System Morpheme Principles. In EL islands, while well-formedness conditions conform to those of the EL, such constituents are under the control of the ML in various ways. Most notably, their placement conforms to ML requirements. In addition, while internal EL islands must be well-formed in the EL, their structure also must meet ML requirements for the constituent in question. The phrase structure of internal EL islands in CS corpora is sketched in *DL* (Chapter 5, pp. 151–4); such islands are discussed again in *Matching* with emphasis on their structural relation to ML requirements. Example [3] illustrates an internal EL island from Moroccan Arabic/French CS. The NP *la régulation* is a well-formed maximal constituent in the EL French, but it is part of a larger NP constituent in the ML Arabic.[6] In Arabic, demonstrative NPs require definite articles; i.e. the demonstrative NP is an N-triple bar which selects a definite N-double bar.

[3] tajʒiw   tajdiru   dak *la régulation*   djal
  T-A/IMPF/come/3P T-A/IMPF/take/3P that the regulation of
les naissances bhal daba tajbʁiw   jħaddu   nsel, . . .
  the births   like now T-A/IMPF/want/3P SUBJ/limit/3P birth/P, . . .
'They come and do that [the] limitation of the births, for example, they want to limit births'

(Moroccan Arabic/French; Bentahila and Davies, 1992: 450, morpheme gloss added to original)

---

[6] Bentahila (1995) questions the ability of researchers to identify the ML on the basis of a single sentence from corpora which they have not themselves collected. In spite of this caveat, it is often possible to identify the ML in single CPs. Also, in the interests of comprehensiveness, it is necessary to test hypotheses against any available data, whether or not it meets ideal conditions for identifying the ML.

The Construct of the Matrix Language

As should be evident from the discussion above, the idea that explaining configurations in CS requires the distinguishing of one of the participating languages as the ML and the other(s) as the Embedded Languages (ELs) remains central to the MLF model. Yet, the ML as a construct needs additional comment now because of misunderstandings which have arisen and because all aspects of the earlier discussion of the ML now seem less on the mark than they did earlier.

First, some readers have misunderstood where the concept of an ML would apply. Some have tried to apply the ML concept to all CPs in discourse samples consisting of not just mixed CPs, but also monolingual CPs. However, the ML versus EL opposition is only relevant within a CP showing CS. That is, the ML versus EL opposition only applies when at least two codes are present in the same CP. Perhaps the reason the concept of an ML confused some researchers may be that they have confounded it with a designation which applies to discourse as a unit, such as 'dominant language' (e.g. Lanza, 1992) or 'unmarked choice' (Myers-Scotton, 1993*b*). While the ML may well coincide with a dominant language or unmarked choice in discourse, this is a separate issue from its role in the grammatical analysis of a mixed CP.

Second, the discussion in Chapter 3 of *DL* of the ML (pp. 66–9) is misguided in some ways and apparently also misleading. The major problem is that this discussion attempts to identify the ML empirically. I now realize that the ML is only identified implicationally through its operations. That is, the ML is a theoretical construct, not an element which is empirically-realized; therefore, it is not subject to definition or directly falsifiable. Further, evidence from previously unexamined data sets shows that the empirically-based definition of the ML offered in Chapter 3 of *DL* does not always hold or is difficult to apply unambiguously; therefore, it should be abandoned. (Recall the claim there is that the ML is 'the language of more morphemes in interaction types including intrasentential CS'.)

Within Linguistics, examples of other theoretical constructs are 'sentence' or 'word'. Like the ML, they are not easy to define in any absolute sense; yet, they are essential in formulating characterizations of linguistic structure. As a theoretical construct, the ML is used in expressing hypotheses which are subject to falsifiability. If the hypotheses which a theoretical construct generate are supported, this indirectly supports the efficacy of the construct. For example, the ML's role as a theorectical construct in CS is supported by testing the hypotheses in which it figures in the MLF model: the Morpheme Order Principle and the System Morpheme Principle. In all the original examples cited in *DL* and in those in this new afterword, the language which corresponds to the ML of these principles is labelled the ML, while the other participating language is labelling the EL.

Another way of looking at the ML is to characterize it as a theoretic principle. The role of such principles is to pose problems, with other parts of a theory designed to solve them. Thus, a major 'problem' which the ML poses is this: in reference to a mixed constituent in CS, if the grammatical frame (i.e. function words and inflections as system morphemes, as well as morpheme order) is attributed to one and only one of the participating languages (labelled the ML), does this characterization capture an important generalization? The answer is 'yes'; the generalization achieved is that only one language (designated the ML) sets the frame of all mixed constituents within a CP showing CS. Furthermore, in the typical CS data set, the prediction that the same language is the frame-setting ML for all such CPs (at least for the same speaker) is generally upheld (although the dynamic nature of the ML is discussed in *DL* in Chapter 3 and in this afterword as well).

Note that such generalizations would not be possible without a construct which applies to the entire CP in question. Other models or discussions recognize that there is a matching between what are called functional elements (i.e. system morphemes) within a single maximal projection; in fact, their main hypotheses generally embody this idea (e.g. Belazi *et al.*, 1994; Santorini and Mahootian, 1996). Yet, such models do not structure their hypotheses around the construct of the ML. The result is that they overpredict possible utterances since—without an ML— they allow for the possibility of the source of system morphemes to change from one constituent to another within the same CP.

Perhaps these researchers are choosing to characterize CS as a narrower phenomenon than it actually is.[7] Their predictions are so phrased that they seem to assume that one language *always* provides the functional elements and therefore that making reference to an ML versus the

---

[7] The converse of this is viewing the structure of CS as socially determined, a position argued against in Chapter 8 in *DL* and in Myers-Scotton (1993*c*). Which option is taken up from the set of structural options *available* can be under the influence of locally-based social (e.g. degree of integration of speakers into the community) or psycholinguistic factors (e.g. degree of proficiency). Yet the set of options itself is based on universally-present linguistic competence.

EL is irrelevant. They do not realize that by not formalizing the construct of ML, they are, in fact, making predictions. If CS took place in a static social situation and if one language were always clearly dominant, it is true that characterizing CS would be simpler.

Recall that the motivation for CS in the first place is largely social; briefly, speakers switch languages because the additional code enables them to project another dimension of their personae or to negotiate a change in their relations with co-participants in conversation (cf., e.g. Gardner-Chloros, 1991; Heller, 1988; Myers-Scotton, 1993*b*).[8] Speakers can so use languages to index attitudes and relations because linguistic codes acquire social and psychological values, thanks to who their typical speakers are, and where and when they are typically used. Generally, one language dominates in CS from a discourse point of view and which language assumes this role depends on the values carried by linguistic choices which conversational participants wish to make salient in the given interaction. In most cases, this discourse-dominant language is also the ML of mixed CPs. Yet, such dominance is dynamic; it is subject to change when social factors and attitudes change over time, or when language proficiency changes, whether on an individual or community-wide basis, as discussed in Chapter 3. Also, the fact that discourse dominance is dynamic may contribute to the possibility of the ML changing within a conversation containing CS; a satisfactory model of CS must allow for that possibility.

Complex Lexical Structure

That congruence (or lack of it) between languages across abstract lexical structure explains CS data is an idea clearly introduced in *DL*; the Blocking Hypothesis relies on this idea and it is also mentioned as an explanation for other phenomena, such as bare forms or 'do constructions'. However, as the model has evolved, it has become clearer and clearer what a central role such congruence plays in explaining permissible CS

---

[8] Not surprisingly, some researchers use terminology which implies that they perceive relations between languages in CS as related to language dominance. They refer to 'host' and 'guest' languages in their discussion of structural constraints on CS (e.g. Sridhar and Sridhar 1980) or they label the participating languages in psycholinguistic experiments as the 'base' and 'guest' languages (e.g. Grosjean and Miller 1994).

structures. Recall that the Blocking Hypothesis (Chapter 5) blocks any EL content morpheme which is not congruent with the ML in certain ways. First, the EL morpheme must have an ML content morpheme as its counterpart; second, it must match that morpheme in terms of thematic role assignment; and third, it must match 'in tems of their discourse or pragmatic functions' (pp. 120–1). The idea of congruence is made both more general and more specific in *Matching* where my colleague and I refer to levels or subsystems of complex lexical structure. The three levels are: lexical–conceptual structure (semantics and input for pragmatic readings), predicate–argument structure (relations between verbs and prepositions and their arguments) and morphological realization patterns (surface requirements for well-formedness, including word order). (Such ideas about lexical structure are motived by Talmy, 1985 and Jakendoff, 1990, inter alia.) The three levels are present simultaneously although not necessary activated at the same time.

Thus, in ML + EL constituents within mixed CPs, such as those illustrated in [4], there is sufficient congruence at the lemma level (where the check of matching lexical structure is made) between the EL elements and ML counterparts so that several EL content morphemes can be morphosyntactically integrated into the ML frame as singly-occurring lexemes. Example [4] illustrates how congruence is played out in a typical conversational exchange from the Nairobi corpus. EL material in this example includes several singly-occurring EL (English) lexemes (a noun *secretary*, a verb *complain*, and an adverb *late*) and an EL island (*any letter*). As the MLF model is now conceptualized, the possibility for singly-occurring EL lexemes to be inserted into an ML frame, integrated from a morphosyntactic point of view, exists because their match with ML counterparts is sufficient at all levels of abstract lexical structure.[9] The EL island (*any letter*) is selected over its Swahili counterpart (*barua yo yote*); the major stylistic advantage which *any letter* offers is that the initial position of the quantifier emphasizes its message. In this example, the claim is that EL lexical material is chosen instead of an ML counterpart because it satisfies the speaker's semantic/pragmatic intentions better than the corresponding ML form. Below, additional reasons for selecting EL islands are discussed.

---

[9] Note, however, that *secretary* could be considered a bare form: while Swahili has no determiners as such, nouns typically occur with a demonstrative as a modifier, but this case is ambiguous since *secretary* could be considered as a title.

[4] Setting: Conversation in a Nairobi office

SPEAKER 1:   . . . Hesbon ha-ja-pat-a   *any letter*
    . . . Hesbon NEG/3S-not/yet-get-FV any letter
    ha-tu-ju-i   kama *secretary*
    NEG-1P-know-NEG/PRES if   secretary
    ha-ku-andik-a
    NEG/3S-NEG/PAST-write-FV
    'Hesbon hasn't yet received any letter. We don't know whether [the] secretary wrote [it].'

SPEAKER 2:   Wa-tu   we-ngi   wa-me-*complain*   juu
    NC2-people NC2-many NC2-T/A-complain about
    ku-to-pat-a   barua ama
    INFIN-NEG-get-FV letter or
    ku-zi-pat-a   *late.*
    INFIN-NC10/OBJ-get-FV late
    'Many people have complained about not receiving letters or receiving them late.'

(Swahili/English; Myers-Scotton, Nairobi Corpus No. 23)

What is said about EL islands in *DL* needs revision. EL islands are treated under two hypotheses, the EL Island Trigger Hypothesis (p. 139) and the EL Hierarchy Hypothesis (p. 144). The 'trigger' hypothesis suggested that EL islands are obligatorily created when an EL morpheme 'not licensed under the ML' (and therefore including either an EL system morpheme or an EL content morpheme which should have been blocked by the Blocking Hypothesis) is accessed. Whether this accessing is 'by error' or not is left open. The 'hierarchy' hypothesis covers what were thought to be optional EL islands. This hypothesis sets up a hierarchy of likely optional islands, beginning with formulaic expressions and idioms as the most likely such islands. I now think that *all* EL islands are obligatory. Thus, I propose the following new EL Island Hypothesis to replace both of the earlier ones:

> EL Island Hypothesis: When there is insufficient congruence between the lemma underlying an EL content morpheme and its ML counterpart at one or more of the three levels of lexical structure, the only way to access the EL element is in an EL island.

(Note that the EL content morpheme is projected at the conceptual level, but would not be accessed, of course, until the surface level. Also, note that what constitutes 'insufficient congruence' needs more study. Current research indicates it is language pair-specific, although it has become clear that similar 'sites' of incongruence certainly occur cross-linguistically.)

The remainder of this section discusses the role of incongruence in EL island formation. However, it does not replace what is said about EL islands in Chapter 4. Rather, it offers more precise motivations for EL islands. To date, three main sources of incongruence resulting in EL islands have been identified.

In some data sets, the most frequent islands will result from lack of congruence at the lexical–conceptual level, either in terms of semantic or pragmatic implications (as is spelled out in *Matching*). Thus, the most frequent EL island may well be that which the 'hierarchy' hypothesis had put at the top of its list: formulaic expressions or idioms, or at least regularly collocated expressions, such as *from a good family* in example [5]. This is because such expressions often do not translate across languages with exactly the same semantic-pragmatic import.

[5] I-ngeyo en pe tye [$_{PP}$*from a good family*] tutwal
    2S-know 1S NEG COP from a good family really
   'You know [that] she is not really from a good family'

(Acholi/English; Myers-Scotton and Bernsten, 1995, Rashid 3.1)

Incongruence at the level of morphological realization patterns accounts for many EL islands. For example, consider [6], as discussed in *Matching*. The EL (English) lemma projecting the morphosyntactic structure of *bring up* calls for the pronominal object of English to occur before the 'satellite' particle. In Spanish an equivalent concept would be conveyed by *no lo van a sacar*, which includes a verb without a satellite (*sacar*) and which places the pronominal object (*lo*) immediately preceding a finite verb or following a non-finite verb. Assume that the speaker felt that *bring up* (with a pronominal object) best conveyed his/her intentions; then, the only way to realize *bring up* and still maintain Spanish as the ML in a mixed CP would be in an EL island.

[6] no va-n a *bring it up*
    no go-3P to bring it up
   'They aren't going to bring it up'

(Spanish/English; Pfaff, 1979: 296; cited in Myers-Scotton and Jake, 1995: 996)

A third source of EL islands seems to be lack of congruence regarding what information about morphological realization patterns is entered in the lemma which supports the content head of a phrase. This is first discussed in Jake and Myers-Scotton (1996). For example, consider [7].

Although Arabic and English verbs may be congruent at the level of lexical-conceptual structure, English verbs typically cannot be inflected with Arabic verbal morphology when Arabic is the ML. Two other structures occur. In the data sets examined for Jake and Myers-Scotton (1996), IP EL islands are the most common. In the Arabic/English corpora in the database, 86 (79 per cent) of all English verbs (including participles) occur in IP EL islands. The relevant bilingual CP consists of an Arabic element in COMP or Specifier of COMP position, followed by a well-formed IP entirely in English. As will be made clear in the section on system morphemes, my associates and I now argue that the prevalence of English IP EL islands in Arabic/English CS can be explained by the distinction of system morpheme types. In [7], a subordinator in COMP, agreeing with the third person subject of the IP, *li?anuhum* 'because/3P', precedes an EL (English) IP.

[7] huma butudfa?ooli   kul haga [_{CP}li?anuhum
    they HAB/IMPF/pay/3P/to/1S all thing   because/3P
[_{IP}*they can afford it*]]
    they can afford it
'They pay for everything for me because they can afford it'

(Palestinian Arabic/English; Okasha, 1995: 3.34)

A second example, from Zulu/English CS, also illustrates an IP EL island. An EL (English) discourse emphatic element *so* and a topicalized NP (a mixed constituent consisting of a mixed NP (*i-language* '[the] language') modified by a relative clause (*e-khuluny-w-a a-ma-gangs* 'spoken [by] [the] gangs', also a mixed constituent) occur in SPEC of CP, before the English IP. This example is interesting because, although the EL provides many surface morphemes, the only EL system morphemes which occur are in an EL island. In mixed constituents, all system morphemes come from just one language, the ML. Thus, Zulu contributes system morphemes to the mixed NPs *i-language* and *a-ma-gangs*, and to the inflected ML verb, *e-khuluny-w-a*.

[8] [_{CP}*so* [_{NP}*i-language* [_{CP}e-khuluny-w-a   a-ma-*gangs*]]]
    So NC9-language NC9/REL-speak-PASS-FV PREP-NC6-gangs
[_{IP}*it differs from one gang to another*]]
[_{IP}it differs from one gang to another]]
'So the language which is spoken by [the] gangs, it differs from one gang to another.'

(Zulu/English; Finlayson *et al.*, 1996)

A New Way of Considering System Morphemes

Such CS data as the English IP EL islands in Arabic/English CS motivate the hypothesis that there are two different types of system morphemes.[10] These are those which are 'indirectly-elected' at the conceptual level (Bock and Levelt, 1994) and those which are 'structurally-assigned'. Directions for those which are indirectly-elected either are included in the lemma which supports the content morpheme selecting them, or this lemma 'points to' the lemma underlying the indirectly-elected system morpheme. Generally, such system morphemes 'flesh out' the content of their head content element in some way necessary to convey the intended meaning. In contrast, rules of the language-specific grammar determine the nature and form of structurally-assigned system morphemes. They typically involve cross-phrasal specifications (e.g. subject–verb agreement). While, of course, structurally-assigned system morphemes also add to the meaning of their head content element, what they add is often redundant. In mixed constituents, EL content morphemes are inflected with these structurally-assigned system morphemes from the ML. They may or may not be so inflected with indirectly-elected ML system morphemes; what happens needs further study, but seems to depend on the particular grammatical category.[11]

For clarification, consider the case of Arabic/English CS. The claim is that EL IP islands can be explained by the distinction of system morpheme types. The hypothesis is that in English, tense/aspect is structurally-assigned. This means that the lemma underlying an English verbal entry does not include tense/aspect. (It would include directions to activate the necessary procedures to structurally-assign tense/aspect in the formulator

---

[10] The idea that there may be differences among system morphemes regarding links to their heads is at least raised in *DL* (p. 53).

[11] For example, it now seems that noun class prefixes in Bantu languages are indirectly-elected system morphemes. When the Bantu languages of a CS pair is the ML, while EL nouns often occur in mixed constituents framed by the ML, these nouns often occur as bare forms (i.e. without Bantu noun class prefixes) and/or are placed in nouns classes with zero allomorphs as minimal prefixes. Class membership is obvious from the agreement prefixes on other elements in the constituent, such as the subject prefix on the verb.) At the same time, in most data sets, at least some EL plural nouns take the class six (plural) prefix, *ma-*. Possibly this prefix has been bleached of some of its indigenous 'pointing functions' and has become simply a mechanism for morphologically integrating plural EL nouns into the ML frame. As indicated in *DL*, many of these EL nouns with the *ma-* prefix also receive the EL plural suffix, also an indirectly-elected EL system morpheme. That these EL doublets are accessed because of 'mis-timing' seems even more plausible if these doublets are distinguished as indirectly-elected system morphemes because of the close attachment of indirectly-elected system morphemes to their heads (both are conceptually-activated at the same level).

where the morphosyntax is set.) In contrast, in Arabic, tense/aspect is indirectly elected *along with* the content morphemes specifying them. This means that the lemma entry underlying an Arabic verbal entry necessarily includes tense/aspect. In fact, there is no such thing as an Arabic verb 'stem' without tense/aspect specified.

Thus, when a speaker 'decides' to use an English verb in an Arabic-framed CP, the English lemma supporting this verb does not 'qualify' as containing the necessary specifications (which are contained in the lemma underlying the Arabic verb) to receive Arabic verbal inflections. Because of this incongruence between Arabic and English regarding the abstract status of tense/aspect system morphemes, the only way to 'realize' a semantically and pragmatically congruent English verb is as a verb with English verbal morphology. This means that system morphemes under INFL must come from English, and the result is a constituent completed entirely in English, i.e. an EL IP island.[12]

The Content versus System Morpheme Distinction Revisited

One of the major innovations of the MLF model was to formalize an asymmetry in co-occurrence restrictions on morphemes: while EL content morphemes may appear in mixed constituent (provided they are sufficiently congruent with an ML counterpart), syntactically active EL system morphemes may not. As is duly noted in *DL*, many earlier researchers commented anecdotally on this asymmetry and Joshi (1985) discussed it extensively. In *DL*, the System Morpheme Principle captures the relevant generalization of these insights, and a lengthy discussion in *DL* (pp. 98–102) offers ways to distinguish what it refers to as system morphemes versus content morphemes. That exposition deserves some support here, but also needs some revision.

First, why does the MLF model use the term 'system morpheme' rather than 'closed class item' (which Joshi used and which many psycholinguists use) or 'functional element' which GB-inspired models use (e.g. Belazi *et al.*, 1994)? The simple answer is that these terms do not cover the same morphemes and therefore do not achieve the same generalizations. The distinction of open versus closed class refers to the ease with which lexical categories (i.e. words, not morphemes) accept new members, either neologisms or borrowings. Like-wise, the notion 'functional' (versus thematic) is a category-defining feature. Approaches to CS adopting either the

---

[12] Additional minor strategies to allow for English verbs in Arabic frames include uninflected or bare English verbs or an English verb in a 'do' construction.

notion of closed versus open class or functional versus thematic category make predictions assuming that all members of these classes/categories behave identically in CS. In contrast, system versus content morpheme is not a syntactic or lexical category-defining feature.

After studying, thinking, and writing about types of morphemes in bilingual speech for a number of years, I remain convinced that the content versus system morphemes distinction captures a generalization which other designations for morphemes miss. First, the problem with 'functional elements' as a cogent category in explaining CS is that not all members of such categories (e.g. pronouns, prepositions) behave the same way cross linguistically. For example, Jake (1994) demonstrates empirically that not all pronouns may occur in the same CS configurations. She addresses the research question, why do EL pronouns occur much more freely in some CS data sets than in others? Recognizing that the more freely occurring ones are content morphemes in their respective languages while those with a more limited occurrence are system morphemes explains this difference. Second, using the content versus system morpheme distinction as a theoretical construct illuminates the differential roles of morpheme types and their relationship to each other in a way which the other characterizations do not achieve. Content morphemes 'relate' the lexicon to P-markers, and system morphemes grammaticize this relationship. To put it another way: in the composition of linguistic structures, content morphemes contribute whatever semantic and pragmatic messages the speaker wishes to convey and, in this initiating role, they project directions selecting the system morphemes which are the nuts and bolts—the grammatical system—which give the constituent its form.

One major addition to the discussion of morpheme types in *DL* which is relevant to explaining CS is provided by the 1995 article *Matching*. In this, my colleague and I expand the notion of thematic roles to include discourse-thematic roles. We argue that speaker intentions can set up or project grammatical structures reflecting *discourse thematic elements* such as Topic, Focus, or Contrast. Operating at the discourse level, these thematic roles are not necessarily related to the theta grid of CP/IP parse structures. Thus, because discourse markers assign such discourse-thematic roles, we classify them as content morphemes at the discourse level. For example, in the sentence *He arived late; therefore, he missed the plane*, *therefore* is a discourse-level content morpheme. Its discourse-level thematic role is to restrict the range of possibly relevant implicatures of the following CP. Following this discussion, I now argue that such discourse markers as *so* in example [8] (above) are content morphemes.

Similarly, certain other lexemes, such as emphatic pronouns, also are content morphemes. Such pronouns have the discourse-relevant role of Topicalizer. (In most syntactic analyses, topic or emphatic pronouns are considered as occurring in Specifier position of COMP of CP.)

A remaining problem regarding the content versus system morpheme distinction is what to do with complementizers. It now seems clear that their characterization in *DL* as system morphemes is generally wrong (although in some languages, such as Arabic, some complementizers are multi-morphemic and include an inflectional element which is a system morpheme). Rather, in general, complementizers pattern like discourse markers; that is, they assign discourse-relevant thematic roles to the CPs which they head. Note that two different predictions which state that COMP must come from only one of the participating languages are not universally supported. First, the prediction in *DL* (p. 130) that if COMP is realized, it will come from the ML does not always hold. This has become clear as more data sets were studied following the publication of *DL*. Still, this constraint does hold categorically in many data sets (e.g. Egyptian Arabic/English CS in Eid, 1992; Palestinian Arabic/English in Okasha, 1995; Chicheŵa/English in Simango, 1995). Second, the prediction about the language 'feature' of COMP of the Functional Head Constraint of Belazi *et al.* (1994) is even less often supported. The claim there is that COMP matches the language of the following CP; yet, there are many counter-examples (e.g. Spanish/English CS in Milian, 1996; Hungarian/English CS in Bolonyai, 1996). Of course, when COMP is a content morpheme, as I now suggest it can be, it should be able to come from either the ML or the EL, as long as there is sufficient congruence. In such cases, COMP need not match the language of its CP. Why it often must come from the ML obviously needs further study.

Singly Occurring Content Morphemes as CS Lexemes or Borrowed Lexemes

Chapter 6 discusses the relation of lexical borrowing to singly-occurring CS lexemes. The argument is that there is little or no difference in their morphosyntactic integration into the grammatical frame of a recipient language (= ML in the case of CS data). Accordingly, there is no motivation to separate out borrowed lexemes if the researcher is proposing to account for the occurrence of EL material in an ML frame in CS data sets. Further, related constraints (i.e. those in the MLF model) can account for the participatory roles of the two (or more) languages in CS data sets, whether singly occurring lexemes or full constituents are at issue. Thus, even though others continue to set aside (some) singly-occurring lexemes when they propose constraints on CS (e.g. Meecham and Poplack, 1995; Belazi *et al.*, 1994), the facts call for no revision of the position taken in *DL*.

The Matrix Language as a Composite

A major argument developed in Chapter 7 of *DL* is that a turnover of the ML is the mechanism resulting in most, if not all, of the cases of 'structural borrowing' (i.e. system morphemes are 'borrowed'). Such an explanation offers a unified way to explain what may have been considered unrelated language contact phenomena, such as mixed languages, language shift, language death, and the development of pidgins/creoles. This chapter includes the cautionary remark that such a claim is only a hypothesis and would have to be tested empirically.

As I have become aware of more data sets for related phenomena (e.g. Kuhberg, 1992 and Kaufman and Aronhoff, 1992, which provide evidence of an ML turnover in child language bilingual production; Savić (1995) and Fuller (1996), which deal with an ML turnover in convergence), I am more and more convinced that the hypothesis can be supported. However, I have also refined the hypothesis to take account of my current ideas that lexical structure is complex (as discussed above). In monolingual proficient speech, or in 'classic' CS (i.e. when speakers are proficient in the ML), the lexical structure framing a relevant CP comes from the relevant single language. However, in bilingual speech where speaker proficiency is problematic in the 'target' ML, lexical structure may have multiple sources.

Thus the new hypothesis is that, in bilingual speech, lexical structure can be split such that all of its subsystems need not come from the same language system. This idea is developed most fully in Myers-Scotton (forthcoming 1997*a*; 1997*b*) for language attrition and convergence and in even more detail by Jake (1996) for interlanguage in second language acquisition. For example, parts or all of the lexical–conceptual structure supporting a content morpheme may come from one language, with the morphological realization patterns coming from another language. For example, in example [9], there is not a single language as the ML. Even though all the morphemes in the verb in this example come from

Pennsylvania German (PG), parts of its lexical structure come from English. PG *bringe* subcategorizes for an NP object and a PP *mit sich* 'with it/themselves'. Yet, it appears in [9] with the morphological realization pattern of its English cognate *bring*; i.e. an English verbal pattern occurring in a PG frame.

> [9] Die   *seid effects* oefters bring-e   *giddiness*
>   DET side effects often   bring-3P giddiness
> Std. Ger.: Die   Neben-wirkung-en bring-en oft   Schwindigkeit mit
>   DET side-effect-P   bring-3P often giddiness   with
> sich
> REFL
> 'The side effects often bring giddiness.'
>
> (Pennsylvania German/English; Enninger, 1979: 348)

In line with this hypothesis that lexical structure can come from multiple sources in language contact phenomena, my associates and I refer to the components from two or more linguistic systems which provide grammatical structure for a relevant constituent as the *composite ML*. For example, in Myers-Scotton (1997*a*) I develop the notion that a composite ML structures constituents when language attrition takes place; also, in Myers-Scotton (1997*c*) I speculate that the best way to describe the components structuring constituents in pidgin/creole development is as a composite ML.

The basic constructs of the MLF model are being extended to explain the structures of language contact phenomena other than 'classic' CS phenomena in which a single language does not fill the role of ML and an ML turnover may well be in progress. In various publications (e.g. Myers-Scotton, 1996*a*; 1997*b*), I propose that there is a 'Matrix Language Recognition Principle' which states that the lexical structure of bilingual CPs is constrained by the lexical structure of an ML and that there is always an ML, and only one ML at a time, even if this is a composite ML. I also propose a 'Morpheme Sorting Principle' which states that content and system morphemes are subject to different constraints on occurrence in all language contact phenomena, and that when there is not sufficient access to the grammatical system of the preferred ML, system morphemes may be left out or reanalysed as part of their lexical (i.e. content morpheme) head. Further, in the later stages of ML turnover, system morphemes may come from several sources. Thus, rather than just hypothesizing that an ML turnover 'happens' (as I do in Chapter 7 of *DL*), I now attempt to predict its particulars in an explanatory way.

This 'Afterword' is written in the spirit of clarification. As is evident, the MLF model is a work in progress. In addition to my own research, the work of others has aided me in my attempts to characterize further what happens in CS and how the principles structuring CS apply to other language contact phenomena. The extent of recent and ongoing research by many others is evidence of the robustness of our enterprise.

References

ANJUM, T. (1991), 'Urdu–English Code-Switching in the Speech of Pakistani Women in Texas'. Ph.D., Univ. of Texas, Austin.

ANNAMALAI, E. (1989), 'The Language Factor in Code Mixing', *International Journal of the Sociology of Language*, 75: 47–54.

ANSRE, G. (1971), 'The Influence of English on West Africa Languages', in J. Spencer (ed.), *The English Language in West Africa*, 145–64. London: Longman.

APPEL, R., and MUYSKEN, P. (1987), *Language Contact and Bilingualism*. London: Edward Arnold.

ASHTON, E. O. (1944), *Swahili Grammar*. London: Longman.

AZUMA, S. (1991*a*), 'Processing and Intrasentential Code-Switching'. Ph.D., Univ. of Texas, Austin.

——(1991*b*), 'Two Level Processing Hypothesis in Speech Production: Evidence from Intrasentential Code-Switching', paper presented at the 27th Chicago Linguistic Society Meeting, May.

BACKUS, A. (1990), 'Turkish–Dutch Codeswitching and the Frame Process Model', paper presented at the International Workshop on Ethnic Minority Languages in Europe, Tilburg, Netherlands, Dec.

BAETENS-BEARDSMORE, H. (1982), *Bilingualism: Basic Principles*. Clevedon, Avon: Multilingual Matters.

BENTAHILA, A., and DAVIES, E. D. (1983), 'The Syntax of Arabic–French Code-Switching', *Lingua*, 59: 301–30.

————(1992), 'Code-Switching and Language Dominance', in R. J. Harris (ed.), *Cognitive Processing in Bilinguals*, 443–58. Amsterdam: Elsevier.

BERG, T. (1987), 'The Case against Accommodation: Evidence from German Speech Error Data', *Journal of Memory and Language*, 26: 277–99.

BERK-SELIGSON, S. (1986), 'Linguistic Constraints on Intrasentential Code-Switching: A Study of Spanish–Hebrew Bilingualism', *Language in Society*, 15: 313–48.

BERNSTEN, J. (1990), 'The Integration of English Loans in Shona: Social Correlates and Linguistic Consequences'. Ph.D., Michigan State Univ., East Lansing.

——(1992), Personal communication.

——and MYERS-SCOTTON, C. (1993), 'English Loans in Shona: Consequences for Linguistic Systems', *International Journal of the Sociology of Language*, 100.

BICKMORE, L. S. (1985), 'Hausa–English Code-Switching'. MA, Univ. of California at Los Angeles.

BIERWISCH, M. (1971), 'Linguistics and Language Error', repr. in A. Cutler (ed.), *Slips of the Tongue*, 29–72. Amsterdam: Mouton, 1982.

BLOM, J. P., and GUMPERZ, J. J. (1972), 'Social Meaning in Structure: Code-Switching in Norway', in J. J. Gumperz and D. Hymes (eds.), *Directions in Sociolinguistics*, 407–34. New York: Holt, Rinehart, and Winston.

BOCK, J. K. (1987), 'Coordinating Words and Syntax in Speech Plans', in A. W. Ellis (ed.), *Progress in the Psychology of Language*, iii. 337–90. London: Erlbaum.

——(1989), 'Closed-Class Immanence in Sentence Production', *Cognition*, 31: 163–86.

——(1991), 'A Sketchbook of Production Problems', *Journal of Psycholinguistic Research*, 20: 141–60.

——and CUTTING, J. C. (1990), 'Production Units and Production Problems in Forming Long-Distance Dependencies', paper presented to Psychonomic Society, New Orleans.

——and LOEBEL, H. (1990), 'Framing Sentences', *Cognition*, 35: 1–39.

BOESCHOTEN, H. (1991), 'Asymmetrical Code-Switching in Immigrant Communities', in *Papers for the Workshop on Constraints, Conditions, and Models*, 85–100. Strasbourg: European Science Foundation.

BOKAMBA, E. (1987), 'Are There Syntactic Constraints on Code-Mixing?', in K. Denning (ed.), *Variation in Language*, 35–51. Stanford, Calif.: Stanford Univ. Press.

——(1988), 'Code-Mixing, Language Variation, and Linguistic Theory: Evidence from Bantu Languages', *Lingua*, 76: 21–62.

——(1989), 'Are There Syntactic Constraints in Code-Mixing?', *World Englishes*, 8/3: 277–92.

BOLINGER, D. (1968), *Aspects of Language*. New York: Holt, Rinehart, and Winston.

BRENZINGER, M. (1987), 'Die Sprachliche und Kulturelle Stellung der Mbugu (Ma'a)'. MA, Univ. of Cologne.

BRESNAN, J. (1978), 'A Realistic Transformational Grammar', in M. Hale, J. Bresnan, and G. Miller (eds.), *Linguistic Theory and Psychological Reality*, 1–59. Cambridge, Mass.: MIT Press.

——(1982), *The Mental Representation of Grammatical Relations*. Cambridge, Mass.: MIT Press.

BROWN, B. (1986), 'Cajun/English Code-Switching: A Test of Formal Models', in D. Sankoff (ed.), *Diversity and Diachrony*, 399–406. Amsterdam: Benjamins.

BURKI-COHEN, J., GROSJEAN, F., and MILLER, J. L. (1989), 'Base-Language Effects on Word Identification in Bilingual Speech', *Language and Speech*, 32: 355–71.

BUTTERWORTH, B. (1983), 'Lexical Representation', in B. Butterworth (ed.), *Language Production, Development, Writing and other Language Processes*, ii. 257–94. London: Academic Press.

BUTTERWORTH, B. (1989), 'Lexical Access in Speech Production', in D. Marslen-Wilson (ed.), *Lexical Representation and Process*, 108–35. Cambridge, Mass.: MIT Press.

CAMPBELL, L. (1987), 'Syntactic Change in Pipil', *International Journal of American Linguistics*, 53: 253–80.

——(forthcoming), 'On Proposed Universals of Grammatical Borrowing', to appear in R. Jeffers (ed.), *Proceedings of the Ninth International Conference of Historical Linguistics*. Amsterdam: Benjamins.

CANONICI, N. N. (1990), 'Subclasses of Zulu Nouns', *South African Journal of African Languages*, 10: 52–8.

CARTER, H. (1991), Personal communication.

CHOMSKY, N. (1981), *Lectures on Government and Binding*. Dordrecht: Foris.

——(1986), *Barriers*. Cambridge, Mass.: MIT Press.

CLYNE, M. G. (1967), *Transference and Triggering*. The Hague: Nijhoff.

——(1982), *Multilingual Australia*. Melbourne: River Seine.

——(1987), 'Constraints on Code-Switching: How Universal Are They?', *Linguistics*, 25: 739–64.

COMRIE, B. (1989), 'Genetic Classification: Contact, and Variation', in T. J. Walsh (ed.), *Synchronic and Diachronic Approaches to Linguistic Variation and Change*, 81–93. Washington, DC: Georgetown Univ. Press.

CONTINI-MORAVA, E. (1991), Personal communication.

CRAWHALL, N. (1990), Shona/English Data. Unpublished.

CUTLER, A., and ISARD, S. (1980), 'The Production of Prosody', in B. Butterworth (ed.), *Language Production, i: Speech and Talk*, 245–69. London: Academic Press.

DAWKINS, R. M. (1916), *Modern Greek in Asia Minor: A Study of the Dialects of Silli, Cappadocia, and Pharasa with Grammars, Texts, Translations, and Glossary*. Cambridge: Cambridge Univ. Press.

DELL, G. S. (1990), 'Frame Constraints and Phonological Speech Errors', paper presented at CUNY Conference on Human Sentence-Processing, New York.

DENISON, N. (1977), 'Language Death or Language Suicide?', *International Journal of the Sociology of Language*, 12: 13–22.

DISCIULLO, A. M., MUYSKEN, P., and SINGH, R. (1986), 'Government and Code-Mixing', *Journal of Linguistics*, 22: 1–24.

DORIAN, N. C. (1977), 'The Problem of the Semi-Speaker in Language Death', *International Journal of the Sociology of Language*, 12: 23–32.

——(ed.) (1989), *Investigating Obsolescence: Studies in Language Contraction and Death*. Cambridge: Cambridge Univ. Press.

——(1990), Personal communication.

DORON, E. (1983), 'On Formal Models of Code-Switching', *Texas Linguistic Forum*, 22: 35–59.

DOWTY, D. (1979), *Word Meaning and Montague Grammar*. Dordrecht: Reidel.

DZAMESHIE, A. (1989), 'Codeswitching in Ewe and English', paper presented at African Linguistics Conference, Urbana, Ill.

——(1992), Personal communication.

EID, M. (1992), 'Directionality in Arabic–English Code-Switching', in A. Rouchdy (ed.), *The Arabic Language in America: A Sociolinguistic Study of a Growing Bilingual Community*, 50–71. Detroit: Wayne State Univ. Press.

ELIASSON, S. (1989), 'English–Maori Language Contact: Code-Switching and the Free-Morpheme Constraint', *Reports from Uppsala University Department of Linguistics*, 18: 1–28.

——(1991), 'Models and Constraints in Code-Switching Theory', in *Papers for the Workshop on Constraints, Conditions, and Models*, 17–50. Strasbourg: European Science Foundation.

ENNINGER, W. (1980), 'Syntactic Convergence in a Stable Triglossia Plus Trilingualism Situation in Kent Country, Delaware, US', in P. Nelde (ed.), *Sprachkontakt und Sprachkonflikt*, 343–50. Wiesbaden: Franz Steiner.

EWING, A. (1984), 'Polish–English Code-Switching: A Clue to Constituent Structure and Processing Mechanisms', in J. Drogo *et al.* (eds.), *Papers from the Regional Meeting of the Chicago Linguistic Society*, 52–64. Chicago: CLS.

FAY, D. (1980), 'Transformational Errors', in V. Fromkin (ed.), *Errors in Linguistic Performance: Slips of the Tongue, Ear, Pen, and Hand*. New York: Academic Press.

FORSON, B. (1979), 'Code-Switching in Akan–English Bilingualism'. Ph.D., Univ. of California at Los Angeles.

FROMKIN, V. (1971), 'The Non-Anomalous Nature of Anomalous Utterances', *Language*, 47: 27–52.

——(ed.) (1973), *Speech Errors as Linguistic Evidence*. The Hague: Mouton.

GARDNER-CHLOROS, P. (1985), 'Choix et alternance des langues à Strasbourg'. Ph.D., Université Louis Pasteur, Strasbourg.

——(1987), 'Code-Switching in Relation to Language Contact and Convergence', in G. Lüdi (ed.), *Devenir bilingue–parler bilingue*. Tübingen: Niemeyer.

——(1991), *Language Selection and Switching in Strasburg*. Oxford: Oxford Univ. Press.

GARRETT, M. F. (1975), 'The Analysis of Sentence Production', in G. Bower (ed.), *Psychology of Learning and Motivation*, 9: 133–77. New York: Academic Press.

——(1982), 'Production of Speech: Observations from Normal and Pathological Language Use', in A. W. Ellis (ed.), *Normality and Pathology in Cognitive Functions*. London: Academic Press.

——(1988), 'Process in Sentence Production', in F. Newmeyer (ed.), *The Cambridge Linguistics Survey*, iii. 69–96. Cambridge: Cambridge Univ. Press.

——(1990), 'Sentence Processing', in D. Osherson and H. Lasnik (eds.), *An Invitation to Cognitive Science*, i/1: 133–75. Cambridge, Mass.: MIT Press.

GIBBONS, J. (1987), *Code-Mixing and Code Choice: A Hong Kong Case Study*. Clevedon, Avon: Multilingual Matters.

GINGRAS, R. (1974), 'Problems in the Description of Spanish–English Intrasentential Code-Switching', in G. D. Bills (ed.), *Southwest Areal Linguistics*, 167–74. San Diego, Calif.: UCSD Institute for Cultural Pluralism.

GIVÓN, T. (1979), *On Understanding Grammar*. New York: Academic Press.

——(1989), *Mind, Code, and Context: Essays in Pragmatics*. Hillsdale, NJ: Erlbaum.

GOODMAN, M. (1971), 'The Strange Case of Mbugu', in D. Hymes (ed.), *Pidginization and Creolization of Languages*, 243–54. Cambridge: Cambridge Univ. Press.

GREEN, D. W. (1986), 'Control, Activation, and Resource: A Framework and a Model for the Control of Speech in Bilinguals', *Brain and Language*, 27: 210–23.

GROSJEAN, F. (1982), *Life with Two Languages*. Cambridge, Mass.: Harvard Univ. Press.

——(1988), 'Exploring the Recognition of Guest Words in Bilingual Speech', *Language and Cognitive Progress*, 3: 233–74.

——and SOARES, C. (1986), 'Processing Mixed Language: Some Preliminary Findings', in J. Vaid (ed.), *Language Processing in Bilinguals: Psycholinguistic and Neurolinguistic Perspectives*, 145–79. Hillsdale, NJ: Erlbaum.

GUMPERZ, J. J. (1982), 'Conversational Code-Switching', in *Discourse Strategies*, 55–99. Cambridge: Cambridge Univ. Press.

——and WILSON, R. (1974), 'Convergence and Creolization', in D. Hymes (ed.), *Pidginization and Creolization*, 151–67. Cambridge: Cambridge Univ. Press.

HAMERS, J., and BLANC, M. (1989), *Bilinguality and Bilingualism*. Cambridge: Cambridge Univ. Press.

HANCOCK, I. (1980), Personal communication. Cited in Thomason and Kaufman (1988).

HANKAMER, J. (1989), 'Morphological Parsing and the Lexicon', in W. D. Marlsen-Wilson (ed.), *Lexical Representation and Process*, 392–408. Cambridge, Mass.: MIT Press.

HANNAN, M. (1974), *Standard Shona Dictionary*. Salisbury: Rhodesia Literacy Bureau.

HAUGEN, E. (1950), 'The Analysis of Linguistic Borrowing', *Language*, 26: 210–31.

——(1953), *The Norwegian Language in America: A Study of Bilingual Behavior*. Philadelphia: Univ. of Pennsylvania Press.

——(1969), *The Norwegian Language in America*. Bloomington, Ind.: Indiana Univ. Press.

——(1973), 'The Analysis of Linguistic Borrowing', in E. Haugen (ed.), *The Ecology of Language*, 80–109. Stanford, Calif.: Stanford Univ. Press.

——(1992), 'Borrowing', in W. Bright (ed.), *Oxford Encyclopedia of Linguistics*, i: 197–9. New York: Oxford Univ. Press.

HEATH, J. (1981), 'A Case of Intensive Lexical Diffusion: Arnhem Land, Australia', *Language*, 57: 335–67.

——(1989), *From Codeswitching to Borrowing: A Case Study of Moroccan Arabic*. London: Routledge & Kegan Paul.

HELLER, M. (ed.) (1988), *Codeswitching: Anthropological and Sociolinguistic Perspectives*. Berlin: Mouton de Gruyter.

HILL, J. H., and HILL, K. C. (1986), *Speaking Mexicano*. Tucson: Univ. of Arizona Press.

HOPPER, P., and THOMPSON, S. (1984), 'The Discourse Basis for Lexical Categories in Universal Grammar', *Language*, 60: 703–52.

HYLTENSTAM, K. (1991), 'Language Mixing in Alzheimer's Dementia', in *Papers for the Workshop on Constraints, Conditions and Models*, 221–54. Strasbourg: European Science Foundation.

JACOBSON, R. (1977), 'The Social Implications of Intrasentential Codeswitching', in R. Romo and R. Paredes (eds.), *New Directions in Chicano Scholarship* (special issue of *The New Scholar*), 227–56. Univ. of California at San Diego.

——(1990), 'Socioeconomic Status as a Factor in the Selection of Encoding Strategies in Mixed Discourse', in R. Jacobson (ed.), *Code-Switching as a Worldwide Phenomenon*, 111–40. New York: Peter Lang.

JAKE, J. L., and MYERS-SCOTTON, C. (1992), 'Testing the Fit: Syntactic Theory and Intrasentential Codeswitching', presented at Annual Meeting of the Linguistic Society of America, Jan.

JAKENDOFF, R. (1977), *X-Bar Syntax: A Study of Phrase Structure*. Cambridge, Mass.: MIT Press.

JOSHI, A. (1981), 'Some Problems in Processing Sentences with Intrasentential Code-Switching', paper presented at Univ. of Texas Parsing Workshop, Austin.

——(1985), 'Processing of Sentences with Intrasentential Code Switching', in D. R. Dowty, L. Karttunen, and A. Zwicky (eds.), *Natural Language Parsing*, 190–205. Cambridge: Cambridge Univ. Press.

KACHRU, B. B. (1978), 'Code-Mixing as a Communicative Strategy in India', in J. E. Alatis (ed.), *International Dimensions of Bilingual Education*, 107–24. Washington, DC: Georgetown Univ. Press.

KAMWANGAMALU, N. M. (1989*a*), 'Theory and Method of Code-Mixing: A Cross-Linguistic Study'. Ph.D., Univ. of Illinois, Urbana.

——(1989*b*), 'Some Morphosyntactic Aspects of French/English–Bantu Code-Mixing', in B. Music *et al.* (eds.), *Parasession on Language Contact: Regional Meeting of the Chicago Linguistic Society*, 157–70. Chicago: CLS.

——(1990), 'Bilingual Code-Mixing: Syntax and Constraints', rev. version of paper given at African Linguistics Conference, Univ. of Georgia, Athens, Apr.

——and LEE, C. L. (1991), ' "Mixers" and "Mixing": English across Cultures', *World Englishes*, 10: 247–61.

KARTTUNEN, F. (1985), 'Nahuatl and Maya in Contact with Spanish'. Texas Linguistic Forum 26, Univ. of Texas Dept. of Linguistics, Austin.

KARTTUNEN, F. and LOCKHART, J. (1976), *Nahuatl in the Middle Years: Language Contact Phenomena in Texts of the Colonial Period*. Berkeley and Los Angeles: Univ. of California Press.

KEMPEN, G., and HOENKAMP, E. (1987), 'An Incremental Procedural Grammar for Sentence Formulation', *Cognitive Science*, 11: 201–58.

KITE, Y. K. (1990), Personal communication.

KLAVANS, J. L. (1983), 'The Syntax of Code-Switching: Spanish and English', *Proceedings of the Linguistic Colloquium on Romance Languages*, xiv. Amsterdam: Benjamins.

KOOPMAN, A. (1990), Personal communication.

LADISLAV, Z. (1971), *Manual of Lexicography*. The Hague: Mouton.

LAHLOU, M. (1989), 'Arabic–French Codeswitching in Morocco', paper presented at African Linguistics Conference, Univ. of Illinois, Urbana.

LEECH, G., and SHORT, M. (1981), *Style in Fiction*. London: Longman.

LEONARD, R. (1982), 'The Semantic System of Deixis in Standard Swahili'. Ph.D., Columbia Univ., New York.

LEVELT, W. J. M. (1989), *Speaking: From Intention to Articulation*. Cambridge, Mass.: MIT Press.

LIPSKI, J. (1977), 'Code-Switching and the Problem of Bilingual Competence', in M. Paradis (ed.), *Aspects of Bilingualism*, 250–63. Columbia, SC: Hornbeam Press.

LÜDI, G. (1983), 'Aspects énonciatifs et fonctionnels de la néologie lexicale', *Tranel*, 5: 105–30.

——(1986), 'Forms and Functions of Bilingual Speech in Pluricultural Migrant Communities in Switzerland', in J. A. Fishman *et al.* (eds.), *The Fergusonian Impact*, ii. 217–36. Berlin: Mouton de Gruyter.

——(1992), Personal communication.

——and PY, B. (1984), *Zweisprachig durch Migration: Einführung in die Erforschung der Mehrsprachigkeit am Beispiel zweier Zuwanderergruppen in Neuenburg (Schweiz)*. Tübingen: Niemeyer.

————(1986), *Être Bilingue*. Berne: Peter Lang.

McCLURE, E. (1981), 'Formal and Functional Aspects of the Code-Switched Discourse of Bilingual Children', in R. Duran (ed.), *Latino Language and Communicative Behavior*, 69–92. Norwood, NJ: Ablex.

MADAKI, R. O. (1983), 'A Linguistic and Pragmatic Analysis of Hausa–English Code-Switching'. Ph.D., Univ. of Michigan, Ann Arbor.

MENOVŠČIKOV, G. A. (1969), 'O Nekotoryx Social'nyx Aspektax Èvoljucii Jazyka', *Voprosy Social'noj Lingvistiki*. Cited in Thomason and Kaufman (1988). Leningrad: Nauka.

MILLER, W. R. (1971), 'The Death of Language of Serendipity among the Shoshoni', *Anthropological Linguistics*, 13: 114–20.

MOHAN, P., and ZADOR, P. (1986), 'Discontinuity in a Life Cycle: The Death of Trinidad Bhojpuri', *Language*, 62: 291–319.

MORAVCSIK, E. (1978), 'Language Contact', in J. H. Greenberg (ed.), *Universals of Human Language*, i. 93–122. Stanford, Calif.: Stanford Univ. Press.

MOUGEON, R., and BENIAK, E. (1987), 'The Extralinguistic Correlates of Core Lexical Borrowing', in K. Denning *et al.* (eds.), *Variation in Language: New Ways of Analyzing Variation*, xv. 337–47. Stanford, Calif.: Stanford Univ. Press.

————(1991), *Linguistic Consequences of Language Contact and Restriction.* Oxford: Oxford Univ. Press.

MPHANDE, L. (1989), Personal communication.

MÜHLHÄUSLER, P. (1985), 'Patterns of Contact, Mixture, Creation and Nativization: Their Contribution to a General Theory of Language', in C.-J. Bailey, and R. Harris (eds.), *Developmental Mechanisms of Language*, 51–87. Oxford: Pergamon.

MUYSKEN, P. (1981), 'Halfway between Quechua and Spanish: The Case of Relexification', in A. Highfield and A. Valdman (eds.), *Historicity and Variation in Creole Studies*, 52–78. Ann Arbor, Mich.: Karoma.

——(1990), 'Concepts, Methodology, and Data in Language Contact Research: Ten Remarks from the Perspective of Grammatical Theory', in *Papers for the Workshop on Concepts, Methodology and Data*, 15–30. Strasbourg: European Science Foundation.

——(1991), 'Needed: A Comparative Approach', in *Papers for the Symposium on Code-Switching in Bilingual Studies: Theory, Significance and Perspectives*, i. 253–72. Strasbourg: European Science Foundation.

MYERS, S. (1990), *Tone and the Structure of Words in Shona.* New York: Garland.

MYERS-SCOTTON, C. (1989), 'Code-Switching with English: Types of Switching, Types of Communities', *World Englishes*, 8: 333–46.

——(1990), 'Elite Closure as Boundary Maintenance: The Evidence from Africa', in B. Weinstein (ed.), *Language Policy and Political Development*, 25–41. Norwood, NJ: Ablex.

——(1991*a*), 'Intersections between Social Motivations and Structural Processing in Codeswitching', in *Papers for the Workshop on Constraints, Conditions and Models*, 57–82. Strasbourg: European Science Foundation.

——(1991*b*), 'Whither Code-Switching? Prospects for Cross-Field Collaboration: Production-based models of Code-Switching', in *Papers for the Symposium on Code-Switching in Bilingual Studies: Theory, Significance and Perspectives*, 207–32. Strasbourg: European Science Foundation.

——(1992*a*), 'Constructing the Frame in Intrasentential Codeswitching', *Multilingua*, 11: 101–27.

——(1992*b*), 'Comparing Codeswitching and Borrowing', *Journal of Multilingual and Multicultural Development*, 13: 19–39.

——(1992*c*), 'Codeswitching as a Mechanism of Deep Borrowing, Language Shift and Language Death', in M. Brenzinger (ed.), *Language Death in East Africa*, 31–58. Berlin: Mouton de Gruyter.

MYERS-SCOTTON, C. (1993), *Social Motivations for Codeswitching: Evidence from Africa*. Oxford: Oxford Univ. Press.

——(forthcoming *a*), 'A Lexically-Based Production Model of Codeswitching', to appear in G. Lüdi, L. Milroy, and P. Muysken (eds.), *One Speaker, Two Languages: Cross-Disciplinary Perspectives on Codeswitching*.

——(forthcoming *b*), 'Building the Frame in Codeswitching: Evidence from Africa', to appear in S. Mufwene and L. Moshi (eds.), *Studies on African Languages: Papers from the Twenty-First Annual Conference on African Linguistics*. Amsterdam: Benjamins.

——and AZUMA, S. (1990), 'A Frame-Based Process Model of Codeswitching', in M. Ziolowski, K. Deaton, and M. Noske (eds.), *Proceedings from the 26th Regional Conference*, 307–21. Chicago: CLS.

NARTEY, J. (1982), 'Code-Switching, Interference or Faddism? Language Use among Educated Ghanaians', *Anthropological Linguistics*, 24/2: 183–92.

NGARA, E. A. (1982), *Language Planning: Proposals for Language Use and Language Teaching in Zimbabwe*. Gwelo, Zimbabwe: Mambo Press.

NISHIMURA, M. (1986), 'Intrasentential Code-Switching: the Case of Language Assignment', in J. Vaid (ed.), *Language Processing in Bilinguals: Psycholinguistic and Neuropsychological Perspectives*, 123–44. Hillsdale, NJ: Erlbaum.

NORTIER, J. (1990), *Dutch–Moroccan Arabic Code Switching*. Dordrecht: Foris.

NURSE, D. (1988), 'The Borrowing of Inflectional Morphology: Tense and Aspect in Unguja', *Afrikanistische Arbeitspapiere*, 15: 107–19.

——and HINNEBUSCH, T. (1993), *Swahili and Sabaki, a Linguistic History*. Los Angeles: Univ. of California Press.

——and SPEAR, T. (1985), *The Swahili: Reconstructing the History and Language of an African Society 800–1500*. Philadelphia: Univ. of Pennsylvania Press.

NZWANGA, M. (1991), Personal communication.

OLORUNTOBA, Y. (1990), Personal communication.

PANDHARIPANDE, R. (1990), 'Formal and Functional Constraints on Code-Mixing', in R. Jacobson (ed.), *Codeswitching as a Worldwide Phenomenon*, 15–32. New York: Peter Lang.

PANDIT, I. (1990), 'Grammaticality in Code-Switching', in R. Jacobson (ed.), *Codeswitching as a Worldwide Phenomenon*, 33–69. New York: Peter Lang.

PARADIS, M. (ed.) (1978), *Aspects of Bilingualism*. Columbia, SC: Hornbeam Press.

PARK, J. E., TROIKE, R., and MUN, M. R. P. (1989), 'A Preliminary Study of Constraints on Korean–English Code-Switching', paper presented at Second Language Research Forum, Univ. of California at Los Angeles.

PARKIN, D. (1974), 'Status Factors in Language Adding: Bahati Housing Estate in Nairobi', in W. H. Whiteley (ed.), *Language in Kenya*, 147–66. Nairobi: Oxford Univ. Press.

PETERSEN, J. (1988), 'Word-Internal Code-Switching Constraints in a Child's Grammar', *Linguistics*, 26: 479–93.

PFAFF, C. (1979), 'Constraints on Language Mixing: Intrasentential Code-Switching and Borrowing in Spanish/English', *Language*, 55: 291–318.

POPLACK, S. (1980), ' "Sometimes I'll start a sentence in Spanish y terminol Espanol": Toward a Typology of Code-Switching', *Linguistics*, 18: 581–618.

——(1981), 'Syntactic Structure and Social Function of Code-Switching', in R. Duran (ed.), *Latino Language and Communicative Behavior*, 169–84. Norwood, NJ: Ablex.

——(1988*a*), 'Contrasting Patterns of Code-Switching in Two Communities', in M. Heller (ed.), *Codeswitching: Anthropological and Sociolinguistic Perspective*, 215–44. Berlin: Mouton de Gruyter.

——(1988*b*), 'Language Status and Language Accommodation Along a Linguistic Border', in P. Lowenberg (ed.), *Language Spread and Language Policy*, 90–118. Washington, DC: Georgetown Univ. Press.

——(1990), 'Variation Theory and Language Contact: Conceptions, Methods and Data', in *Papers for the Workshop on Concepts, Methodology, and Data*, 33–66. Strasbourg: European Science Foundation.

——and MILLER, C. (1988), 'The Social Correlates and Linguistic Processes of Lexical Borrowing and Assimilation', *Linguistics*, 26: 47–104.

——and SANKOFF, D. (1988), 'Codeswitching', in A. Ulrich *et al.* (eds.), *Sociolinguistics/Soziolinguistik*, 1174–80. Berlin: Mouton de Gruyter.

——WHEELER, S., and WESTWOOD, A. (1987), 'Distinguishing Language Contact Phenomena: Evidence from Finnish–English Bilingualism', in P. Lilius and M. Saari (eds.), *Proceedings of the 6th International Conference of Nordic and General Linguistics*, 33–56. Helsinki: Univ. of Helsinki Press.

PÜTZ, M. (1991), Personal communication.

RAMAT, A. (1991), 'Code-Switching in Dialectal Communities: Effects on Language Shift', *Papers for the Workshop on Impact and Consequences: Broader Considerations*, 189–224. Strasbourg: European Science Foundation.

REYES, R. (1974), 'Studies in Chicago Spanish'. Ph.D., Harvard Univ., Cambridge, Mass.

——(1976), 'Language Mixing in Chicano Bilingual Speech', in J. D. Bowen and J. Ornstein (eds.), *Studies in Southwest Spanish*, 182–8. Rowley, Mass.: Newbury House.

ROMAINE, S. (1989), *Bilingualism*. Oxford: Blackwell.

ROSENBERG, B., ZURIF, E., BROWNELL, H., GARRETT, M., and BRADLEY, D. (1985), 'Grammatical Class Effects in Relation to Normal and Aphasic Sentence Processing', *Brain and Language*, 26: 287–303.

SANKOFF, D., and POPLACK, S. (1981), 'A Formal Grammar for Code-Switching', *Papers in Linguistics*, 14: 3–43.

————and VANNIARAJAN, S. (1990), 'The Case of the Nonce Loan in Tamil', *Language Variation and Change*, 2: 71–101.

SCHWANENFLUGEL, P. J., and REY, M. (1986), 'Interlingual Semantic Facilitation:

Evidence for a Common Representational System in the Bilingual Lexicon', *Journal of Memory and Language*, 25: 605–18.

SCOLLON, R., and SCOLLON, S. (1979), *Linguistic Convergence*. New York: Academic Press.

SCOTTON, C. M. (1979), 'The Context is the Message: Syntactic and Semantic Deletion in Nairobi and Kampala Varieties of Swahili', in I. Hancock (ed.), *Readings in Creole Studies*, 111–28. Ghent: Story-Scientia.

—— (1982*a*), 'The Possibility of Code-Switching: Motivation for Maintaining Multilingualism', *Anthropological Linguistics*, 14: 432–44.

——(1982*b*), 'An Urban–Rural Comparison of Language Use among the Luyia in Kenya', *International Journal of the Sociology of Language*, 34: 121–36.

——(1983), 'The Negotiation of Identities in Conversation: A Theory of Markedness and Code Choice', *International Journal of the Sociology of Language*, 44: 115–36.

——(1986), 'Codeswitching and Diglossia', in J. A. Fishman *et al.* (eds.), *The Fergusonian Impact*, ii. 403–15. Berlin: Mouton de Gruyter.

——(1988*a*), 'Codeswitching as Indexical of Social Relationships', in M. Heller (ed.), *Codeswitching: Anthropological and Sociolinguistic Perspectives*, 151–86. Berlin: Mouton de Gruyter.

——(1988*b*), 'Code-Switching and Types of Multilingual Communities', in P. Lowenberg (ed.), *Language Spread and Language Policy*, 61–82. Washington, DC: Georgetown Univ. Press.

——(1988*c*), 'Differentiating Borrowing from Code-Switching', in K. Ferrara *et al.* (eds.), *Linguistic Change and Contact: New Ways of Analyzing Variation*, xvi. 318–25. Austin: Univ. of Texas Press.

——and OKEJU, J. (1973), 'Neighbors and Lexical Borrowings', *Language*, 49: 871–89.

SEUREN, P. A. M. (1990), Personal communication.

——(1991), Personal communication.

SHAFFER, D. (1977), 'The Place of Code-Switching in Linguistic Contact', in M. Paradis (ed.), *Aspects of Bilingualism*, 265–74. Columbia, SC: Hornbeam Press.

SIMANGO, S. R. (1991), Personal communication.

SOARES, C., and GROSJEAN, F. (1984), 'Bilinguals in a Monolingual and a Bilingual Speech Mode: The Effect on Lexical Access', *Memory and Cognition*, 12: 380–6.

SOUTHWORTH, F. C. (1980), 'Indian Bilingualism: Some Educational and Linguistic Implications', in *Studies in Child Language and Multilingualism, Proceedings of the New York Academy of Sciences*, 345: 121–46.

SRIDHAR, S. N., and SRIDHAR, K. (1980), 'The Syntax and Psycholinguistics of Bilingual Code-Mixing', *Canadian Journal of Psychology*, 34: 407–16.

STEMBERGER, J. P. (1985), 'An Interactive Activation Model of Language Production', in A. W. Ellis (ed.), *Progress in the Psychology of Language*, 143–86. Norwood, NJ: Erlbaum.

SWIGART, L. (1992), 'Practice and Perception: Language Use and Attitudes in Dakar', Ph.D. Seattle: Univ. of Washington.

SWINNEY, D., ZURIF, E. B., and CUTLER, A. (1980), 'Effects of Sentential Stress and Word Class upon Comprehension in Broca's Aphasia', *Brain and Language*, 10: 132–44.

THOMASON, S. G. (1983), 'Genetic Relationship and the Case of Ma'a (Mbugu)', *Studies in African Linguistics*, 14: 195–231.

——(1988), Personal communication.

——and KAUFMAN, T. (1975), 'Toward an Adequate Definition of Creolization', paper presented at the 1975 International Conference on Pidgins and Creoles, Honolulu.

————(1988), *Language Contact, Creolization and Genetic Linguistics*. Berkeley: Univ. of California Press.

TIMM, L. (1975), 'Spanish–English Code-Switching: *El Porque y how-not-to*', *Romance Philology*, 28: 473–82.

TOSCO, M. (1990), Personal communication.

——(1992), 'Dahalo as an Endangered Language', in M. Brenzinger (ed.), *Language Death in East Africa*, 137–56. Berlin: Mouton de Gruyter.

TREFFERS-DALLER, J. (1991a), 'Towards a Uniform Approach to Code-Switching and Borrowing', in *Papers for the Workshop on Constraints, Conditions and Models*, 259–79. Strasbourg: European Science Foundation.

——(1991b), 'French–Dutch Language Mixture in Brussels'. PhD, Univ. of Amsterdam.

VAID, J. (1980), 'The Form and Function of Code-Mixing in Indian Films: The Case of Hindi and English', *Indian Linguistics*, 41: 37–44.

VAN COETSEM, F. (1988), *Loan Phonology and Two Transfer Types in Language Contact*. Dordrecht: Foris.

VAN NESS, S. (1992), Personal communication.

WALTERS, K. (1989), Personal communication.

WEINREICH, U. (1953), *Languages in Contact*. The Hague: Mouton; repr. 1967.

WENTZ, J., and MCCLURE, E. (1976), 'Ellipsis in Bilingual Discourse', *Papers from the Regional Meeting of the Chicago Linguistic Society*, 656–65. Chicago: CLS.

WHISTLER, K. (1988), *Kwic-Magic*. Richmond, Calif.: LST Software.

WHITELEY, W. H. (1960), 'Linguistic Hybrids', *African Studies*, 19: 95–7.

——(1969), *Swahili: The Rise of a National Language*. London: Methuen.

WOLFF, J. U. (1983), 'The Indonesian Spoken by the Peranaka Chinese of East Java: A Case of Language Mixture', in F. Agard and G. Kelly (eds.), *Essays in Honor of Ch. F. Hockett: Linguistics Contributions*, iv. 590–601. Ithaca, NY: Cornell Univ. Press.

WOOLFORD, E. (1983), 'Bilingual Code-Switching and Syntactic Theory', *Linguistic Inquiry*, 14: 520–36.

ZGUSTA, L. (1971), *Manual of Lexicography*. The Hague: Mouton.

ZURIF, E. B. (1990), 'Language and the Brain', in D. Osherson and H. Lasnick (eds.), *An Invitation to Cognitive Science*, i. 177–98. Cambridge, Mass.: MIT Press.

References in the Afterword

BELAZI, H. M., RUBIN, E. J., and TORIBIO, A. J. (1994), 'Code Switching and X-Bar Theory: The Functional Head Constraint', *Linguistic Inquiry*, 25: 221–37.

BENTAHILA, A. (1995), 'Review of *Duelling Languages*', *Language*, 71: 135–40.

——and DAVIES, E. E. (1992), 'Code-Switching and Language Dominance', in R. J. Harris (ed.), *Cognitive Processing in Bilinguals*, 443–58. Amsterdam: Benjamins.

BHATIA, T. K., and RITCHIE, W. C. (1996), 'Bilingual Language Mixing, Universal Grammar, and Second Language Acquisition', *Handbook of Second Language Acquisition*, 627–88. London: Academic Press.

BOCK, K., and LEVELT, W. (1994), 'Language Production: Grammatical Encoding', *Handbook of Psycholinguistics*, 945–84. New York: Academic Press.

BOLONYAI, A. (1996), 'Turning It Over: L2 Dominance in Hungarian/English Acquisition'. Unpublished paper.

EID, M. (1992), 'Directionality in Arabic–English Code-Switching', in A. Rouchdy (ed.), *The Arabic Language in America: A Sociolinguistic Study of a Growing Bilingual Community*, 50–71. Detroit: Wayne State University Press.

ENNINGER, W. (1979), 'Language Convergence in a Stable Triglossia Plus Trilingualism Situation', in P. Freese, K. Feywald, W. Paprotte, and W. Read (eds.), *Anglistik Beitrage sur Fachwissenschaft und Fachdidaktik*, 43–63. Munster.

FINLAYSON, R., CALTEAUX, K., and MYERS-SCOTTON, C. (1996), 'Orderly Mixing: Codeswitching in a South African Township', submitted for publication.

FULLER, J. (1995), German/English Data. Unpublished.

——(1996), 'When Cultural Maintenance Means Linguistic Convergence: Pennsylvania German Evidence for the Matrix Language Turnover Hypothesis', *Language in Society*, 25: 493–514.

GARDNER-CHLOROS, P. (1991), *Language Selection and Switching in Strasburg*. Oxford: Oxford University Press.

GROSJEAN, F., and MILLER, J. L. (1994), 'Going in and out of Languages: An Example of Bilingual Flexibility', *Psychological Science*, 5: 201–6.

HELLER, M. (ed.) (1988), *Codeswitching: Anthropological and Sociolinguistic Perspectives*. Berlin: Mouton de Gruyter.

KAUFMAN, D., and ARONHOFF, M. (1991), 'Morphological Disintegration and Reconstruction on First Language Attrition', in H. W. Seliger and R. M. Vago (eds.), *First Language Attrition*, 175–88. Amsterdam: Benjamins.

KUHBERG, H. (1992), 'Longitudinal L2 Attrition versus L2 Acquisition, in Three Turkish Children, Empirical Findings', *Second Language Research*, 8: 138–54.

JAKE, J. L. (1994), 'Intrasentential Codeswitching and Pronouns: On the Categorial Status of Functional Elements', *Linguistics*, 32: 271–98.

——(1996), 'Constructing Interlanguage: Building a Composite Matrix Language', submitted for publication.

——and MYERS-SCOTTON, C. M. (1996), 'Verbs in Arabic/English Codeswitching and Lexical Structure', paper presented at Symposium on Codeswitching and Lexical Structure, Linguistic Society of America, annual meeting, January.

JAKENDOFF, R. (1990), *Semantic Structures*. Cambridge MA: MIT Press.

JOSHI, A. (1985), 'Processing of Sentences with Intrasentential Code Switching', in D. R. Dowty, L. Kartunnen, and A. Zwicky (eds.), *Natural Language Parsing*, 190–205. Cambridge: Cambridge University Press.

LANZA, E. (1992), 'Can Bilingual Two-Year-Olds Code-Switch?', *Journal of Child Language*, 633–58.

MAHOOTIAN, S., and SANTORINI, B. (1996), 'Code Switching and the Complement/ Adjunct Distinction', *Linguistic Inquiry*, 27: 464–79.

MEECHAM, M., and POPLACK, S. (1995), 'Orphan Categories in Bilingual Discourse: Adjectivization Strategies in Wolof-French and Fongbe-French', *Language Variation and Change*, 7: 169–94.

MILIAN, S. H. (1996), 'The Sociopragmatics of Codeswitching: Multifunctionality and Ambiguity of Codeswitching in Family and Peer Interactions'. MA, University of South Carolina, Columbia.

MYERS-SCOTTON, C. M. (1993a), *Duelling Languages: Grammatical Structure in Codeswitching*. Oxford: Oxford University Press.

——(1993b), *Social Motivations for Codeswitching: Evidence from Africa*. Oxford: Oxford University Press.

——(1993c), 'Common and Uncommon Ground: Social and Structural Factors in Codeswitching', *Language in Society*, 22: 475–504.

——(1996a), 'Code Switching', in F. Coulmas (ed.), *Handbook of Sociolinguistics*, 217–37. Oxford: Blackwell.

——(1997a), 'A Way to Dusty Death: The Matrix Language Turnover Hypothesis', in L. Grenoble and L. Whaley (eds.), *Endangered Languages*. Cambridge: Cambridge University Press.

——(1997b), 'Compromise Strategies in Codeswitching', in G. Extra and L. Verhoeven (eds.), *Processes of Language Change in an Immigrant Context*. Tilburg: University of Tilburg Press.

——(1997c), 'Matrix Language Recognition and Morpheme Sorting as Possible Structural Strategies in Pidgin/Creole Formation', in A. Spears and D. Winford (eds.), *Pidgins and Creoles: Structure and Status*. Amsterdam: Benjamins.

——and BERNSTEN, J. (1995), Acholi/English Data. Unpublished.

——and JAKE, J. L. (1995), 'Matching Lemmas in a Bilingual Language Competence and Production Model: Evidence from Intrasentential Code Switching', *Linguistics*, 33: 981–1024.

OKASHA, M. (1995), Arabic/English Data. Unpublished.

PFAFF, C. (1979), 'Constraints on Language Mixing: Intrasentential Code-Switching and Borrowing in Spanish/English', *Language*, 55: 291–318.

SAVIĆ, J. M. (1995), 'Structural Convergence and Language Change: Evidence from Serbian/English Code-Switching', *Language in Society*, 24: 475–92.

SCHÜTZE, C. (1996), *The Empirical Base of Linguistics*. Chicago: University of Chicago Press.

SIMANGO, S. R. (1995), Chichewa/English Data. Unpublished.

SRIDHAR, S. N., and SRIDHAR, K. (1980), 'The Syntax and Psycholinguistics of Bilingual Code-Mixing', *Canadian Journal of Psychology*, 34: 7–16.

TALMY, L. (1985), 'Lexicalization Patterns: Semantic Structure in Lexical Form', in T. Shopen (ed.), *Language Typology and Syntactic Description III*, 51–149. New York: Cambridge University Press.

Index